Alatai Sm

Risk and Society

D1421829

Risk and Society

David Denney

SAGE Publications

London ● Thousand Oaks ● New Delhi

© David Denney 2005

First published 2005

Apart from any fair dealing for the purposes of research or
private study, or criticism or review, as permitted under
the Copyright, Designs and Patents Act, 1988, this publication
may be reproduced, stored or transmitted in any form, or
by any means, only with the prior permission in writing of
the publishers, or in the case of reprographic reproduction,
in accordance with the terms of licenses issued by the
Copyright Licensing Agency. Inquiries concerning
reproduction outside those terms should be sent to
the publishers.

SAGE Publications Ltd
1 Oliver's Yard
55 City Road
London EC1Y 1SP

SAGE Publications Inc.
2455 Teller Road
Thousand Oaks, California 91320

SAGE Publications India Pvt Ltd
B-42, Panchsheel Enclave
Post Box 4109
New Delhi 110 017

British Library Cataloguing in Publication data

A catalogue record for this book is available
from the British Library

ISBN 0 7619 4739 6
 0 7619 4740 x

Library of Congress control number available

Typeset by C&M Digitals (P) Ltd., Chennai, India
Printed on paper from sustainable resources
Printed and bound in Great Britain by Athenaeum Press, Gateshead

Contents

Tables and Boxes

Acknowledgements

My interest in risk developed during the course of an ESRC project 'Violence Against Professionals in the Community'. This was part of the Violence Research Programme which was funded between 1997 and 2002 to explore violence against the person. The programme was directed by Professor Betsy Stanko, who was generous with both her time and her immense knowledge. I am also indebted to my co-researchers Jonathan Gabe, Maria O'Beirne, Mary Ann Elston and Ray Lee for carrying forward the research into violence, which motivated me to write this book. Some of our work is mentioned in Chapter 5 on risk and professional practices. My colleague Professor Jane Tunstill always offered encouragement and support.

I would also like to acknowledge the understanding and endless patience of Chris Rojek, Kay Bridger and Mila Steele at Sage, and I am indebted to the anonymous reviewer who spent a considerable amount of time in giving incisive and detailed criticism. Many of the suggestions offered have now been included. I would also like to thank Bedfordshire County Council for allowing me to reproduce their job advertisement 'Head of Risk Management Group'. I also wish to acknowledge the kind permission of Solo Syndication to reproduce the articles 'Chips may cause cancer, warns top food expert' and 'Alert as GM pollen spreads', which were both published in the *Daily Mail* on 28 June 2002.

Shirin Denney has lived with the writing of this book, for which I am very grateful.

I dedicate this book to my children, Joe and Eve.

Introduction

Risk has come to dominate individual and collective consciousness in the twenty-first century. Although global insecurity has been created by terrorism, pollution, global epidemics, and famine, risks involved in aspects of everyday life such as food, sunlight and travel have become major preoccupations. Seemingly innocuous objects, including – carpets, footwear, televisions, vacuum cleaners, personal stereos can create a potential risk to health. In one case recorded by Britain's Department of Trade and Industry, a tea cosy was listed as being the cause of an accident (Spicker, 2001: 17). Research and theory in social science has produced a plethora of risk related literature during the last two decades. Academic interest in risk has been accompanied by a burgeoning expansion of professional risk management activities. In 1995 it was estimated that the risk industry employed 1.5 million people in the United Kingdom (UK) alone (Adams, 1995). It would now be impossible to estimate the numbers of people involved in risk evaluation and risk management in its multifarious guises worldwide.

Rationale

Ideas about risk can seem complex and inaccessible, seemingly unrelated to life in the social world. In order to help make sense of what is emerging from the growing corpus of risk related literature, this book has two principal aims. Firstly, it will critically examine the social construction of risk from a number of theoretical positions. Secondly, ideas about the nature of risk will be related to aspects of daily life. Given the eclectic nature of the notion of risk, materials from diverse areas within the social sciences will be utilised, although it has been necessary to be selective in addressing particular substantive areas. The problems, which are examined, reflect contemporary social practices, all of which are contested at a global level.

Social science cannot provide conclusive answers as to the nature of risk in contemporary society. Social science can help to understand how risk constitutes an important aspect of the social world. The book aims to provide an accessible bridge between ideas about risk, the workings of social institutions, and social practices.

Structure of the book

The book will be divided into three sections. Part I will examine the meanings which have been ascribed to risk. Here, differing ideas about risk will be critically examined. Part II of the book combines a consideration of major life events and risk within everyday aspects of living. Attention in Part III is turned towards overarching themes, by examining the risks posed by terrorism, global regulation, governance, and developments within international relations. Chapter One examines the nature and development of the concept of risk. Chapter Two is a substantial longer chapter which critically examines some of the major theoretical positions which have been taken by social scientists with respect to discussions about risk. Chapter Three is concerned with the way in which decisions about risk are an integral part of everyday experience in relation to the family, housing, employment, and education. Chapter Four concentrates more specifically on risk and health containing discussions related to immunisation, eating and drinking, smoking and public health. Chapter Five focuses upon risk and the changing nature of professionalism. The communication of risk through the media in television, film, and the printed word is discussed in Chapter Six. Social welfare and risk is examined in Chapter Seven with a focus upon child protection, mental health interventions, older people and the relationship between risk and the contract culture in welfare. The preoccupation with the relationship between risk and crime forms the basis for discussions in Chapter Eight. Chapter Nine examines the idea that a new form of terrorism has emerged following the attacks of 11 September 2001. In Chapter Ten the implications of the regulatory state and systems designed to control risk in organisations are discussed. Chapter Eleven is concerned with some of the global efforts which have been made to regulate and protect the environment. Chapter Twelve develops some of the themes in Chapter Eleven by examining the possibility that risk can be avoided through global governance. Chapter Thirteen develops discussions in Chapters Nine and Twelve, and explores the possibility that risk underpins a new approach to international relations, which in itself poses a new risk to peaceful co-existence. Chapter Fourteen concludes by developing some of the over-arching themes which have emerged.

Each chapter begins with a short outline. Suggestions for further reading will be made at the end of each chapter. Full references for further reading are included in the bibliography.

Part I   Understanding Risk

ONE   The Nature of Risk

Outline

This chapter examines the development of the concept of risk. First, the idea of risk is distinguished from that of danger. The chapter then examines how the concept of risk has developed since the premodern period. Risk is presented as both a positive and a negative concept. The chapter also suggests that risk has become a globalised idea. However, as the world becomes more complex in its relations, it is difficult to reach any consensus as to what constitutes risk.

Changing views of danger

The distinction between the words 'risk' and 'danger' is one which has moved beyond the realm of semantics. Some writers have suggested that 'risk' could well be dropped from political discourse, since the word 'danger' would work as well. 'Risk' carries a menacing tone when it enters public debate (Douglas, 1992).

In the premodern period, dangers were associated with disease, war, epidemic and failing harvests. More specifically, the dangers posed by demons, wild dogs, highwaymen, the night, crossroads, lepers and evil portents have been replaced by other different, although equally potentially lethal, dangers (Lupton, 1999a). However, during the nineteenth century the notion of 'dangerousness' was crystallised in the idea of the 'dangerous classes'. Some of the earliest theories relating to crime claimed that criminal behaviour was to some extent biologically determined. The work of early criminologists reflected this approach to potential danger. For example, Lombroso argued that the danger of criminality could be associated with particular physical features. These included large hands and feet, and distinctive torsos (Lombroso, 1897). As criminology and psychiatry developed through the nineteenth and twentieth centuries, governments endowed professional experts with the power to define who was, and who was not, dangerous. Whether a person was a danger to society could therefore be judged by those qualified to measure such physical attributes. Throughout this period the person acclaimed as the 'expert' began a long upward path of ascendancy.

'Danger' has also been linked to the concepts of 'nation' and 'culture' throughout history. In the nineteenth century, Irish people were portrayed as being dangerous and particularly prone to social disorganisation (Croall, 1998). Black people have been variously conceptualised in dangerous terms. The populist myth of black people posing a risk to the established order has been present throughout history. In the late 1970s young black people in Britain were seen as constituting a new 'mugging class' (Hall et al., 1978; Solomos, 1988). Urban riots in the early 1980s were also portrayed by the media as challenging and disturbing to a law-abiding country.

Since the mid-1980s other dangers created by new technology have dominated populist presentations of danger. Nuclear radiation, chemical waste, asbestos and lead poisoning have structured much public debate.

Some single acts carried out by individuals have led to the perception that the world is a far more dangerous place. The murder of two-year-old James Bulger by two other children and in 1996 the murder of children by a lone gunman in a primary school at Dunblane are examples in the UK of such acts. The shooting of young children by their peers in Columbine High School in Littleton, Colorado, in 1999 resulted in the construction of unique discourses of threat and danger (Vanderveen, 2002). These events, as we will see later, are often presented by the media as examples of moral disintegration. The reporting of the Bulger case suggested that a new level of moral degeneracy, which was a threat to society, had been reached. Moreover, the reporting of the case led to 'parents everywhere asking themselves and their friends if the Mark of the Beast might not be imprinted on their offspring'. At the end of the trial, the judge described the two defendants as 'wicked and cunning' and as having 'committed acts of unparalleled evil and barbarity' (The Times, 24 November 1993, cited in Muncie, 1999b, quoting from The Times, 24 November 1993).

The dangers posed by terrorism have existed over a long period. The activities of the Bader Meinhof group during the 1970s, of the IRA in Northern Ireland and on the British mainland over the last 30 years, and the current activities of ETA in Spain have generated dangers of apparently unimaginable proportions. Each outrage seems more shocking than the last, both in its scale and its ferocity.

Development of the concept of risk

The term 'risk' is a concept which developed in the sixteenth and seventeenth centuries and was first coined by the early western explorers. The word was assimilated into the English language through its usage in Spanish and Portuguese, and referred to sailing in unchartered waters. Risk, then, originally had a spatial connotation. Later, risk became more closely associated with the temporal when it came to be used by business and commerce (Giddens, 1991). The term was then widened to refer to other situations of uncertainty. Some traditional cultures had no need of the concept (Douglas, 1992).

Elderidge (1999) has shown how the founding fathers of sociology were, in their own ways, concerned with questions related to risk. Marx drew attention to the instabilities and misery created by the capitalist mode of production. The consequences of the Industrial Revolution brought new risks as the population became urbanised and worked with often dangerous machinery. Durkheim was concerned with the danger of society disintegrating as an over-emphasis on economic development led to the breakdown of moral regulation. Weber analysed risks that were associated with the growth of bureaucratic organisations which emerged as a result of industrialisation.

The anticipation and prevention of danger has now given rise to an industry of risk assessors and risk analysts. Ewald (1991) noted that rather than notions of danger, risk should be more closely associated with chance, hazard, probability, eventuality and randomness on the one hand, and loss and damage on the other.

The rise of an increasing societal concern with uncertainty has resulted in the development of a 'risk community' emanating from government, industry, trade unions, the public and their representatives (McQuaid, 1998; Beck, in Adam et al., 2000b). From this position, the 'risk community' appears to comprise almost the total population. The evaluation of risk is now a multidimensional continuum, ranging from the acceptable to the unacceptable. Risk, according to Colledge and Stimpson (1997), exists in basic configurations of given circumstances. A risk is said to exist when an individual is in the presence of a definable physical agent with a known effect, for example, radiation. Risk also exists when a society elects to take a course of action while knowing there are risks involved. The pre-emptive declaration of war on the basis of a risk to the safety of the nation in itself constitutes a risk. Risk can also be seen when the specific dangers of a particular environment become known, whether this is the pollution of heavily urbanised area or the dangers of a remote wilderness. Risk also exists where there is uncertainty about the acceptability of social activities and specified illnesses, as in the case of cigarette smoking and the socially accepted use of alcohol (Colledge and Stimpson,

1997). Lupton emphasises the manner in which risks are socially constructed. She describes risks not as realities lying outside, but as 'assemblages of meanings, logics and beliefs around material phenomena giving phenomena form and substance' (Lupton, 1999a: 30).

Risk has taken on differentiated meanings that are used in both moral and political discourse.

Risk as a negative force

Risk carries an added, more negative meaning, which is 'beyond danger':

> Descriptions of risk are typically stated in terms of the likelihood of harm or loss from a hazard, and usually include identification of what is at risk and may be harmed or lost (e.g. health of human beings or an ecosystem, personal property, quality of life, ability to carry on an economic activity); the hazard that may occasion this loss; and a judgment about the likelihood that harm will occur. (National Research Council, 1996; see also Gostin, 2000)

Risk, in this sense, is concerned with the likelihood of mass exposure to physical or psychological harm, as distinct from the danger and hazard to an individual. Thus, if one takes aviation as an example, the danger lies in the very nature of the technologically based activity, which defies gravitational pull. Modern air travel involves the danger of many tons of metal flying through the atmosphere at high altitudes carrying hundreds of people, powered by potential kerosene bombs. The risk lies in the remote possibility that, given the congruence of circumstances or human error, the machine may fall out of the sky, creating loss of life on a huge scale.

This pessimistic view of risk is reflected in Lupton and Tulloch's empirical study of risk perception. They found that participants in their study tended to categorise risk in negative terms: 'The emotions of fear and dread were associated with interpretations of risk as danger of the unknown' (Lupton and Tulloch, 2002: 325).

Some conceptions of risk are negative to the point where they merge with the notion of hazard. An important distinction needs to be made between the two. A hazard can be defined as an agent of harm, for example HIV. The perceived risk is the subjective estimate that exposure to the hazard will be harmful (Ferguson et al., 2001).

Risk as a positive force

Although most people appear to experience risk in negative terms, risk can be presented from a more positive position. Giddens (1998) is not alone in arguing that active risk-taking is a core element in the creation of a dynamic economy and innovative society. As well as deriving its dominance from links with danger, risk has also been characterised as the driving force behind global capitalist development, a dynamic positive force for good, and a prerequisite to participation in a technologically based global era. Those who advocate risk from this position claim that the development of western society has been based upon risk. The age of exploration, which began in fifteenth-century Italy, Spain, England and Portugal, and continues to this day, would not have occurred without a propensity to risk. Zey (1998: 313) argues that Christopher Columbus actually represents the prototypical risk-taker. Motivated by both his vision of a round earth, and the need to establish a trading route with the Indies, Columbus spent the better part of his life convincing the world that he was correct. Zey goes on to argue that the propensity to take risks underwrote scientific endeavour in the eighteenth and nineteenth centuries. This spirit of adventurous risk, he argues, is reflected in the work of quantum physicists and genetic engineers.

In an article in the journal *Business*, entitled '10 Risks Businesses Must Take To Succeed', entrepreneurs are warned: 'Of course, you could just sit back and employ a risk-free strategy, but then you'd always be wondering what could have happened. Risks are what makes the difference between just another company and an industrial player' (*Business*, 2001: 19). The article goes on to describe the key risks which businesses must take so as not to stand still. These include investment in technology, forming alliances with other businesses, investment in customer care, being prepared to fail, stretching the business to find new ways of trading, talking to competitors, decentralising power within a business which is already leading the market, and taking radical strategy decisions.

Taking risks can also be culturally acceptable, as when children 'take dares' or people parachute for charity (Green, 1997). From this position, risk becomes a driving force for change in a world where anything may happen. Risk-taking reflects the undying and heroic quest to create wealth.

Some commentators, writing from an individualist position, have argued that particular risks are essential in creating a desired social identity and consumption patterns. The association with risk can make a particular occupation appear attractive (Kikbusch, 1988; Bunton and Burrows, 1995; Green, 1997). The question as to why certain risky occupations, such as flying for the Air Force, attract such large numbers of applicants is debatable. This could be associated with the intrinsic pleasure derived from flying (Jones, 1986). Other explanations include the manner in which professional risk-taking is portrayed in the media as heroic. Civil aviation is still an experience which is associated with hedonism and risk.

Conclusion

In attempting to understand risk, it is important to make a distinction between what is real and what is possible. In other words, risk represents a world state in which there is a conjunction between uncertainty of outcome and human concerns about outcome (Rosa, 1998). Uncertainty can be seen as a state of mind resulting from a process of assessment of a number of alternative predictions of the future. Uncertainty is the product of a form of 'computation' based upon existing knowledge and new information (Bradac, 2001). Contemporary notions of risk appear to contain an illusory searching to conquer uncertainty itself. The certainty of security in all aspects of experience appears now to be a desirable and marketable commodity.

Further reading

P. Slovik's *The Perception of Risk* (Earthscan, 2000) provides an excellent introduction to the manner in which risk can be understood. Deborah Lupton's *Risk* (Routledge, 1999a) has some excellent background to the development of the concept of risk. Boyne's book, also entitled *Risk* (Open University Press, 2003), contains an excellent section on risk and uncertainty. Peter Bernstein's remarkable book, *Against the Gods: The Remarkable Story of Risk* (John Wiley, 1996), traces the concept of risk from the Greeks through the role of the dice in 1200 to the technologically created contradictions of the mid-1990s. Not only is this book well researched, but it is also eminently readable. Frank Furedi's *Culture of Fear* (Cassel, 1998) examines society's fear of taking risks.

TWO   Theoretical Positions

Outline

As risks become complex and unknowable, the formalised systems for assessing and managing them become more pervasive. Although the dominant definition of risk in contemporary society adheres to a positivistic notion of validity, risk theory presents often competing ideas as to what constitutes risk. The differentiated forms of discourse, which have been developed in relation to risk, are based upon a number of theoretical positions. So much material, both empirical and theoretical, now exists on risk that it has become possible to make conceptual distinctions between the various approaches that have been taken. This chapter examines ideas about risk from a number of positions. Individualistic, culturalist, phenomenological and regulationist perspectives will be examined. Explanations based upon the 'risk society' thesis and governmentality will also be discussed. Writers from all positions recognise that risks are variable in origin and format. This chapter will also consider some of the problems that have been identified with the models of risk.

'Ideal types' and approaches to risk

Attempts have been made to characterise the different theoretical approaches to risk. Lupton (1999a) has developed theoretical matrices, which distinguish between differing levels of risk discourse, usefully identifying three broad epistemological positions. Whereas 'Realists' define risk as an objective hazard, which exists independent of other social and cultural forms of social action, 'weak constructionists' conceptualise risk in terms of an objective reality mediated through social and cultural processes. A third 'strong constructionist' or 'poststructuralist' position, in which risk is socially and politically contingent upon 'ways of seeing' the social world, also emerges. This position concentrates more closely on the nature of the discourses which construct ideas about risk (Foucault, 1965, 1972). All these models, as Lupton points out, are highly differentiated and constitute ideal types, each position encompassing an enormous range of theoretical terrain. Weber described an ideal type as a:

> ... one-sided accentuation of one or more points of view and by the synthesis of a great many diffuse, discrete, more or less present and occasionally absent individual phenomena, which are arranged according to those one-sidedly emphasised viewpoints into a unified analytical construct. In its conceptual purity, this mental construct cannot be found empirically anywhere in reality. (Weber, 1949: 90)

The views of risk presented in this chapter are not descriptions of what exists in reality, but an aid to interpretation and explanation (Lee and Newby, 1981). Nevertheless such ideal typifications of risk form an important starting point in assisting in understanding the vast and complex theoretical literature which has emerged over the last 30 years with respect to risk. What follows in this chapter is a development of these ideas, which are more closely associated with specific social practices. This chapter explores a number of possible ways of viewing risk from six perspectives (see Table 2.1). Some of the frameworks described here contain overlapping elements. It is therefore important to distinguish between prevailing populist notions of risk and differences in approach reflected in risk theory. Although the theoretical positions described below may be viewed as 'ideal typical', they will serve to demonstrate the tensions and contradictions that characterise discourses of risk.

The individualist position

The justification for making an attempt to individualise and quantify the likelihood of specific risk from an individualist position simply is that index-aided risk decisions are more accurate than unaided judgements (Gottfredson and Gottfredson, 1986). Index linked risks relate particular situations to the likelihood of undesirable things happening. Thus in the field of education, the number of children who can be supervised by one teacher on school trips is linked to a number of factors. The age, ability, and number of children, and previous experience of teachers all form part of an index of risk factors which are used to decide upon an appropriate teacher/pupil ratio. More supervision is required for situations engaging in outside school activities which are deemed risky (ROSPA, 2004). In the event of anything going wrong in the activities of governments

Table 2.1 Theoretical positions and risk

	Theoretical base	Definers of risk	Policy implications	Explanation of emergence of risk	Criticisms of position
Individualist position	Probability theory Cognitive psychology Engineering actuarialism	Qualified experts	Need for individual risk assessments to be structured into institutional activities	Risk is an independent variable	Socially and culturally decontextualised
Culturalist position	Social anthropology Structural functionalism Social constructionism	Ideas about risk and danger are culturally created by communities	Policies must take account of cultural understandings of risk	Objective reality is mediated through political need for a forensic approach to risk	Static structural functionalism Too little attention is paid to future social developments
Phenomenological position	Phenomenology	Individual construction	Strategic intervention is required in relation to phenomena designated as constituting highly relevant risk, e.g. AIDS/HIV	Cognitive events produce a recipe for risk management	Can be used for the purposes of analysis only
Risk society position	Risk society High modernity	Experts	Third Way combination of private with public State should provide protection against risks according to need Socially inclusive to reduce risks	Emergence of traditional and post-traditional society High modernity Reflexivity	Essentialised over-emphasis on risk

(Continued)

Table 2.1 (Continued)

	Theoretical base	Definers of risk	Policy implications	Explanation of emergence of risk	Criticisms of position
Postmodern position	Poststructuralism Postmodernity Governmentality	Experts	Increased use of surveillance to govern individuals and aggregate population groups	The tendency to deconstruct the subject, and the creation of calculable heterogeneous elements which constitute risk	There is an over-concentration on deconstructing what exists and an under-emphasis of the real risks
Regulatory position	Systems Organisational theory	Bureaucrats Politicians Media	Creation of systematic mapping and describing of risks	Differentiated causation, including natural, social and manufactured	There is an over-emphasis on systems Decontextualisation

and public or private organisations, there appear to be no institutionalised blame-avoidance mechanisms. Scientific risk analysis can be seen as providing a barrier between hazard and blame. This has given rise to the emergence of a new semi-profession of risk assessment managers, and the adoption of numerous anticipatory risk procedures that are designed to ensure that every effort has been made by the organisation to avoid a known potential risk. Such an approach to risk has considerable global credence, which appears to link explanation, and the moral imperative of risk, with prevention. It also has the virtue of being easy to understand and is built upon empirical research rather than theory.

All six theoretical positions described in Table 2.1 emphasise the predominance of individualised quantitative forms of risk assessment. Those adhering to an individualistic position operate on the basis that the likelihood of risk can be calculated by measuring a number of predetermined disposing factors.

Box 2.1   Risk and probability

Risk is:

> The probability that a particular adverse event occurs during a stated period of time, or results from a particular challenge. As a probability in the sense of statistical theory risk obeys all the formal laws of combining probabilities. (The Royal Society, 1992: 2)

The definition of risk in Box 2.1 reflects the dominant positivistic notion of validity. This popular conception contrasts with 'risk theory', in which different perspectives compete. Risks from this position are usually regarded as being multifactorial, each factor having a potential weighting which can be calculated. It then becomes possible to develop a form of risk assessment which indicates the likelihood of a particular number of circumstances accumulating to create danger and hazard to an individual group or aggregate population. Likelihoods of danger are measured, and in some cases predicted by experts. Individualised risk assessments draw most heavily on positivistic science and the disciplines which are derivative of natural sciences. Evidence to assist in the prediction of risk can be drawn from statistics, natural science, physics, chemistry, biology, geology and engineering. Individualised risk theorists also utilise the harder social sciences, like psychology, economics, and empirical quantitative studies of social phenomenon. Central to the individualist position is the idea that it is possible to calculate the probability of risk. Drawing on the hypothetico-deductive method, risk can be located in particular scenarios in which independent variables are concrete and statistically measurable. Those at risk are both autonomous actors and members of aggregate populations.

This approach to risk has affected the way in which the insurance industry assesses risks. According to Ewald (1991), insurantial risk has three characteristics. First, risk is calculable. For an event to be a risk it must be possible to establish the regularity of certain events, and the like-lihood of that event occurring. Secondly, risk is a collective concept in that it only becomes calculable when the likelihood of a particular event occurring is calculated with respect to a population. Lastly, risk is capital in that 'what is insured is not the injury that is actually lived, suffered and resented by the person it happens to, but as capital against whose loss the insurer offers a guarantee' (Ewald, 1991: 204). One does not replace a close relative or a limb. The insurer offers compensation for the loss. For Ewald, insurance represents an attempt to master time and discipline the future, and is not resignation to fate.

Through the incorporation of individualist forms of analysis, it becomes possible to assess risks in a manner which is based upon probability and 'science'.

Some writers in the area of risk have attempted to be more quantita-tively accurate when approaching risk. Drawing on the writings of the Reverend Thomas Bayes, MacDonald and MacDonald (1999) offer a clear account of what to many can be a bewilderingly complicated formulation. In essence, like Bayes, MacDonald and MacDonald argue that beliefs about risk should be modified by information about the world. The kernel notion depends upon taking some expression of our beliefs about an unknown quantity before the data is available (our prior probabilities) and modifying them in the light of that data to arrive at our posterior proba-bilities. MacDonald and MacDonald argue that presenting probabilities should be regarded in terms of 'odds'. Thus if the probability of a horse winning a race is 0.75, in other words three quarters, a losing probability or risk of losing is 0.25 or one quarter. The odds or probability of winning are three to one (MacDonald and MacDonald, 1999).

Individualised risk and blame

Box 2.2   Risk assessment

Risk Assessment is:

The process of identifying hazards which may cause an accident, disaster or harm. (Manthorpe, 2000: 298)

Individualised risk assessment has become a managerial device to both avoid and apportion blame. The outline of risk assessments in relation to educational (school) trips signifies that the managing authority has done everything to ensure safety. Any risk which then occurs becomes an unforeseen risk, which could not have been envisaged by the education authority. Blame can then be apportioned elsewhere, for example, as incompetence on the part of the individual teacher. The reliance on universal truths about the nature and possibility of calculating risks is well suited to the needs of managers and governments (Castel, 1991; Luhman, 1991). All accidents have to be attributable to an individual or organisation (Douglas, 1992). Risk and the imagined ability to calculate risk can also represent a powerful impetus to the expansion of managerial activities.

Clark and Newman (1997: 152) argue that, managerially, risk constitutes 'an imperialist logic of its own which turns the problems of the new organisational settlement into opportunities for its own enlargement'.

Following Douglas, Kemshall (1997) links the seemingly endless expansion of individualised risk assessment to a 'blame-laden culture' in which organisations and individuals who are responsible for assessing risks attempt to protect themselves from potential litigation. Risk procedures are thus seen by managers of organisations as replacing professionally based judgements (Kemshall et al., 1997). Crucially, for Douglas, individualistic perceptions of risk also fail to explain why some phenomena are regarded as risky while others are not.

The over-dependence and unchallenged organisational dependency on risk assessments can result in punitiveness if linked to the ascription of blame. Risk assessments of an individualised kind also have the potential to disempower sometimes vulnerable individuals. Clear and Cadora (2001: 55) argue that: 'In instances where risk instruments are now used, they clarify, standardise, and objectify the criteria for judgements previously made on the basis of the raters' own opinions and skills'.

The voice of the service user, patient, client or customer can become smothered within a swathe of quantified and standardised risk assessments designed to protect them. Socio-legal scholars concerned with the erosion of human rights have also criticised individualised notions of risk assessment. Concerns about the unsafe society have now displaced concerns about equality. Regarding contemporary moral panics, Hudson (2001: 159) argues:

Contemporary events show us – if we need to be shown – that events such as the German extermination of the Jews cannot be looked at as one-off aberrations. There may be differences in scale and scope but the instinct to describe the stranger, who may simultaneously be one's neighbour, as a dangerous alien other is strong and ever-present.

Risk assessments emanating from the individualist position do not have due regard or the conceptual apparatus to consider wider structurally based risks, which involve discrimination against particular groups. Racial differences are particularly important here given that black defendants in court can be at greater risk of earlier incarceration as a result of the subjective interpretations of events by criminal justice personnel (Denney, 1992). Comparative criminological evidence suggests that these risks of institutionalised discrimination are global in proportion (Ontario Commission, 1995).

Knowledge and perceptions of individualised risk

Often, the more recent the information relating to the risk, the more bias is introduced into the judgement processes. Recent occurrences tend to distort the perception of the scale of the danger. Accidents which occur with great frequency are judged by the general population to cause as many deaths as disease globally. In fact, the opposite is the case since disease causes 16 times as many deaths as accidents. The most over-estimated causes of death include all accidents, pregnancy, childbirth, abortion, flood, tornadoes, cancer, fire and homicide. Individuals also have a propensity to believe that they are personally immune from risky events. The 'it won't happen to me' phenomenon applies to many individuals when they drive a motorcar or smoke a cigarette. The most under-estimated causes of death include smallpox vaccination, diabetes, lightning, stroke, tuberculosis, asthma and emphysema (Colledge and Stimpson, 1997).

Dimensions of risk and the danger of oversimplification

Individual risk perception does not fall along a unidimensional continuum from low risk to high risk. Slovic (1987) describes variations in individual's perceptions of the dimensions of risk. First, so-called 'dread risks' are perceived as being uncontrollable and possibly resulting in death. The second form of risk is described as the 'unknown risk' and has three essential elements: it is perceived as being observable; it has an immediate effect; and it is known to science. DNA technology fulfils these criteria because it is observable and known to science while also having an immediate impact.

Individualist studies of risk concentrate on the manner in which knowledge of risk is perceived. Ferguson (2001) has concluded that the relationship between knowledge and risk perception is complex. There are two forms of knowledge used by individuals when they assess risk: there is raw knowledge, which is what people know; and there is 'calibrated knowledge', which refers to what people think they know about a risk (Ferguson, 2001). It is the latter that will tend to guide individual action.

Young (1999) argues that an actuarial approach in calculating risk is not concerned with probabilities or justice, but with harm minimisation. Risk management has created a series of 'gated havens in a hostile world' (Young, 1999: 6). Mary Douglas, one of the most outspoken critics of this mode of risk analysis, also takes up the theme of over simplicity (Douglas, 1992). In much of his writing, Beck recognises that an individualistic approach is necessary to risk analysis, in that scientific measurement and observation are required if the existence of risks are to be acknowledged. Like Douglas, Beck sees the weakness of individualised risk assessment as failing to take account of how scientific objectivity is situated in cultural and political contexts. Beck argues that nuclear, chemical and genetic technology makes actuarial calculation of risks extremely complex. It is now impossible to understand the nature of many of the risks that human beings face either individually or collectively (Beck, 1992).

There are thus numerous difficulties in approaching risk from an individualist position and always a danger of reducing the complexity of risk to unsubstantiated certainty. The idealised risk assessment paradigm avoids some complex questions. The importance of individualist forms of risk assessments appears now to have an unprecedented dominance within society. Such assessments are attractive to various arms of the media, which are able to dramatise risk by associating it with a particular individual, group or isolated social situation. Each risk can be conceptualised as being unique and unrelated to any other. Risks can be presented as possessing their own individual complexities, which can be best understood through the application of exhaustive probability calculations. The specific nature and the promise of scientific success in predicating and possibly reducing risk have made individualised risk assessments attractive to government and non-governmental organisations and social institutions. Individualised risk assessments provide individuals and organisations with an illusion of security. Many organisations are now required to undertake risk assessments in an attempt to avoid and control risks. The application of individualised risk assessments are fundamental to the operation of commercial and public organisations. Everything has to be done to ensure protection from potential hazard through standardised procedures which are routinely carried out. Within commerce, the emerging profession of risk manager marks the establishment of a role in helping an organisation to manage business risk. In medicine, individualised risk assessments are made to identify how specific predisposing factors can form the basis for the creation of a professional opinion. Social welfare risk assessments form an important part of the care of children, older people and the mentally ill.

The culturalist position

Mary Douglas has made one of the most significant contributions to studies of risk over the last four decades. Her work has been variously characterised as constituting an anthropological or 'culturally-based' approach to risk. Her early writing focuses upon bodily rituals (Douglas, 1966). Here, Douglas argues that rituals of cleanliness, which are related to the body, can be viewed as creating order out of chaos. Her study of the Coorgs, a Hindu caste, suggests that this group police their own bodies in a manner that is reflected in the fear they experience in dealing with the outside world. *Risk Acceptability According to the Social Sciences* (Douglas, 1985) and *Risk and Culture* (Douglas and Wildavsky, 1982) have both been influential in the creation of a framework for understanding risk in contemporary society. In these works, Douglas focuses upon the impossibility of a form of analysis which does not take into account the uniqueness of the community in which the perceived risk occurs. Each community is typified by forms of authority, commitment, boundaries and structures that determine the manner in which risk is constructed and acted upon.

Douglas separates herself from individualistic interpretations by insisting that risk is not an objective, measurable concept, but is socially, culturally and politically constructed. Drawing on the functionalist approach taken by Durkheim, Douglas argues that societies, like bodies, have entrances and exits that embody the idea of internality, externality, and boundary. The complexities of the body, with each having its different but interrelated functioning parts, can be used as a way of understanding how human societies operate (Douglas, 1966). Douglas demonstrates how the margins of the body can be perceived as marking the point at which potential barriers to danger can be broken down. Risk can be seen as the equivalent to being sinned against, since it implies being vulnerable to the events caused by others. Instead of isolating risk as a technical problem, Douglas argues that the moral and political implications need to be considered. Whereas the language of sin appeals to a religious authority, the language of risk, for Douglas, appeals to the authority of scientific experts and what Wilkinson (2001a: 4) has referred to as the 'prophetic powers of modern rationality'. The theoretical framework in which risk is analysed needs to transcend the culture in which risks occur (Douglas, 1992).

Douglas has suggested that risk can also be seen in terms of what she calls 'grid' and 'group' indices. The grid group indices represent and explain the barriers that people have created around themselves and the outside world. 'Grid' describes a situation in which there is strong agreement on the meaning and scope of risk (Douglas, 1973). Hargreaves Heap and Ross (1992: 9) describe grid as: 'The set of rules which govern individuals in their personal interactions. Strong or "high" grid means strongly defined roles which provide a script for individual interaction. Towards the weak end of the axis, the public signals of rank and status fade and ambiguity enters relationships'. Grid therefore, represents a form of restriction which results from social stratification as between, for example, men and women.

The term 'group' refers to the amount of control over risk an individual can exert within a system. It is:

> The extent to which an individual's interactions are confined within a specific group of people who form a sub-group within the larger community. Where group is strong there is a clear boundary between members and non-members, and though it may be possible for an individual to leave the group, that will have high costs in that membership of the group confers many benefits. As a result, members of the group are able to exert considerable pressure on the individual to conform to its requirements. (Hargreaves et al., 1992: 9)

Grid and group represent a taxonomy of cultures that assist in an understanding of how an individual's experience can impact on the way in which risk is perceived. A market-led society can be classified as low grid/low group since in such a society an individual has few constraints and individual freedom is highly valued. A hierarchical society can be characterised as high grid/high group since individuals in such a society experience constraint, while the regulations surrounding social actions are also highly defined and regulated. Douglas also argues that some societies are low grid/high group, as is the case in communes and therapeutic communities, whereas high grid/low group represents societies where those who are excluded from all groups have restricted opportunities for social interactions, for example, older people in some societies can be described in these terms (Hargreaves et al., 1992).

The articulation of grid and group helps determine how individuals within particular cultural sub-systems perceive accidents and dangers. Where both grid and group are strong, and there is a high degree of consensus about norms, then disease and accidents are attributable to moral factors or the general metaphysical scheme of life (Green, 1997). When grid and group are weak, there is little consensus as to what constitutes risk.

Lupton (1999b) has combined grid and group with respect to risk. She argues that four ideal types can be identified.

1　A hierarchical group (high grid/high group) shows respect for authority and conforms to the dominant norms in a society.

2　Egalitarians are characterised by low grid/high group and tend to identify with the group holding outsiders responsible for risk.

3　Individualists with low grid/low group characteristics are individualistic and entrepreneurial, wishing to regulate risk themselves. They also see the positive benefits of taking risks, often in profit-making terms.

4　Fatalists (high grid/low group) are those whose approach to risk lacks any affiliation to group. Fatalists will tend to trust in fate or luck. If hazards are present in the social world, there is very little an individual can do to control them.

Like Giddens and Beck, Douglas takes cognisance of globalisation, arguing that risk has now acquired a new prominence, serving the 'forensic needs' of a global culture. Globally, the language of risk combines abstractness with a 'scientific' authenticity, endowing the concept of risk with an aura of assumed objectivity. However, the global development of objectified, quantifiable assessments runs contrary to the idea of risk being grounded in cultural sub-systems, as described by Douglas. Thus, for Douglas, risk is not a neutral, measurable term, as suggested by those who subscribe to individualist ideas about risk. Rather, risk serves a particular function within the community at a particular time. Risk cannot be isolated from the moral, aesthetic and political foundations of a community. Instead of isolating the risk as a technical problem, Douglas argues that we should formulate, so as to include however crudely, its moral and political implications (Douglas, 1992: 51).

For Douglas, political issues arise when risk is used to apportion responsibility. The more culturally individualised a society becomes, the more significant becomes the forensic potential of risk. Risk becomes a mechanism for holding individuals to account within a culture of risk (Kemshall, 2000). Risk thus becomes central to the process of accountability and the production of blame trails. Wynne (1992) has argued in similar terms that definitions, knowledge and responses to uncertainty are ultimately based upon the maintenance of familiar identities.

Limitations of the culturalist model

This model, although immensely influential in academic circles, has had little influence in practical political terms. This may have resulted in the work of Douglas being subject to less scrutiny than the dominant individualised scientism described above. Some have argued that Douglas approaches the question of risk from a static position which could stem from a structural functional starting point in understanding the relationship between culture and risk. This is particularly true of the grid group indices which locate individuals within fairly rigid categories. Wilkinson (2001a) has argued that individual experiences of social processes like risk are unclear and often contradictory. Any approach which attempts to oversimplify the complexity of risk perception by placing experience within rigid categories obfuscates understanding of the day-to-day reality of risk. It has also been suggested that Douglas appears to give little attention to how conceptions of risk might change in the future. She is more cognisant of environmental and structural issues such as poverty in her analysis (Lupton, 1999a).

Lupton also argues that the other danger in Douglas's work is that it has been incorporated into the conceptualisations of individualist risk experts. Douglas's writings have shown how cultural and political pressures taint lay perceptions of risk. Others have, according to Lupton, used Douglas's work to suggest that the state should not attempt to impose its views of risk reduction, given the subjective nature of risk assessment. Lupton has suggested that Douglas's position on risk seems to reflect a conservative approach, on occasions making global businesses appear like victims: 'In representing industry and big business as singled out as scapegoats and inappropriately blamed for risk, Douglas may herself be criticised for failing to recognise the cultural underpinnings of these institutions' (Lupton, 1999a: 57).

Rosa has argued that Douglas, in her famous work with Wildavsky (1982), does not distinguish between the world of ontology and the epistemology of risk. Ontology concerns the belief that human beings have in the continuance of their own identity and capacity for social action (Giddens, 1990). Ontology is concerned with the way in which people make sense of their own being and existence within the world. The reappearance of the sun each morning is a form of ontological security for human beings. For some prescientific societies an eclipse of the sun represented a threat to their security (Jaeger et al., 2001). Epistemology refers to the way in which individuals and groups of individuals come to understand and know risks. This results in Douglas and Wildavsky conceptualising risks in collective terms, which are too broad. In post-traditional societies, Rosa has described a dualism in the perceptions of the way in which risk is understood. Risk is inextricably linked to the notion of fate and probability. Both are important in considering how individuals and organisations make judgements about risks. The failure of Douglas to recognise such dualism camouflages the distinction between modern and traditional societies. For Rosa, this places culturalists like Douglas and Wildavsky at an extreme relativistic end of a risk continuum, with positivistic, individualised risk assessment at the other. This could make culturalists almost oblivious to the reality of real risk (Rosa, 1998).

Some work in the area of race relations has suggested that an over-emphasis on culture can serve to de-politicise racism and discrimination (Bourne and Sivanandan, 1980). In a critique of culturalist discourse on HIV/AIDs in Africa, Seidel and Vidal (1997) have argued that culturalist discourse often fails to take account of the changing and innovatory prac-tices which are emerging in response to the disease. The effect of the overlapping arguments, and especially the culturalist discourse which constructs 'Africa' as incapable of change, including adapting to condom use, and which 'explains' this in terms of certain immutable 'cultural traits' and 'cultural facts', would seem to have a negative impact on international funding (Seidel and Vidal, 1997: 77).

Beck disagrees with the idea, ascribed to Douglas and Wildavsky (1982), that there are no substantive differences between dangers posed to individuals in early history and those experienced in later, more advanced societies. The only distinctions made by Douglas and Wildavsky (1982) according to Beck, are located within the cultural domain. Cultural per-ceptions of danger have changed while the dangers remain the same.

True and important though this view may be, it is still not satisfactory. For, among other things, we know that people in the Stone Age did not have the capacity for nuclear and ecological annihilation, and that the dangers posed by lurking demons did not have the same political dynamic as the man-made hazards of ecological self-destruction (Beck, 1996: 4).

It would be unfair to regard Douglas as engaging in a naïve anthropo-logical travelogue that distances her from the reality of structural inequality. Her work incorporates a critical analysis of risk in historical, political and cultural terms. Significantly, other major figures within the study of risk, like Beck, do not fully consider the approach taken by Douglas, although he owes much to her theoretical groundwork.

The phenomenological position

Drawing on the work of phenomenologists like Alfred Schutz (1964), attempts have been made to develop an alternative account of risk based upon phenomenology. Schutz drew a fundamental distinction between two bases for social action. At one level there are routinised activities, while other forms of social action are based upon calculated action. This distinc-tion represents the extremes of possible actions across a continuum. Bloor (1995), drawing on the work of Schutz, has constructed what he refers to as a system of 'relevancies' to assist understanding of 'risk behaviour'.

Phenomenological approaches analyse routinised practices of risk behaviour. The model outlined by Bloor also usefully focuses upon a sequence of cognitive events that lead to a 'recipe' for risk management

Box 2.3 Phenomenological approach to risk (adapted from Bloor, 1995: 26)

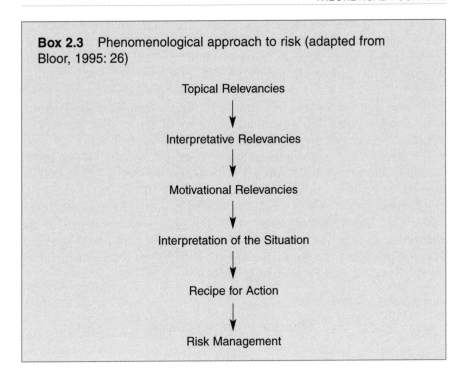

Topical Relevancies

↓

Interpretative Relevancies

↓

Motivational Relevancies

↓

Interpretation of the Situation

↓

Recipe for Action

↓

Risk Management

(see Box 2.3). However, it can provide no more than the beginnings of the creation of a conceptual framework which some might argue is far removed from how risks are experienced in the social world. From a phenomenological standpoint, it is not the task of the sociologist to ascertain what is real. Schutz (1964), one of phenomenology's most ardent proponents, argued that perceptions of the world are socially constructed. Meanings are constructed socially with other individuals. Phenomena, in this case risk, are real, that is, they are defined as real through social interaction. One of the major problems here is that although risk may be over- or understated, risk has a reality which is becoming more pervasive.

Topical relevance determines whether or not a situation is problematic for an individual. Interpretative relevancies constitute the individuals knowledge, which can be drawn upon to understand the situation. This cognitive process will often involve an attempt to compare past situations with a potentially risky situation which presents itself. Once the interpretation of the relevance of an event has occurred, a number of possible strategies for action may have been evolved. At each stage of this process of the development of 'intrinsic topical relevancies' volition and constraint are conceptually separated. Relevancies are differentiated from this theoretical position. Bloor's 'intrinsic topical relevancies' are situations defined as being problematic on the basis of selection by the subject. Imposed topical relevancies are situations which are rendered problematic by the actions and interpretations of others. Bloor does not claim that this approach does anything more than provide an 'heuristic framework for the description of various diversities of risk practices and risk reduction' (Bloor, 1995: 27). Bloor does not present any predictive model of risk behaviour, but argues that this approach offers a form of analysis which focuses upon immediate situations where social action takes place. This approach encourages a concentrated focus upon what he refers to as 'automatic activity' and 'rational weighting of costs and benefits' (Bloor, 1995).

Bloor and others have applied the phenomenological approach to a number of contemporary sites of risk, including HIV/AIDs infection and the construction of risk in predictive testing of particular diseases (Bloor, 1995; Cox and McKellin, 1999). It is the least well developed of the theoretical approaches to risk. One of the major problems of this approach is that it provides the means whereby real risks can be socially constructed away (Gramling and Freudenberg, 1996).

The risk society position

Probably no one writer was more influential in the field of risk theory than Ulrich Beck. Although the idea of the 'risk society' cannot be ascribed to one contribution, Beck's *Risk Society: Towards a New Modernity* (1992), first published in German, has now been reprinted five times and has become a seminal text. *Risk Society* reflects a swathe of writing which seeks to demonstrate that at some point in the last 30 years, traditional capitalist societies have changed towards what has been variously characterised as 'late modernity', 'postmodernity' or the 'post-traditional society'. In order for societies to develop they must become more reflexive. Reflexivity is already becoming visible in the critique of science, which is developing in the Green movement and in other areas of social life (Lash and Wynne, 1992).

Beck argues that in the 1960s and 1970s, welfare and an increased access to education produced the emergence of the language of rights. Many of the criticisms which resulted from rights-based perspectives were directed towards technology. Global anti-nuclear protests also developed at this time. The environmental movement, which drew attention to the global risks created by technology, emerged partly in response to these changes (Beck, 2001).

Table 2.2 shows the major changes which characterised the transition from traditional to post-traditional social formations. In the traditional society, processes of socialisation were partially unconscious, due to the power of old role models which are no longer dominant. Traditional values

Table 2.2 Movement from traditional to post-traditional society

	Traditional	Post-traditional
Values	Universal	Atomised
Professional knowledge	Distinction between lay and professional	Competing expert systems of knowledge
Political control	Minimal	Centralised incompetence in the face of increased danger

also tended to be universally applicable. In the post-traditional society, values become more atomised and fragmented, while the distinction between lay and professional becomes less defined. Although lay people are forced to be reliant on experts, there is a growing understanding that experts often disagree and make errors when calculating risk. Lay people see science and industry as producing the risks about which they are concerned. Individuals constantly seek to come to terms with uncertainty through the application of a form of rationality based upon science. Concomitantly, science no longer has any privileged claim to rationality since the critics of science come from outside and within itself. Despite the reliance on a logic based upon technology, uncertainty now forms the basis for the formation of a post-traditional society. Technology has resulted in the need to cope with risk situations which are different in character from those of the past.

In the traditional society, political control at both the cultural and the local level is institutionalised in the form of technical competence. This is seen in the form of governmental directives, law and administrative procedures. In the post-traditional society political control is more disjointed and fragmented. Beck also describes a change in values in the post-traditional society. In the traditional class society, ideas relating to the value of equality constituted a central dynamic, whereas in the post-traditional society safety becomes an overriding imperative guiding debates related to values. Beck argues that:

> The place of the value system of the 'unequal' society is taken by the value system of the 'unsafe' society. Whereas the utopia of equality contains a wealth of substantial and positive goals of social change, the utopia of the risk society remains peculiarly negative and defensive. Basically one is no longer concerned with attaining something 'good' but rather preventing the worst. (Beck, 1992: 49)

Beck argues that collective patterns of life, full employment and exploitation have now been undermined by five related processes. He lists these as globalisation, individualisation, the gender revolution, under-employment and global risks. For Beck, what all these processes have in common is that they are consequences of industrial modernisation. The political challenge is that society must respond to these challenges simultaneously (Beck, 1999).

What Beck refers to as radical modernisation undermines the foundations of the first modernity. Any notion of certainty collapses in a new kind of capitalism and a new global order. The speeding up of modernisation has produced a gap between quantifiable risks and unquantifiable risk. The new technology is releasing unpredictable and incommunicable consequences that can endanger life on earth (Beck, 2002a). Thus the distribution of risks has displaced conflict between social classes. According to Beck, the transition from traditional to post-traditional society has changed people's apprehension of risk. The post-traditional political economy transports risk out of the sphere of things that visit people through natural events and into the sphere of outcomes that are the result of collective conscious and unconscious decisions. Beck focuses upon the social interventions, including those made by professionals and politicians, which generate risks (Taylor-Gooby, 2000: 6). Consequently, in the post-traditional society, identifying who has responsibility for risk management and prediction becomes elusive as risk becomes politicised. As the impact of manufactured risk becomes pervasive, political incompetence and inactivity becomes widespread, raising the possibility that risks are no longer amenable to political intervention. Beck thus makes his distinctive contribution to ideas about risk based upon the debates surrounding social transformations. He describes a longer-term process that has been occurring in western societies over a period of 400 years from premodernity, through classical modernity, to reflexive modernity (Boyne, 2003).

The technisisation of risk also derives from the proliferation and omnipresence of technology. In the risk society individuals are waiting for the latest technological development to catch up with the negative consequences of the previous innovation. For Beck, the scientific institutions which symbolised progress have brought the planet to the point of near catastrophe (Wilkinson, 2001b).

Box 2.4   Risk and technology

In advanced modernity the social production of wealth is systematically accompanied by the social production of risks. Accordingly, the problems and conflicts relating to the distribution in a society of scarcity overlap with the problems and conflicts that arise from the production, definition and distribution of techno-scientifically produced risks. (Beck, 1992: 19)

Under these conditions, risk management becomes an impersonal quasi science which conceals a range of social and moral judgements. This challenges trust in governments and all forms of professional expertise. Beck defines risk in a way which, on first inspection, would appear to be simple, but when explored can be bewilderingly complex.

Box 2.5　Beck's definition of risk

Risk may be defined as a systematic way of dealing with hazards and insecurities induced and introduced by modernisation itself. (Beck, 1992: 21)

Boyne (2003) suggests that Beck identifies two kinds of risk. First, there are physical hazards that can destroy life. These would include radioactivity and toxins. Secondly, there are the social and cultural risks associated with marriage and childhood. Science is reflexive in that it both solves and produces problems. The results of scientific endeavour produce pollution, while also creating the potential to make the globe a cleaner, healthier place. In this situation the rationality of the scientist, technocrat and citizen collide (Dingwall, 2000). Beck describes reflexive modernisation in terms of changing patterns of social experiences in which old certainties provided by traditional institutions like the Church and the professions are being fundamentally challenged (Beck, 1998). Individuals in the risk society are required to make major decisions about employment education and self identity in a world in which beliefs about social class, gender, and the family are being overturned (Mythen, 2004). The individualised nature of these decisions creates new forms of risk which can act back upon themselves in a reflexive manner. For instance, making the decision to take up a university place in a situation in which students require substantial loans carries a long-term risk. The decision to go to university impacts on other life decisions over a longer period. Having a major debt may affect employment and housing possibilities after graduation. Equally the decision not to take up higher education may appear to be less risky in the short term, but may make an individual less employable if made redundant.

For Beck, the more knowledge that is available, the more it becomes possible to break down complex social actions into their constituent parts. This leads to a knowledge-dependent society, mediated through global reconstruction and the restructuring of social institutions (Beck, 1998).

Criticisms of Beck

Beck's writings have been enormously influential in defining the parameters of debates about risk. His work has theoretical offshoots into many areas, and it is difficult to think of a sociological text in the last two decades that has created as much controversy as *Risk Society* (1992). Beck has probably had more detractors than supporters, and criticising Beck has, in itself, become a significant sociological preoccupation.

One of the most common criticisms of his approach is that it fails to take full cognisance of the complexities of specific risk situations. An important feature of the 'risk society' thesis is that it is based upon a form of 'value consensus' which presupposes a shift from mass concerns about survival to those related to risk and insecurity. As with Giddens, Beck appears to assume that concerns about material poverty and discrimination in the western world have been replaced by insecurity and fear of new forms of risk. Beck's thinking has also influenced the development of a theoretical base for a 'new' approach to politics. This particularly applies to risk and 'third way' politics, where in the UK the ideas of Giddens in the late 1990s formed a significant backdrop to the development of policies. In Britain, 'Third Way' politics claims to address new risks created by technology, while combining social solidarity with a thriving and dynamic economy. 'Third Way' polices in the UK, and the new democratic principles which preceded the election of President Bill Clinton in the USA, appear to have been built on an assumption that individuals currently think of their lives in terms of managing uncertainty and danger, not major structural inequality. Although 'Third Way' politics emphasise the importance of developing strategies which will lead to greater social inclusivity, the idea of structural inequalities of any kind being symptomatic of present structural arrangements are presented as being outmoded (Jordan and Jordan, 2000).

Some commentators might find such a position difficult to recognise, given the continued existence of social divisions based upon race, class, gender and sexuality, and disability. Dingwall (2000) has argued that Beck appears to regard need as being an absolute rather than a relative concept. It is, he argues, too crude to equate need with subsistence. Elderidge (1999) regards Beck's emphasis on the instability of risk as misplaced, given the evidence of global suffering, genocide and torture.

Beck has also been challenged on historical grounds. O'Malley (2000) has argued that there is a danger in focusing too heavily on risk, which is but one aspect of the social world. Risk societies are contingent in their origins, and variable in format. It is dangerous to regard the current risk-conscious condition as the inevitable result of an historical logic. Risk has been uppermost in the minds of citizens and policy-makers throughout history. Impersonal and unobservable risks in the past, such as plagues, were global and striking all strata of society.

Beck has been regarded as being unduly pessimistic about risk. Lash and Wynne (1992) point out that Beck does not become as pessimistic as Weber or Foucault. Although Beck can assist in understanding the nature of some of the origins of the ascendancy of risk management, and the way in which the nature of risk has changed, his arguments have some limitations. Risk is not experienced in the same way by different groups of people in the community. The idea of a risk society fails to take into consideration the subtle differences in the way people experience and explain risk. 'Risk society' theories fail to capture the fluidity of risk, which is elusive and constantly changing its form (Brown, 2000). Some risks are knowable, understandable and predictable, while others are not. Underlying all these explanations of risks is a complex set of often conflicting ideas about the nature of human motivation. An attempt to reduce these distinctions to the emergence of a 'risk society' can lead to oversimplification. Given that the threat of risk is often overestimated, Luhmann (2000) has shown how the rhetoric of public protection is now greater than the real risk faced by individuals. Kemshall (1997, 2002) in a similar vein, argues that perceptions of risks, particularly in the area of crime, have been exaggerated.

The contribution of Giddens

Although Beck's name is most often used synonymously with the 'risk society' thesis, it is important to acknowledge that other theorists have made significant contributions from a similar viewpoint. Anthony Giddens (1990, 1994, 1998), in a number of influential publications, has developed ideas about risk along a similar theoretical trajectory to Beck. Giddens has argued that although the 'risk society' has its roots in a post-feudal Europe, it has in the twentieth century progressed to become more global (Giddens, 1991).

Both Giddens and Beck share a theoretical starting point in that they see risk as being central to the development of postmodern or post-traditional societies, although Giddens prefers the term 'high modernity' or 'late modernity' to characterise the changes which have occurred following the period of modernity. The notion of risk, for Giddens, comes into use in forward-looking societies. Traditional societies such as the Roman Empire or Chinese society trusted in fate and the will of the gods. The post-traditional society has replaced such beliefs with the far less certain world of risk. According to Giddens, one of the central features of high modernity is the uncertainty about truth, and claims to truth. This has been accompanied by a growing scepticism about the ability of experts to predict complex risks. These doubts, according to Giddens, increase mass anxiety (Giddens, 1991).

Although the work of Giddens and Beck share a number of common positions, their work on risk is distinctive. Giddens parts company with Beck when he distinguishes between external risks, which are created by tradition or nature, and manufactured risk. The latter is created by the impact of technology, science and a developing knowledge of the world. The present age, however, in essence, is no riskier or more dangerous than previous periods of history. Risks are now more likely to be manufactured (Giddens, 1994, 1998, 1999). Giddens also provides an analysis of risk that is in many respects more programmatic and more directly applied to the post-traditional world than the work of Beck. Consequently, Giddens has had far more influence on politicians, particularly in Britain, than has Beck.

Risk and governmentality

Although Michel Foucault did not specifically deal with the concept of risk in his writing, a number of writers have drawn upon his work with respect to risk. In *Discipline and Punish* (1977), Foucault analyses forms of state sovereignty based on the monarchy and absolute power. He contrasts this with what he refers to as disciplinary power, which is more pervasive and operates on individuals, not through coercive force, but through mundane, everyday activity. This approach to social regulation developed through the eighteenth century and by the nineteenth century, according to Foucault, required the formation of particular forms of governmental controlling interventions. During the nineteenth century risk became 'a kind of omnivorous, encyclopaedizing principle for the objectification of experience – not only the hazards of personal life and private venture, but also of the common venture of society' (Gordon, 1991: 38).

The success of nineteenth-century individualism and enterprise depended to some degree on the ability of the insurer to remove the risk. The development of such controlling forms of 'governmentality' came to constitute a rationality which dominated western political ideas by the twentieth century. The state became involved in the surveying and training of individuals to conform to norms which emphasised productivity. Governments involved themselves with irrigation, fertility, habits of acting, ways of thinking, crime and welfare (Foucault, 1972). Risk management forms an integral part of governmentality, incorporating modes of thinking through which the state claims to be working to protect the population from risk (Crawford, 2002b).

Box 2.6 The idea of governmentality

The main concerns of the governmentality school have been described as:

The shifting forms of rule traversing older boundaries between statutory, voluntary and commercial institutions in liberal politics, and the new ways in which populations are rendered thinkable, measurable, differentiated and sorted into hierarchies for the purposes of government. (Stenson and Edwards, 2001: 74)

In an influential essay, Castel (1991) has described the process whereby the subject is becoming almost indistinguishable from the risk. New preventative policies transform individuals into 'factors, statistical correlations of heterogeneous elements. They deconstruct the concrete subject of intervention, and reconstruct a combination of factors liable to produce risk. Their primary aim is not to confront a concrete dangerous situation, but to anticipate all possible forms of irruption of danger' (Castel, 1991: 288). Preventative strategies within the area of social policy are now dominated not by the individual subjects needing services provided by the state, but by combinations of 'factors' which have come to constitute risk assessment. This makes for the emergence of a new mode of surveillance, which focuses on risks faced by aggregate populations and not individuals. Such state activities are based upon the supposed possibility of using risk science as a basis for reducing harm occurring to civilians (Castel, 1991).

Unlike centralised state power, as reflected in the notion of the post-traditional society, a fracturing occurs between the state, the economy and social policy. One of the most important developments within this fracturing process has been the deconstruction of the subject. New policies of risk prevention in the areas of crime, health and welfare represent a transfer from the assessment of dangers posed by individuals, and the vulnerability of individuals to danger, towards statistical calculations of hazards based upon the probability of risk to entire communities. To be assessed as being at risk requires the individual to be located within a complex series of calculated probabilities. The control of these probabilities, and protection of individuals from risk, becomes the responsibility of interlocking agencies with varying levels of direct connection with the state.

The notion of 'governmentality' reflects a situation in which the state becomes increasingly concerned with the government of populations as an end in itself rather than the consolidation of state power. Through the government's desire to govern the conduct of individuals, a series of social practices are developed which subject individuals to particular modes of subjugation. People are either incited or invited to recognise and act upon their moral obligation. The avoidance of risk constitutes such a form of moral obligation.

Theories based upon governmentality have made an important contribution in understanding the relationship between risk and the development of new modes of mass surveillance. This approach raises the important possibility that risk is a convenient vehicle for creating a justification for increased and technologically sophisticated governance.

Technology has resulted in the need to cope with risk situations which are different in character from those of the past. Various forms of risk management, and the accompanying 'moral technology', form the basis for managerialised, scientifically based, risk assessment and management (Ewald, 1991).

The governmental position has gained less attention due to its emphasis on the importance of fragmentation. It is difficult to base any form of social practice upon this position. The expert is presented by governments and organisations, and often by individual themselves, as having an ability to understand danger, and so they are in a strong position to predict risk. This gives the expert and the expert opinion increasing power. Although the governmental position draws attention to new forms of governance and networked forms of security, it might be argued from a Marxist position that such explanations fail to recognise the central source of risk. This would lie within the capitalist mode of production, in which one social class, through its ownership of the means of production, is able to expropriate surplus value from the labour of impoverished groups.

The machinations of international capital also create risks for those who are more prosperous and not included within the underclass. In the UK, for instance, the inability of endowment morgages to yield enough funds to pay off the principal loan, despite promises to the contrary, has created serious risk for an unknown number of people. This risk was directly attributable to conditions pertaining in global markets and the operations of international capital. Risk from this perspective is conceptualised in terms of an individual's capacity for self-government, and not from the extent to which the risks they face are attributable to a mode of production, which will inevitably create risks for those who do not own the means of producing wealth.

Garland (1990) has argued that there is a danger in taking the disciplinary argument too far. An over-emphasis upon structures, surveillance, control and correction tends to produce accounts of modernity which can appear monolithic. Methods of control are not perfectly administered and are often inefficient. The utilisation of the idea of risk by governments contains contradictions, which make any uniform application of social control through risk problematic.

Risk regulation

Authors writing from a regulatory position attempt to capture what is absent from the risk society approach at the same time as trying to understand the manner in which social systems manage risk. A comparative approach, which can best be described as scientific, is adopted by moving beyond the telescopic 'risk society' and microscopic individualised explanations of risk. Risk regulation theorists would argue that the individualist approach explains too little, while 'risk society' and governmental explanations attempt to explain too much.

Box 2.7   Risk regulation regimes

The notion of risk regulation regime is meant to denote the:

Complex of institutional geography, rules, practice, and animating ideas that are associated with the regulation of a particular risk or hazard. (Hood et al., 2001: 9)

Writers arguing from the risk regulation position (see Box 2.7) use the term 'regime' to link risk with the regulatory systems that are designed to signify the manner in which risk is regulated within a particular risk domain. There is some overlap with the other risk positions described above in that these theorists are interested in professional and expert views of risk, and variations in the perception of risks. They also combine the approaches of organisational theorists and cultural theorists to describe risk regulation frames.

Fatalist risk regulation regimes, drawing on the work of Wildavsky (1988), stress the unpredictability of risks, which evoke a minimal *ad hoc* response from government. Hierarchical risk regulation regimes rely on the role of experts who not only forecast risk, but also play a part in constructing anti-risk policies. The egalitarian risk regulation regime model stresses the importance of community participation in decision-making, the role of government here being to encourage community participation.

Writers in the regulatory school create risk categories which bear some resemblance to the approach taken by those in the individualist and phenolenological schools described earlier. Individuals in situations where they can exercise some level of choice take voluntary risks, while compulsory risks are taken within scenarios where individuals have little or no control.

Risks can be caused by:

- natural phenomenon, e.g. earthquakes;
- social movements, e.g. revolution;

- state imposition, e.g. the unintended impact of government policies;
- corporate risks, e.g. those emanating from the machinations of private enterprise; and
- the use of technology which is too sophisticated or not sophisticated enough for the task (Hood et al., 2001).

The study of risk regulation regimes, it is argued, facilitates the identification of questions which do not become apparent from any of the other positions. Such a form of analysis is also used as a basis for the development of regulative policy.

Variations in risk regulation regimes are not readily explained by over-arching theories about how modern societies construe risk. A more conservative approach to risk regulation is required, it is argued, which emphasises the importance of microanalysis of regime regulation variations. This form of explanation concentrates on the analysis of organised group activity, the transactional nature of goods, and accounts of variations in public attitude and opinion (Hood et al., 2001: 58).

Limitations of the regulatory model

Although exponents of the regulatory school claim that it does cut a middle way between macroanalyses of risk society theorists and individualist approaches, there are inherent problems with an approach which is so eclectic in nature. Risk regime analyses contain disparate elements, including aspects of cultural explanation, while also sharing some of the concerns of risk society theorists. This approach relies most heavily upon attempting to understand the systems and organisational theory underlying risk regimes.

There are important distinctions between descriptions of what exists and an analysis which seeks to explain risk in all its complex manifestations. Wider questions relating to the socio-historic basis of risk are not considered within this approach. The questions posed by risk regime theorists are in some respects partial. The danger with this approach to risk is that it attempts to analyse risk from an organisational systems position, which can be seen as providing a particular pointer. Although advocates of the 'middle way' claim that this approach focuses on questions which would not otherwise be asked, the answers to these questions, and the implications for future regulatory practices, are not always clear.

The regulatory approach to risk has also been criticised as being based on an inappropriate emphasis on anticipation. Over-prescription and standardisation can be costly and ultimately self-defeating. All situations cannot be predicted, and constant monitoring and regulation is time consuming (Kemshall, 2002). Turner (1997) has referred to this over-emphasis on anticipation as the 'McDonaldisation of risk'.

Conclusion

The forms of analysis described above present the notion of risk from distinctive standpoints and lead to the formulation of a number of only partially answered questions. Individualists will ask how people perceive the frequency of risk. Are these perceptions accurate? Are errors in judgement about the likelihood of risk predictable? Is it possible to understand the cognitive processes underlying such judgements? (Colledge and Stimpson, 1997).

Douglas widens the discussion of risk to encourage the consideration of some basic questions. Since her early writings in the mid-1960s, Douglas would ask why some communities regard some social phenomena as constituting a risk while others are not (Douglas, 1966). Phenomenological analysis encourages questions to be asked about how events are interpreted as being relevant to risk management. Beck (1992) asks how risk impacts on all levels of social interaction. In the risk society, individuals are constantly seeking to come to terms with uncertainty, through a contested form of scientific rationality. Why have individuals become responsible for anticipating and negotiating risks? Why are risks unknowable and unpredictable as technology takes a global grip? How safe is a particular drug? Can I believe the expert who tells me that it will be effective and safe? What are its side-effects? Insecurity from this perspective now forms the basis for the formation of a society in which the distribution of risk has to some extent displaced conflict between social classes. Governmentalist theory asks how competing discourses of risk determine what it is possible and not possible to say about risk. This approach focuses on the relationship between 'moral technology', power and risk. Risk regulation analysts emphasise the importance of combining approaches and ask how social systems attempt to control risk.

This chapter has drawn attention to some of the limitations in all these approaches to understanding the social construction of risk. There are limitations to all contemporary forms of risk analysis. Quantitative forms of risk assessment conceptualise risk within stark individualist terms. Risk assessment is concerned with the assessment of probabilities of uncertain events. Risks are pre-existent in nature and identifiable only by experts who base their assessments on rational choice and probability theory. Such attempts to assess risks are fraught with dangers because there are numerous sources of error. These include insensitivity to sample size since smaller samples frequently have wider variance. Individuals expect the global characteristics of a process to be present in a small sample (Colledge and Stimpson, 1997). While the individualistic approaches fail to take account of the complexity of risk, cultural and phenomenological explanations have not taken sufficient cognisance of the environmental and structural problems within which risks are conceptualised. There are dangers in regarding the emergence of a risk society as the inevitable result of an historical logic, since risk has been uppermost in the minds of citizens and politicians throughout history. Analyses of risk based upon the governmental perspective do not give appropriate recognition to the reality of risk in everyday life.

Explanations of risk based upon the work of Beck have also been criticised for being reductionist and essentialist. Taylor-Gooby (2001b) has argued that ambivalence about the experience of risk and uncertainty exists because individuals find it difficult to differentiate between the progress they experience in living standards and the pressures they feel in other areas of social life.

Further reading

A number of clear accounts have already been given in relation to understanding risk. Discussions of risk-based theories are considered in Stenson and Sullivan's edited volume *Crime, Risk and Justice* (Willan, 2001). Although related to crime, these readings provide an incisive critique of Beck and other risk society theorists from a postmodern perspective. Robert Dingwall offers an extensive critique of Beck in '"Risk Society": The Cult of the Millennium' in Manning and Shaw (eds) *New Risks, New Welfare* (Blackwell, 2000). Some critical observations of the work of Douglas are also made in the same collection. Peter Taylor-Gooby also provides a critical analysis of the risk society theories with respect to social welfare in *Risk Trust and Welfare* (Macmillan, 2000). Deborah Lupton's *Risk* (Routledge, 1999a), provides one of the best accounts of differing theoretical approaches. Boyne's *Risk* (Open University Press, 2003) also contains particularly good coverage of the work of Beck. Elderidge's *Risk Society and the Media* (Longman, 1999) also provides a good critique of Beck. Anthony Giddens addresses post-traditional globalised risk in *The Third Way and its Critics* (Polity Press, 2000). Adam, Beck and Van Loon's edited collection, *Risk Society and Beyond* (Sage, 2000), contains useful sections on risk culture and the technologies of risk. Tulloch and Lupton examine how people respond to and exeprience risk in *Risk and Everyday Life* (Sage, 2003). Through interviews, they explore the meanings and significance of risk for 'lay' people. Ian Wilkinson's *Anxiety and the Risk Society* (Routledge, 2001b) examines the problem of risk in a clear and readable style.

Part II   Living in the Risk Society

THREE   Risk and Everyday Experience

Outline

In this chapter it will be shown how some principle social institutions are rooted within changing ideas about risk. This chapter examines how decisions about risk are woven into the everyday experience of securing basic requirements of living. It will be argued that the management of risk has become more individualised, privatised and pragmatic. Individuals, households and families have become responsible for their own risks yet the institution of the family is under great pressure. The housing market provides the context in which decisions designed to create not only shelter but also maximum profits are made. A bad decision can be costly and, in some cases, disastrous. The labour market provides the resources to finance shelter, which can also be regarded in some societies as a major investment. Education in the risk society can be viewed as a means of aquiring credentials that can enhance and provide longer-term security against unemployment and homelessness. Risks in education, employment and housing are intrinsically linked. This chapter examines the way in which these developments have created the need to make risky decisions, which can have a positive or negative impact on everyday life.

The institution of the family

The institution of the family has been a central plank upon which policies have been constructed by governments of all political complexions. In Germany, Switzerland, Italy, and to some extent in Spain and France, European Christian Democratic ideals link welfare, occupational structure and welfare with the family (Taylor-Gooby, 2001a). In Britain, Margaret Thatcher used the family as a basic unit upon which her 'revolution' was to be created in the 1980s. John Major's 'back to basics' campaign in the 1990s also used the family as the starting point for the evangelical zeal with which his form of conservatism would create a more moral society. For Tony Blair similar ideas are constructed around the family. Social policy reflects values which are designed to create stability within society, through the family. As traditional modes of behaviour, such as the family, begin to break down, so do such institutions which have hitherto provided a vital form of security. Families appear to have to make choices relating to lifestyle, employment, education and housing faster and without the safety net of a state-funded welfare state (Driver and Martell, 2002). In the USA and many parts of Europe, the family also forms the keystone of civil society. The family in the UK is seen by government not as creating a risk-free zone but, as was the case in New Labour's 1998 Green Paper *Supporting Families*, supporting a universal model of 'rational economic man' and the 'rational legal subject'.

Despite the consistent reliance on the family as a source of social cohesion and order, there is strong evidence to suggest that this form of security is collapsing. In the USA, the 1950s image of the happy suburban middle-class family does not correspond to reality. Family structure has become quite diverse within all socio-economic groups. Not only are women more likely to be employed outside the home, but among married couples, dual-earner couples are becoming most prevalent (Hertz and Marshall, 2001).

There is now a strong risk that children will experience their parents' divorce and, in consequence, major changes in family life have increased. According to the Census Bureau in the USA, in 2000 50 per cent of all first marriages ended in separation or divorce within 15 years (see Divorce Reform website at www.divorcereform.org/rates.html). More than 70 per cent of children affected by divorce are under 10 years of age (Wade and Smart, 2002). Divorce and separation are also closely associated with the risk of increased poverty.

In the UK the number of families in households with less than half the national average income after housing costs in 1999 was 14.5 million. This was more than double the number in the early 1980s. Around two-thirds of heads of households in social housing do not have paid work, compared with one-third in other forms of tenure. Significant health inequalities persist, with premature death being more geographically concentrated. Children in the manual social classes are twice as likely to die in an accident as those from non-manual classes. The poorest two-fifths are one and a half times more likely to be at risk of a mental illness than the richest two-fifths. There are other indicators that would suggest, to the contrary, that some risks are diminishing. Fewer children are failing to achieve basic educational standards. Levels of overcrowding and the numbers of households without central heating were, substantially reduced in the late 1990s (Rahman et al., 2000).

Poverty and other factors can in themselves be used as indicators of risk. Notwithstanding problems of verifiability and reliability, which are attendant in what Green (1997) has referred to as the 'social construction of accidents', some studies have suggested that risk factors such as poverty can contribute to increase the risk of accidents. Brown and Davidson (1978) found that children with young working-class mothers diagnosed as having psychiatric disorders were more likely to be involved in accidents than children of mothers from middle-class families without psychiatric disorders. A study of general practitioners suggested that they associate risk of childhood accidents with single parenthood, previous accidental injury, four or more children in a family, socio-economic depression and family stress (Kendrick et al., 1995).

Risks associated with poverty are no longer regarded by policy-makers as being amenable to corrective, state-financed safety nets. Poverty is 'calculated' by applying an actuarially based probability factor. This position is based upon the belief that greater proportions of the population are able to live relatively affluent lives due to technological change. Giddens and Beck do not attempt to explain away poverty, and acknowledge that in many developed western democracies inequalities of income are increasing. Giddens quotes from the work of Leisering and Leibfried, claiming that 70 per cent of the German population have never been poor, 20 per cent have or will be occasionally poor, and 10 per cent are poor in a more chronic fashion (Giddens, 2000: 112). Stenson (2001) has argued that the central dilemma confronting 'Third Way' theorists is how to include the 'truly disadvantaged minority' without alienating the contented majority.

The distinction between those who are socially 'excluded' and those in a state of poverty appears to have become blurred in the risk society. Research carried out by Taylor-Gooby (2001a) suggests that the impact of risk is still differentiated across social groups. New risks are associated with the most basic decisions made by families. According to Beck (1992), technological, social and economic interventions can generate unpredictable side-effects. Using dramaturgical imagery, he describes the family as the 'setting' and not the play. He argues that in marital and extra-marital relationships, conflicts are opened up by the possibility of choice. These choices are related to such factors as the differing professional mobility of spouses, and the division of housework and childcare. Lack of institutional solutions to these problems, for example the lack of childcare facilities, aggravates conflicts within personal relationships (Beck, 1992). People will take risks in a number of areas of social life so as to maximise benefits and minimise loss. The impact of these developments in the postwar period has been the transfer of risk management from the state and state agencies towards the individual.

Ewald (1991) has also emphasised the individualised dimension of risk insurance. Insurance against risk has a number of important dimensions. It reflects an attempt to master time and discipline the future. It is, for Ewald, a 'moral technology' which avoids a resignation to suffering at the hands of fate. Insurance can be understood as an indemnification of damages, maintaining equity, and resulting in the harm suffered by one being borne by the collective. By providing life insurance on behalf of children, and insurance for old age, accidents and a shortage of work, individuals perceive themselves to be liberated from fear (Ewald, 1991).

Housing

The change in the structure of the housing market from rented tenancy to home ownership has been one of the most significant changes in post-war economic and social life. Home ownership is not simply related to the purchase of a home. It has much wider cultural and economic significance. Munro (2001a: 167) writes:

> Even when owners are persuaded of the seductive possibility of large capital gains to be made through trading, it is perhaps not surprising that the main motivation for embarking on a potentially uncertain and costly move is that there is also a strong desire to change consumption characteristics of their home, typically connected with family imperatives.

The growth of individual home ownership has been a common feature in many countries across the developed world. Home ownership is embedded within the American consciousness. More than 90 per cent of American housing stock is privately owned. American families equate home ownership with 'having made it' (Stegman et al., 1995). The expansion of home ownership has also occurred in Hong Kong, New Zealand, Australia, France, Hungary, Japan, and other parts of the developed world. The move away from renting towards home ownership has generally occurred among younger mobile households (Forrest and Murie, 1995).

In the UK one of the most significant changes brought about by the Thatcher government in the early 1980s was the notion of the 'right to buy' policy with regard to council housing. There was a compelling logic to this policy, which had a great attraction to many families during that period (Forrest and Murie, 1992). Buying your own council house gave the tenant a stake in the housing market. It encouraged the acquisition of low-risk capital investment which would increase in value. The government provided every available incentive to encourage individuals to purchase their own homes. Tax incentives were provided to those who had mortgages, while those who rented council property were offered the property at low cost. As this national acquisition of council housing stock progressed through the 1980s, the availability of social housing simultaneously diminished, further increasing the value of the asset.

By 1997, 67 per cent of households in Britain were owner-occupiers, and home ownership became the preferred option for all groups in society. In the 1980s, year-on-year increases were followed by falling numbers of property transactions. At the height of the housing recession in 1991, 74,540 households had lost their property as a result of either court action or voluntary repossession (Ford et al., 2001). Despite the risks involved in the housing market and the widespread publicity given to the growing rate of repossessions during economic recession, the popularity of private home ownership has steadily increased. The number of mortgages advanced increased from 709,000 in 1980 to 1,181,000 in 1999 (Ford et al., 2001). These increases were reflected internationally (Forrest and Murie, 1995).

As the dynamic of home ownership moved inexorably on, it became clear that many individuals had underestimated the potential risks involved. Munro (2000a) has demonstrated how the expansion of the private housing market increased and created new forms of risk for groups of people. Government policy can combine with easy borrowing to propel some groups of people into unsustainable home ownership. In the UK, by 1993/94 households which had purchased their homes from local authorities were 1.8 times more likely to be in mortgage arrears, compared with households which purchased from private sellers. Those with 100 per cent mortgages were also twice as likely to face arrears than those with mortgages representing a lower proportion of the purchase price (Ford et al., 2001).

Drawing on Beck, it is possible to argue that the compulsive dynamic of home ownership is another example of the blindness of men and women to the dangers of risks created by modernity. The consequences of the ascendancy of the ideal of home ownership often has a profound impact on daily life. As owner-occupation becomes ever more prevalent, widening participation has increased the risk of mortgage arrears. This results in homelessness as the supply of social housing concomitantly diminishes. Owner-occupation presents families with uncertainties which result directly from the changes and the vicissitudes of the housing and financial markets. Capital gains from housing are dependent upon house price inflation being greater than increases in the prices of other goods and services. Such conditions are not permanently sustainable. The value of the investment, in this case the price of housing, has risen and fallen periodically, as one would expect in any free market situation (Munro, 2000b).

Rising levels of female employment have led to increased numbers of double-income families. Although this may spread the risk of paying a mortgage across two incomes, it may lead to higher levels of borrowing, which further increases the risk of mortgage default (Hogarth et al., 1996).

Ford, Burrows and Nettleton (2001) have argued that home ownership might be 'inserted' into the idea of a risk society at a global and local level. The housing market is itself part of wider processes of globalisation. Developments in global financial markets create uncertainties which can affect the availability of credit for mortgages. Global interest rates, which are themselves related to wider political questions, can have a profound effect on the ability of individuals to repay mortgages. As global interest rates rise, so does the risk of mortgage default.

Risks in the housing market are also related to location. There are important regional and local differences in house prices which are associated with changes in the labour market and employment prospects. In Britain, most notably in the old heavily industrialised areas of the north of the country, the demand for mortgages may be declining (Ford et al., 2001). Families are more likely to enjoy a low-risk return on their income in housing 'hot spots', where property is in particular demand. Such is the trust in the rise in house prices in such areas that the number of individuals engaging in the comparatively risky business of buying properties to let has increased. Trust in the buoyancy of the housing market in the south east of Britain has led to secondary risks, which involve families taking out a second debt, being taken. Within this scenario, home-buyers are dependent upon a precarious income derived from rent in order to pay a second mortgage. If the income from rent is not forthcoming, then the possibility of being unable to pay the second mortgage can lead to severe financial difficulty. Such is the belief in the ability of the housing market to deliver profit that even individuals who have experienced unemployment seem oblivious to the possible risk of extra debt (Ford et al., 2001).

While market conditions and widening participation are factors that have an over-arching influence on the shaping of risks, other, subsidiary risk factors are inextricably linked. In surveys of English housing conducted between 1995 and 1999 the reasons for mortgage arrears appear to fall under three groupings, which can be regarded as secondary to the primary causes of risk in the housing market mentioned above. The three classifications – loss of income, household changes and increases in expenditure – relate to unexpected changes in family circumstances. Thus, loss of earnings through sickness, the failure of a self-employed person's business, redundancy, loss of overtime, divorce, pregnancy and death, are all situations which are seen as significant, if not defining, factors by those who have mortgage arrears.

Variations in choices made by households do not vary with changes in market conditions, as might be expected. Although various financial institutions operate checks and balances to protect their investments, it may be that individuals are not particularly sensitive to the sources of risk in the housing market. Munro reaches the conclusion that, for most people, housing carries with it the idea of a refuge and a locus of family life. The changes in behaviour identified with boom and bust are more likely to be associated with greater fluidity in the housing market, accompanied by the possibility of capital gains. As Munro (2000b) argues, buyers do not 'fine tune' the financial aspects of their decisions to reflect more detailed expectation about housing market risks. It may well be that there are simply too many potential risks which are unknowable for people to make rational calculations as how best to protect themselves from risk. Such risks are perceived as being in the main beyond the control of the individual, and include future job stability, interest rate changes and the future of house prices (Munro, 2000b).

According to Croft (2001), there are a number of factors – a 'pool' of latent risks – that can form a precursor to homelessness. These factors can be collective (such as rises in interest rates) or individual (such as redundancy). The crystallisation of risk factors is a substantive event that transforms a series of events into a major problem. The consequences of the event can interact in a complex manner in a positive or a negative way. Such reactions make any strategic decisions concerning impended homelessness less likely, although planned strategies, for example debt-counselling and saving, can be used to control future events (Croft, 2001).

Education

Beck has argued that 'normal' linear biographies, which characterised traditional societies, have been transformed. Biographies are now constructed through a process of reflexive biography: 'Certainly the scarcity of educational opportunities is a problem that affects everyone, but what does that mean for the forging of my own fate, which nobody does for me' (Beck, 1992: 135). Education, for Beck, becomes a variable that can be 'moderated', 'subverted' and 'suited' to one's sphere of action.

Decisions made with respect to education, like housing and employment, are increasingly risk-laden and individualised. To describe individuals in the risk society as making decisions about education is somewhat inaccurate. Beck contends that in the risk society alternatives, upon which decisions are made, do not exist. Different expectations exist between individuals and nations regarding the nature of educational participation and outcome. Individuals negotiate often complex biographical plans in order to avoid risk, according to Beck. More calculated decisions are made, for example, 'between acquiring a stable job upon leaving school and pursuing further or higher education. One risk posed by education is that it could delay entry into the labour market. Such decisions require careful consideration of risk' (Heggen and Dwyer, 1998).

Basing their evidence on research carried out in Canada and Australia, Dwyer and Wynn (2001) argue that the fears and uncertainties experienced by young people with respect to education are justified. Although parents and teachers place immense faith in the benefits of investment in education, there is a growing concern that those excluded from education, or those who may have had their education disrupted are in danger of constituting an underclass at risk. Although most students do find employment upon graduation, there is some evidence to suggest that graduate unemployment has risen slightly. In the UK, 67.7 per cent of graduates find work within six months of leaving university. Some academic subjects are more risky than others in terms of job prospects. Almost 80 per cent of individuals with degrees in civil engineering or accountancy find jobs within six months of leaving university. The downturn in the computer industry is blamed for the increases in unemployment among information technology graduates (British Broadcasting Corporation, 2002a).

The imposition of student loans adds a further dimension of risk when considering the decision to undertake higher education. In the USA, students are graduating with record levels of debt. Between 1999 and 2000, 64 per cent of students graduating in the USA borrowed money from the federal government for educational purposes. During the same period the average student loan doubled, reaching $16,928. Loans for higher education also appear to be differentially affecting lower-income groups. The ability of graduates to repay borrowed money has become an increasing problem. Some 39 per cent of those borrowing money for educational programmes are unable to manage their loan (Cappannari, 2002).

Working

The world of work has always been risk-laden and uncertain. Risks associated with work have changed in nature as nation states, particularly in western Europe, have moved towards more flexibility in labour markets. This, according to some commentators, has been in response to the process of globalisation (Esping-Anderson, 1996). What Beck has also described as the 'Brazilianisation of the West', will stretch employment flexibility to its limit, creating a situation in which those depending upon a regular wage are in a minority. Most earn their living through selling and moving flexibly between different forms of insecure temporary profit-making activity (Beck, 2000b). Under these conditions of precarious reactive living, the factors responsible for the development of employment-related risks become even more elusive.

A number of examples can be given of the relationship between the risk of unemployment, globalisation and flexible labour markets. In 2003, British Telecom (BT) announced the opening of a new call centre in India. The company said that it would open two new call centres in Bangalore and Delhi and planned to employ 2,000 people. This would be accompanied by a reduction in staff employed in British call centres from 16,000 individuals to 14,000, and a concomitant drop in the number of call centres from 100 to 31 over the same period. BT claimed that this would not lead to any compulsory redundancies in the UK. The Communication Workers' Union responded by saying that this was British work, which should be carried out in Britain. The move contravened the firm's job protection policy, while also destroying British jobs (British Broadcasting Corporation, 2003a).

There is nothing new about companies relocating to less developed countries where they can cut their labour costs. This development in the communications industry could be seen as a reflexive move on the part of BT to increase its diminishing market share. It is also a technologically driven development, which would have been impossible one decade earlier. Until the creation of affordable global communication, most individuals rarely experienced international telephony. The BT move, which was followed by many other companies establishing call centres overseas, has also created a nationalistic reaction to a global employment strategy, fuelled by the perceived risk of unemployment.

In the UK, both Conservative and New Labour governments have adopted an approach to employment policy that appears to have decreased job security in most sectors (although the New Labour government did establish a minimum wage in 1999), emphasising the importance of paid work as the main route out of poverty. Abbott and Quiglers (2001) argue that there is substantial evidence to suggest that in Britain, employment risk has increased with labour market flexibility. Household heads are now more likely to occupy riskier employment positions, and are more likely to be involved in part-time work and/or self-employment. Some 30 per cent of current employees are likely to have experienced some form of unemployment within the last five years (Cebulla et al., 1998). Ford has described two types of risk associated with the flexible labour markets. First, these are direct risks, such as unemployment, poorer terms of employment, variable work hours and volatility of income. Secondly, there are the consequential risks, which include reduced standards of living, a lack of future pension provision, an inability to pay housing costs and possibly prolonged ill-health because people are more likely to continue to work during periods of ill-health due to a lack of eligibility for sick pay.

The development of flexible labour markets has led to the gradual erosion of state safety nets to protect against unemployment. Government action seems to be built upon two assumptions. First, the idea that private insurance markets can effectively protect against the effects of unemployment. Although insurance schemes may offer limited protection against some employment-related risks, such as redundancy, it is more difficult to provide cover for more complex situations, such as temporary mental illness, divorce or caring responsibilities.

The second assumption is that individuals make rational decisions about how they respond to the risk of unemployment. Governments, according to Abbott and Quiglers (2001), assume that people will organise private insurance. While those in paid employment are aware of the potential threat of unemployment, perceptions of their own market position is frequently inaccurate. A large proportion of people in full-time employment fail to see redundancy before it arrives.

'Third Way' politics involves the family taking more responsibility for the risk of unemployment. Yet research indicates that a considerable number of families in the lower socio-economic categories, although aware of the increasing risk of unemployment, are not in a position to protect themselves due to a lack of money. Even when households have some scope for financial planning, a hierarchy of risk means that planning against the risk of unemployment is not possible when higher priorities, such as life insurances and pensions, have to be met. An examination of the financial planning of all socio-economic groups reveals a clear pattern of prioritising some risks over others (Abbott and Quiglers, 2001: 122). Thus, when families attempt to guard themselves against risk, the availability of financial resources makes prioritisation essential. Parents appear to make planning against premature death the most important priority. Planning for the eventuality of illness or accident in an attempt to protect income is prioritised over the risk of unemployment.

While those examining risk from an individualist position would argue that questions relating to the over- or underestimation of risk are of fundamental importance, this research points to the pervasiveness of structural constraints. It is not the case that individuals occupy the relatively luxurious position of making a choice as to what risks they take seriously. Pragmatism, the reality of their own financial position and the unwillingness of government to provide state-funded security may force individuals to take some risks more seriously than others. This constitutes a further structural dimension to the construction of risk in what has now become, to borrow a cliché from 1980s political rhetoric, a 'property-owning democracy'. The experience of risk for many low-income families can become intolerable and unacceptable.

The individualist approach to risk also fails to take into consideration the complexities of the different discourses which give meaning to risk. Subjective meanings in ascribing the scale or severity of a particular risk are fraught with unresolved difficulties, since there can be no universal agreement on what severity means in relation to a potential hazard. One example of this difficulty can be seen in the risk of verbal abuse in the workplace. As there is no universal agreement as to what constitutes verbal abuse, racist and sexist discourse can be camouflaged within the complexity of particular forms of professional language, and even presented as humorous banter (Denney, 1992). The potential impact of verbal abuse as a hazard is even more complicated. Whereas one individual might regard verbal abuse as an inevitable feature of social existence, another might regard it as psychologically damaging (Gabe et al., 2002).

Although the actuarial language of risk assessment has objective and scientistic credibility, the technologies of risk assessment are quite imprecise in predicting hazard and form a weak basis for professional intervention. The values underlying risk assessments are concealed in a veil of scientific mystery, unknown to those whose risk is being assessed.

Individualist forms of risk analysis are epidemiological and can involve individuals in self-regulation. Individualised risk assessment, although seen by public organisations such as the British National Health Service (NHS) as being imperative, are often based upon laudable principles, but utilise precarious technical data. In a document which was produced for health workers in the NHS by psychologists at Nottingham University, both managers and individual workers were exhorted to work in an 'integrated' manner to combat risk (Royal College of Nursing/NHS Executive, 1998). Such an integrated approach to the risk assessment of violence at work required individual employees to address four main areas of risk assessment. These included 'preparation and planning' before any potentially violent incident occurred, 'de-escalating' violence when it occurred, the development of appropriate professional responses to violent incidents, and encouraging employees to learn from violent events in order to know how to deal with possible future events. The document reminds readers that:

> As yet there are no well worked out and validated systems of risk assessment for work-related violence that are easily available. It is therefore necessary for each trust to think carefully about the nature of the evidence that it can collect in relation to workplace violence which will allow the reliable self-identification of hazardous situations and 'at risk' groups, and some assessment of the size of the risk to safety and health involved. (Royal College of Nursing/NHS Executive, 1998: 43)

Within this extract we see the call for quantification, while simultaneously identifying problems in defining what it means to constitute 'evidence' for risk assessment. The need for quantification in an area which may be unquantifiable is a recurring theme in the professional risk assessment literature. The complexities of risk have created ideas that are differentiated and pervasive, forming the basis for the link between risk assessment and state action. The assumption appears to be, according to Ericson and Haggerty (1997), that if a certain number of risk factors are present, then the likelihood of a deleterious outcome is increased to the point where the state must take action. Hence the demand for risk definition and assessment structures social organisation (Ericson and Carrière, 1994).

Conclusion

At key life stages, from birth to death, the experience of risk is becoming more individualised and complex. New risks associated with technology, labour markets and housing markets minimise any sense of a safety net, increasing the number of risk dilemmas that people are forced to manage. The consequences of making the wrong decision, particularly in the area of education, appears to increase the ramifications of risk. Domestic risks are less controllable since they are linked to global markets and technologies. In some areas, most notably housing, individuals appear to adopt an extremely optimistic approach to the possibility of risk.

Further reading

In *Blair's Britain* (Policy Press, 2002), Driver and Martel produce a remarkably lucid account of the development of the Third Way in politics and examine various aspects of risk. Ewald's chapter on insurance and risk in Burchell, Gordon and Miller's collection *The Foucault Effect* (University of Chicago Press, 1991) offers an analysis which is applicable to many aspects of risk in everyday life. Ford, Burrows and Nettleton's edited collection, *Home Ownership in a Risk Society* (Policy Press, 2001) contains excellent chapters on repossession and mortgage arrears. Abbott and Quiglers' chapter in Edwards and Glover's edited volume, *Risk and Citizenship* (Routledge, 2001), provides a useful account of the management of unemployment in the risk society. Dwyer and Wynn's *Youth Education and Risk* (Routledge, 2001) has drawn together international research on the impact of transition periods within families and schools as young people progress towards adulthood. The book usefully examines risk in the educational life chances and lifestyles of young people.

FOUR Health and Risk

Outline

Medical and scientific experts provide the basis upon which health panics are built. Lupton (1993, 1999) has argued that personal health appraisals have been found to have limitations in predicting risk. This chapter examines a number of risk-laden life-stage events in which medical science has particular relevance. Infertility treatment, childbirth, child immunisation, risk prediction and the consumption of food and drink will be discussed. Risks associated with global epidemics will also be examined.

Infertility treatment

Infertility treatment is purposive in that couples are driven by a belief that treatment can lead to pregnancy. Health risks are associated with infertility treatment as procedures become more invasive. As men and women proceed through treatment options, their concerns about possible risks increase. In one study, 15 out of 27 women were concerned about the possible risks involved with infertility surgery (Becker and Nachtigall, 1994). A higher proportion of women, 43 out of 53, were worried about the possible side-effects of fertility drugs, including the possible over-stimulation of the ovaries. Evaluations of risk were not confined to the immediate physical risks, but included the emotional and financial cost. However, medical risk was not a factor which would lead to the cessation of treatment. When initial efforts to conceive had been unsuccessful, the need for a baby was often viewed as a priceless benefit.

Becker and Nachtigall argue that American women take risks in connection with infertility in order to fulfil the 'cultural norm of motherhood'.

Risks become an inevitable by-product of persistence. The need to continue to experiment with their bodies becomes a responsibility as desperation increases. Thus 'doing nothing' is equated with failure. Couples weigh the benefits and risks against the possible outcomes of a procedure. Individual perceptions of risk may be shaped by individual biography, culture and the experience of being a patient (Becker and Nachtigall, 1994). From a cultural position, Becker and Nachtigall draw an important distinction between a balanced, considered approach to risk-taking and a more 'risk-seeking' position. The former is characterised by weighing the value that can be gained by action against the harm that can be done by inaction, whereas the latter contains elements of gambling. Both forms of risk-taking seem to be practised by the physicians who provide the service and the patients who undergo infertility treatment.

In *Risk Society*, Beck provides an extensive discussion of the sub-politics of medicine. With regard to in vitro fertilisation, Beck considers a series of problems: 'The availability of embryos provides science with long hoped for "experimental objects" (language fails) for embryological, immunological and pharmacological research' (Beck, 1992: 206), but who will perform the 'quality control of embryos' and by what right do these experts make judgements? What happens to the low quality embryos which do not satisfy the requirements for prenatal entry into the world?

Childbirth

Although childbirth does, in itself, pose some risks for a minority of women and babies, the major risks associated with the event are socially and historically determined. Low income, poor diet, smoking and medical interventions constitute important risk factors in childbirth. Debates about childbirth, according to Lane (1994), have been dominated by the notion of risk. Obstetricians have been interested in the safety of childbirth, while the experience of the woman having the child has been secondary. Hospital rules and procedures are designed to guard against risk. Childbirth is structured by the need to rationalise the birth process, ultimately to ensure a safe delivery of the child, and also to guard against any possible litigation. However, what follows admission into hospital is a catalogue of treatments which ultimately deny autonomous choice for most women (Lane, 1994).

Beck has argued that medical science discourages self-criticism (1992). With respect to childbirth Lane (1994) contends that Beck assumes the existence of impermeable boundaries. She argues that obstetricians are no longer exempt from criticism and scrutiny from service users. Litigation, and the fear of litigation, has perpetrated professional barriers in obstetrics, as it has in other areas of medicine.

Child immunisation

In a study of mass childhood immunisation, Rogers and Pilgrim (1995) show how two irreconcilable and reflexive questions illustrate the problem of the relationship between expert opinion (and trust in experts) and risk:

- Are unvaccinated children a health risk to themselves and others?
- Are vaccines a health risk to children?

Measles, mumps and rubella (MMR) vaccine, which was introduced in 1988, has been used worldwide. It was meant to herald a new era of protection against these diseases. Yet many pressure groups have linked the MMR immunisation to autism and bowel disorders (www.this-is-health.com). In 1993 the Japanese government decided to stop using the combined MMR vaccine.

For Rogers and Pilgrim (1995), the debates surrounding the programme of mass childhood immunisation, which has been endorsed by successive governments globally, point to a vociferous challenge to expert opinion. They claim that the traditional authority of the expert is breaking down, not only in relation to immunisation, but also in other areas of health. Patients can now consult a number of other sources in search of accurate information, for example the Internet.

Risk of inherited illness and the family

New technology can increase the early detection of inherited diseases. Through an analysis of a person's genetic make-up, it is now possible to predict the probability of that person developing certain medical conditions. This information can then be recorded on a smart card. The rationale behind such technology is that if an individual has a genetic proclivity to a particular disorder, then it might be possible to take steps to avoid the disease occurring. Although such tests may predict the vulnerability of particular groups to some common diseases, there are a number of potentially worrying social developments attached to the technology.

According to some critics, this technological development could lead to the creation of a 'genetic underclass' and to an even greater mass preoccupation with health. One of the most significant possibilities is that of the 'gene ID card', on which the complete genetic code of a newborn child could be recorded. Companies or organisations could then use this information to exclude some individuals from using their services. For example, insurers could refuse life insurance cover therefore also excluding people from applying for mortgages, etc. Employers, too, could use the information to discriminate against employees – all on the basis of a genetic test. Enormous DNA databases could be established, and ultimately used for more sophisticated surveillance and identification systems (British Broadcasting Corporation, 2003b). In other areas, such as mental health, genetic prediction, if ever developed, could also have detrimental effects for those designated as having a predisposition to inherited forms of mental illness. Even though it is estimated that such technology is still two decades away, it is already possible to detect some 200 disorders through genetic testing. There is, therefore, an urgent need to develop legislation to protect citizens against the possibility of genetic discrimination. Indeed, at the time of writing, such legislation is already before Congress in the USA (*Guardian*, 2004b).

Attention has also been focused on the psychological impact and stress on individuals and families of knowing the risks of inheriting genetic conditions and illnesses, and on how people deal with such risks, but little consideration has been given to how individuals construct the social meanings that lie beneath understandings of inherited risk. However, Cox and McKellin (1999) have studied the social construction of hereditary risk of Huntingdon's Disease, a degenerative condition that is characterised by involuntary physical movements, cognitive impairments and changes in personality. Death usually occurs within 15–20 years of onset. Cox and McKellin have adopted a phenomenological approach. Drawing on the theoretical approach of Bloor (1995), they have argued that hereditary risk has a constant high degree of relevance, and is constructed as being both problematic and amenable to strategic intervention. The relevance of risk is fluid, and at certain particular junctures, for instance when a predictive test result is given to a patient, the risk of an inherited disease has a high level of relevance. At other times it has much less importance. The risk of an inherited illness confirmed by an objective scientific test can be contained within the family. Constructions of risk associated with predictive tests are not static or objective but based upon a coherent framework of understanding. Within the family, it is a social and not a biological understanding that shapes everyday conceptions of inherited risks. Some family members, who did not test positive for Huntingdon's Disease, felt a combination of guilt and relief. Other family members were able to separate taken-for-granted understandings of risk with a more objectified assessment based upon the likelihood of risk.

Women interviewed by Hallowell (1999) believe that they had a responsibility to other people not only to determine their own risks, but also to take steps to control those risks. Even though only a small proportion of women are thought to carry genetic mutations that predispose them to cancer, the 'genetisisation' of breast and ovarian cancer has led to the recategorisation of many healthy women as being at risk. As a result of genetic counselling, many healthy women have adopted risk management practices that have had major personal consequences. There is evidence that those attending clinics for genetic counselling conceptualise risk in 'binary' terms. Thus, cancer either will or will not occur. Although geneticists and clinicians distinguish between best- and worst-case scenarios, women frequently overlook this distinction. Of the 46 women interviewed by Hallowell, only one of those defined as having a low risk of cancer chose to do nothing. Six women intended to explore the possibility of major surgery, while the remaining women managed their risks by joining a screening programme. 'In justifying their behaviour, the women in this study, those who were mothers and who were not, drew upon gendered discourses of motherhood and womanhood which position women as responsible for the care of others' (Hallowell, 1999: 115).

Individual understandings of health risks

Douglas often found it helpful to place individuals in groups that were presented as having common worldviews (see Chapter Two). One example of this can be seen in her description of responses to the risk of HIV/AIDS. The first of Douglas's groups describes those who see the body as completely open to the invasion of infection. A second group regards the body as being immune from infection. A third group conceptualises protective layers against infection – the physical skin and the local community – which police exits and entrances. A fourth group sees the body as a machine, which has its own protective layer, that can be pierced by an act of carelessness. Each view of the body affects the way in which individual members of each group conceptualise the disease. Thus HIV/AIDS can be an ever-present danger, a minor problem, or the penetration of protective layers. Blame-worthiness reflects a lack of individual care (Douglas, 1992).

Douglas's model has much to offer, but Lupton (1999) argues that it fails to take account of the diversity of ways in which people understand and deal with HIV/AIDS. In the case of HIV/AIDS, ideas about the human body and HIV/AIDS are connected to political processes. Those infected with the virus have been marginalised by the creation of a *cordon sanitaire*.

Lupton's main criticism of the model is that the categories created by Douglas fail to take account of the diversity of ways in which gay people understand and deal with HIV/AIDS.

Perceptions of risk in many medical contexts are not static and cannot be quantified. It is an ever-changing experience with respect to the individual and family members. Individual constructions of risk, according to Becker and Nachtigall (1994) are often constructed by biographies, knowledge of one's own body, cultural experience and knowledge of the health system. One could add to these factors, knowledge of specific medical risks. Risk-taking is also determined by social stratification in this area. Some procedures are only available within the private sector of health systems. Risk-taking in the area of health is often driven by specific goals, which are perceived as life-threatening. Cancer therapies, for example, while holding out the hope of survival, can in themselves reduce life in both quantitative and qualitative terms. The likelihood of risk-taking can also vary depending on the life stage of an individual. Plant and Plant (1993) argue that some of the psychological characteristics of adolescence in western societies encourage risk-taking. One feature of this is the myth of invulnerability, when young people at their physical peak regard themselves as being indestructible. Such activities associated with this life stage include unprotected sex, experimentation with drugs and the riding of motorbikes.

Eating and drinking

Over the last two centuries, fears about the health risks posed by the consumption of certain foods have come to prominence at particular moments in history. Prior to the mid-nineteenth-century national food policy, the burden of risk assessment lay firmly with the public as far as food was concerned. Debates around food have, since the nineteenth century, focused upon the perception of a largely ignorant public in need of protection from dishonest and negligent food producers (Draper and Green, 2002). In an attempt to feed populations with life-sustaining and health-enhancing foods, strategies of intense and industrialised food production have been adopted. This has particularly been the case since the Second World War. Whereas in the nineteenth century the preoccupation of social reformers like Booth and Rowntree was with mass access to food and the risks involved in poor nutrition, a century later, concern about obesity and weight loss has become an international pastime in the western world. With the development of refrigeration and the postwar availability of meat, tinned fruit, eggs and sugar, individual food consumption increased. By the 1960s, family size most often determined both the quality and quantity of food consumed (Cahill, 2002a). As the popularity of pre-prepared food developed in the 1970s and 1980s, convenience food became a substantial element in the diet of the developed world. Knowledge of food preparation, and the safe preparation of fresh food, concomitantly declined.

By the end of the 1980s there was an ever-increasing list of food-related risks, which posed major problems for governments of all political complexions. Food panics, and the risks to health created by food, have periodically dominated the political agenda. Salmonella, listeria, the safety of microwave ovens, and food irradiation generally have all been identified by 'experts' as being potentially risky. Food additives, the impact of pesticide residues, Bovine Somatotrophin, Alar (a plant growth inhibitor used on apples), the development of genetically modified (GM) foods, Creutzfeldt-Jakob Disease (CJD), swine vesicular disease and, in 2001, foot and mouth disease have all to various degrees raised questions about the relationship between risk and food (Lang et al., 2002). Evidence has mounted since the Second World War to suggest that there is a link between diet and degenerative disease. These diseases include coronary disease, cancers of the breast and colon, diabetes and dental decay. By the 1990s Europe, like the USA, was suffering from the effects of mass obesity.

In the UK in 1999, the Acheson Inquiry into inequalities of health found a greater incidence of premature deaths in lower socio-economic groups from heart disease, stroke and some cancers. Other diet-related disorders, including obesity and hypertension, are clustered in the lower socio-economic groups. The diet of lower socio-economic groups is characterised by foods that provide cheap energy – there is an over-consumption of full cream, sugar, potatoes, cereals and meat products. Such a diet is lower in nutrients such as calcium, magnesium, foliate and vitamin C. Cardiovascular diseases are the chief cause of death in the UK. One-third of deaths from cardiovascular disease before the age of 75 are due to poor nutrition. A similar number of premature deaths are caused by cancer (Lang et al., 2002).

Risk food and panic

Political careers have been destroyed when senior politicians have made public statements about the potential risks posed by food. In 1988, Britain's Junior Health Minister Edwina Curry was sacked when she claimed that most British eggs were infected with salmonella. Salmonella poisoning has increased annually, from 10,000 cases in 1982 to 32,000 cases in 1996. Escherichia Coli (E Coli) is a bacterium that causes serious inflammation of the colon and can have fatal consequences. It can be transmitted in beef and beef products, unpasteurised milk, raw vegetables, yoghurt and cheese. During the 1990s, the incidence of E Coli infection increased from none to 600,000 cases. There has been a similar increase in the number of cases of Campylobacter, which can also produce diarrhoea, vomiting and severe abdominal pain (Meikle, 1998).

In the mid-1980s a new disease appeared among herds of British cattle. Spongiform Encephalopathy, so-called because its victims developed sponge-like holes in their brains, became known as Bovine Spongiform Encephalopathy (BSE), or, more popularly, 'Mad Cow Disease'. The disease was also discovered in US herds in December 2003. There was a strong scientific suggestion that Scrapie, the variation of Spongiform Encephalopathy that was common in sheep, had crossed to cattle through the use of food supplements containing material from sheep carcases. It was never made clear to the public that Scrapie in sheep was not the same as BSE. Some scientific opinion also suggested that the disease could be transferred to humans, and in 1996 the British government concluded that the human form of BSE, Creutzfeldt-Jacob Disease (CJD), posed a risk to public safety (Brouwer, 1998). However, the question of the risk to humans from BSE is difficult to calculate, since the number of infected cattle shown to have been eaten by humans can be computed in various ways. Thus, the BSE crisis provides a clear example of some of the many difficulties in attempting to assess risk. Anderson et al. (1996) claimed that 446,000 infected cattle had been eaten by the start of the ban on specified bovine offal in 1989. Between 1989 and 1995 a further 283,000 infected cattle had been eaten. These results do not take into account the under-reporting of cases that has taken place since 1992 (Dealer, 1998). Dealer and Kent (1995) calculated that the number of infected cattle eaten by 2001 was 1.8 million. Internationally, the incidence of CJD per million of the population is less than 1 per cent (Barclay and Sleator, 1997). It is also possible that BSE in humans has an incubation period which could be as long as 20 years.

In attempting to reassure the public of the almost non-existent risk that BSE could cross the species barrier, the British government placed a heavy reliance upon scientific evidence. The message given out by successive government ministers was that British beef was completely safe to eat. In 1989, the then Minister of Agriculture, in a written reply to a parliamentary question, said: 'The risk of transmission of BSE to humans appears remote and it is therefore most unlikely that BSE will have any implications for public health' (cited in Lang, 1998: 9). By 1995, however, the Ministry of Agriculture, Fisheries and Food conceded that there could be some inaccuracies in the research and diagnosis and, in 1996, the government finally admitted that there may be a link between BSE and CJD. As a result, regulations relating to the removal of bovine offal were tightened (Lang, 1998). The political and diplomatic consequences of the risks posed by CJD became serious in the mid-1990s. The European Union banned British beef products and, in response, the British Prime Minister announced that 'without further progress towards lifting the ban, we cannot be expected to co-operate normally on other Community business' (cited in Barclay and Sleator, 1997: 6).

The BSE crisis illustrates how a questionable scientific assessment of risk to public health exposed the European Union's incapacity to act collectively when national interests were at stake. The response of government to the risks posed by food fall within the regulatory framework discussed in Chapter Two. In 1996 the European Union laid down regulations designed to address the risks to public health caused by British beef. Measures included a selective slaughter programme and the introduction of an effective animal identification and animal recording system with official registration (Barclay and Sleator, 1997). Some European states, including the UK, France and Finland, have subsequently set up food agencies to monitor and regulate food safety at a national level. Greece and the Netherlands are still debating whether to do so. Plans to develop European-wide laws to regulate food safety are currently under discussion (Lang et al., 2002). Britain's Food Standards Agency came into being in April 2000 and is committed to producing a 20 per cent drop in food poisoning within five years.

Beck (1999) has argued that the BSE risk became 'real' through the digitalised imagery of the media. Consumers have no way of testing the adequacy in representations in the media. The origins of BSE are fabricated and their sources connect chemistry and molecular biology, medicine and computer graphics. The 'becoming real' of the risk of BSE, for Beck, is related to this mediation process. However, once an individual is made aware of the risks, the responsibility of whether or not to eat beef becomes an individual one. As Beck argues: 'The sudden accessibility of the "knowledge" regarding the possible relationship between BSE and CJD has thus transformed a hazard into a risk' (1999: 136).

BSE and other political débâcles, including salmonella in eggs and genetically modified organisms, point to an attempt by the government to apply regulation in proportion to the available evidence. This stands in contrast to the precautionary principle (Smith, 2004), where action is not based upon the possession of evidence. Rather, imagined worst-case scenarios form the basis for preventative action by governments. In the case of the BSE crisis, ministers and civil servants were not prepared to take action even though the possible negative implications for human health had been identified 11 years earlier. The major preoccupation was to avoid panic. 'The problem was that the government had little evidence. The government's position was that there was no evidence of a link between BSE and CJD' (Smith, 2004: 322).

Risk and public trust in food safety

The problems related to safe food bring into sharp relief the relationship between risk and trust. Beck's observation that environmental risks cannot be touched, tasted, heard or smelt is particularly apposite here (Beck, 1992). The identification of risk in the case of food was entirely dependent on the interpretation of scientific evidence. The BSE fiasco also reflects the minimal effort made by governments and the food industry to engage public involvement in discussions relating to food safety. This leaves considerable scope to build trust in policies related to food through wider discussion (Macnaughten, 2000). It must be acknowledged that it is difficult to create trust in an area where there is so much disagreement among the experts as to what constitutes risk. Researchers working within an individualist framework have examined perceptions of the potential risks associated with food. Psychologists have concentrated on attempting to understand public attitudes to the dangers posed by food, and the attitudes of individuals to the development of biotechnology and food production (Frewer et al., 1997).

In the main, interest in food has been anthropological in nature, and is more akin to the culturalist position described in Chapter Two (Lèvi-Strauss, 1966). Many of the more recent studies relating to perceptions of food and risk draw upon the work of Beck. Shaw (2000) argues that close parallels to the literature on risk and food exist in studies of the public understanding of science. The idea that the expert has knowledge which is scientifically based is founded on the belief that the views of the consumer are uninformed a 'deficit view' of the consumer. This, it is argued, deflects attention from the 'intuitive' knowledge of lay expertise (Irwin and Wynne, 1996).

Expert knowledge in food and risk assessment

The status of expert knowledge has been challenged in the area of food as it has in other areas, most notably medicine. Experts have exerted a crucial important influence in the construction of policy during food crises. Politicians used expert advice during the BSE crisis in Europe, although the nature of the advice relating to the risk to humans changed over time.

Shaw (2000) has examined the way in which experts view the public's perception of the risks posed by food consumption. She interviewed a number of food experts from the private sector, including food retailers, manufacturers, representatives from food campaigning groups and representatives from the National Farmers' Union. She also interviewed food experts employed by local and central government. Some experts in Shaw's sample acknowledged the limitations of their own knowledge about food. Experts related risk to broader social changes such as the shift from a rural to an urban society, and the production of fast food which has resulted in a reduced knowledge about microbiological food safety. In the post-Second World War period there has, according to experts, been a lack of awareness that food itself is a potentially 'dangerous biological material': 'Eating food is intrinsically dangerous. Food is biological material, it is not stable against microbial attack. ... Our forebears knew this very well [but people] began to lose that intrinsic knowledge' (Shaw, 2000: 141).

Some food experts interviewed by Shaw appear to locate themselves within an individualist position (see Chapter Two). They talked about food risk in technical, actuarial terms, and consequently viewed public knowledge of risk as partial, and the knowledge of some experts as limited. Other experts, most notably from the food campaigning sector, saw the relationship between food and risk in a wider political and social context. Shaw concludes that experts reflect risk as being both subjectively perceived and socially constructed (Shaw, 1999, 2000). In times of crisis, expert opinion is transformed by governments into knowledge which can then be used to inform public safety. Expert opinion tends not to be presented by governments as being undifferentiated and complex, but as containing levels of non-existent certainty. Such expert consensus, according to Shaw, is imagined. We have seen above how selective use of expert advice was used in relation to the BSE crisis. There are other examples in which expert opinion was used in a similar manner. In the UK in 2001, the foot and mouth epidemic resulted in the mass slaughter of animals on the basis of veterinary advice which also prohibited mass inoculation. The immense cost of the mass slaughter has not been fully estimated, although the government has said that it would advise mass vaccination in the event of any future outbreak. The question of transferability of foot and mouth to humans was again shrouded in mystery during the outbreak.

In work carried out in the UK which sought to understand perceptions of risk, Draper and Green (2002) concluded that people use sophisticated strategies to assess the safety or riskiness of food preparation and consumption. Such strategies allow for the routinisation of food choices and for the management of uncertainty. In Draper and Green's qualitative analysis, safety emerged as a factor that was linked to cost. If food was cheap, it was assumed by the public that food producers had cut corners in safety.

A number of competing discourses, which included ideas about socialising, pleasure and convenience, were evident in Draper and Green's research relating to food. Discussion of food largely occurred within a framework of trust, in that food is considered safe unless and until the suppliers have demonstrably breached consumers' trust. Their research concluded, therefore, that food safety appeared to be a matter of intermittent importance (Draper and Green, 2002). Other evidence suggesting that individuals construct dichotomies of safety, counter-posing knowledge and confidence against ignorance and risk, supports these findings. Where the food was purchased and the country in which the food was produced are key factors in the creation of knowledge (Macintyre et al., 1998; Caplan, 2000).

Public health and global epidemics

During the twentieth century there were four great pandemics. In 1918, Spanish influenza killed 20 million people throughout the world. In 1957, Asian 'flu killed tens of thousands of people. In 1968, Hong Kong 'flu, which reappeared briefly in 1970 and 1972 and affected mainly the elderly, killed thousands worldwide. In 1983, the HIV/AIDs virus was identified. Some 42 million people around the world are now thought to be infected, while 3 million people died of AIDs-related illnesses in 2002 alone (Connor, 2003).

Mary Douglas is baffled by the manner in which large numbers of people are impervious to information relating to risks. Those who consider themselves to conform to dominant norms and values within a society direct their attention towards marginalised groups such as gay people and injecting drug-users, who are blamed for the spread of the disease (Douglas, 1992). This approach to risk within public health focuses upon risk as a consequence of lifestyle choices. Here risk appraisals and screening are undertaken with the intended aim of promoting risk awareness and good health.

Lupton (1999a) has described differing discourses within the public health and risk arenas. Pollution, nuclear waste and toxic materials can cause risks to public health. A common lay response to such health risks is anger at governments, feelings of powerlessness and anxiety. Governments design risk communication to defuse panic reactions within the community, and to build trust and credibility in risk regulators and risk analysts. Risk assessments are presented to the public as being based upon scientific quantification (Lupton, 1999a).

Frankenburg (1994) has shown how the field of epidemiology interweaves with what he refers to as 'individuals' social and cultural notions of risk'. Risk enables the medical practitioners to believe, in the face of recurring illness, that they have done their best by pointing out relevant risks to patients. Health promotion programmes tend to distance the culture of the 'risk population' from the general population.

The first global epidemic of the twenty-first century was Severe Acute Respiratory Syndrome (SARS). In its early form, SARS resembles influenza but quickly develops into pneumonia and can prove fatal. There are three inherent factors that give SARS its global risk status:

1　It is highly infectious.
2　It is a serious illness that requires intensive care treatment.
3　Medical staff who provide care are also susceptible to infection, a situation which can lead to large number of seriously ill people receiving no care.

One in 20 of those infected with SARS succumbed to the disease. Most of the deaths occurred among the very young, the old or those who were weakened by other illnesses, although the disease also killed some younger healthy people (Connor, 2003). SARS appeared to originate in the Guandong Province of China in November 2002 and, at the time of writing, has affected 4,600 people worldwide. Most of the cases have been in East Asia, although there were a significant number in Canada.

The response to the risk of contracting SARS has a number of recognisable features, some of which were present in HIV/AIDs epidemic. First, there was a panic reaction in the areas most affected. In Beijing, for example, many people tried to escape risk by leaving the city *en masse*, while others tried to stock up on essential items, fearing that the whole city would be quarantined. Secondly, the civil authorities took preventative action by effectively excluding those who had possibly been in contact with the virus. Some quarantine restrictions were also placed on the city of Toronto, the only epicentre of the disease outside Asia. On 22 April 2003, the World Health Organisation (WHO) advised travellers to avoid Toronto. In India, Singapore, Taiwan and Hong Kong, severe restrictions were imposed upon people who were thought to be at risk of being in contact with the SARS virus. Secondary panics were triggered in Europe. Only six cases were reported in Britain yet children returning to boarding schools in the UK from Far Eastern countries were quarantined. Individuals made risk assessments, some of which had bizarre consequences. In Brussels, a couple were asked to have their wedding ceremony conducted outside the City Hall after fears that the Chinese bride might have caught SARS on a recent trip to the Far East. Following the ceremony, it was reported that the pen used by the couple was destroyed, while staff also washed their hands as a precautionary measure (Connor, 2003). People in Hong Kong wore facemasks to protect themselves even when travelling in cars with closed windows.

The third global reaction to the epidemic was the apportioning of blame. China and Canada were blamed for not acting quickly enough in the face of serious health risks. The authorities in Toronto were severely critical of the WHO for over-reacting to the risk by advising travellers to avoid their city – a decision that had major economic implications. The mayor of Toronto argued passionately that Toronto was safe, although further cases of SARS were reported after the mayor had made his statement.

There is no doubt that panic reactions to the risk of infections like SARS can pose longer-term economic risks. The impact on the airline and tourist industries was immediate, particularly in Hong Kong and Toronto. Some small businesses faced catastrophic consequences. Rumours suggesting that there was a risk of contracting SARS in Chinese Restaurants circulated globally which resulted in a sharp reduction in trade (www.urbanlegends.about.com). They had also been blamed for creating the foot and mouth epidemic among farm animal stock in the UK in 2001. The role played by experts in this case lends weight to Beck's contention with regard to risk – no one is an expert or everyone is an expert (Beck, 1994).

Most cases of SARS were restricted to families, hospitals or hotels, and the mortality rate of 6 per cent would not indicate a particularly high level of infection. On the other hand, the interconnectedness of globalisation has the potential to increase the spread of new diseases and may lead to more frequent global epidemics in the future. The SARS epidemic showed the complex enmeshing of risks which turned into a political struggle between organisations. Pressure to manage risks, as was the case in Toronto, can undermine the ability to manage the problem. Risk as a tool for determining policy decisions is flawed because perceptions of risk are different and represent various interests. The manner in which governments and official organisations intervene will affect the way in which the problem is perceived (Smith, 2004). Different views of risk are based upon moral and political assumptions and can create global conflict between different groups.

Risk, health and individualised behaviour

Hallowell (1999) has argued that a moral imperative is reflected in health risks, and this is connected by experts to people's lifestyles and personal choices. Public health programmes, particularly those connected with HIV/AIDS, stress the importance of protecting oneself and others from the risk of infection.

Models that have been used to understand risk-related behaviour have been individualist in orientation, for example the Health Beliefs Model (HBM), which is one of the most significant psycho-logistic models for understanding risk-related behaviour with respect to HIV/AIDS. From the individualist position, health behaviour, including the practice of safe sex, arises from a number of interrelated perceptions:

1   Individuals must view themselves as being susceptible to a health threat.
2   The threat must be seen as having serious consequences.

3   The preventative measures available must be perceived to be effective.
4   The benefits of taking preventative action must be seen as outweighing any
    losses.

Bloor (1995) criticising from a phenomenological standpoint, argues that this model overlooks the fact that sexual relationships involve two parties in risk behaviour, and can involve constraint. This is particularly evident in studies of both male and female prostitutes, where sex often occurs at the 'punter's discretion'. Also, within marriage and long-term relationships, individuals can feel constrained to engage in sexual activity which can involve a risk of contracting disease.

Sociologists have been concerned with the way in which different discourses of risk have impacted upon individual perception. Allen et al. (1992) conducted research into attitudes towards the risk of HIV infection with respect to the dangers posed by dental practice. While members of the public appeared to take a reasonably relaxed attitude towards the possibility of being treated by a dentist diagnosed as being HIV positive, analysis of comments by other respondents reflected the complexity of different medically related risk discourses. The response of the public to the possibility of contracting HIV from dentists was influenced by media coverage of the risk. It also derived from the individual's perception of the personal qualities of the dentist. Central to the development of personal trust were perceptions of hygiene, trustworthiness and the relationship that had developed between patient and professional.

Discourses of trust and responsibility are inextricably related to perceptions of health risks. Health promotion campaigns are based upon the idea that health risks can be reduced through the creation of greater awareness and education about potential risk. Few writers have drawn attention to what might be referred to as the 'ethics' of health promotion. Lupton (1993) helpfully reminds us of the distinction between informing and persuading, arguing that if the purpose of a health campaign is the latter, then it can easily become coercive. Health education campaigns, she argues, have the potential to manipulate information, and thus appeal to individual feelings of guilt and fear. This is often combined with a naïvety inherent in health promotion messages. Governments in the western world tend to take the view that the public communication of health risk is desirable in most circumstances. Governments justify their involvement on the basis of containing costs and preventing individuals from harming themselves or others. The stated intention of the intervention is ultimately to improve health. Health education that emphasises risk can constitute a form of authoritarian and ideologically based government intervention, which serves only to regulate social activity (Lupton, 1993).

This view is supported by the postmodern view of health campaigns. O'Malley (2002) argues that programme designers appear to assume that campaigns appeal to those who are making rational choices. Health campaigns operate on the assumption that individuals have freedom of choice. This is not always possible. Drug-users who have developed a physiological dependence on a particular substance are not able to simply make a rational decision to desist. Despite this an appeal is made based upon a moral imperative to reduce risk to one self and others. Addiction is conceptualised as the result of making an immoral choice and ignoring obvious risks. Such a basis for action is implausibly oversimplistic. The use of biased or inaccurate information in health campaigns aimed at minimising drug use can also be counterproductive, thus limiting the credibility of the programme (O'Malley, 2002).

Decisions with respect to health and illness are not made on a 'rational' basis. Subjective perceptions of responsibility and trust dominate. For example, a 'good doctor' is likely to be perceived as one whom the patient has known for a considerable period of time. The possibility that such levels of subjectivity lead to miscalculations of risk is high. Individuals seek reassurance from medical professionals that there is some substance to their own judgements about medical risks (Green and Thorogood, 1998).

The smoking of tobacco is an activity which remains culturally acceptable in many western countries and is expanding within the developing world. The numbers of younger people who smoke tobacco is, according to some sources, orchestrated dishonestly by multinational companies based in western societies. Smoking is empirically linked to the risk of developing lung cancer and other fatal illnesses, yet it is an activity which is not punishable by the law. Some five million people have died in the UK in the last 40 years as a result of smoking (see Action on Smoking and Health at www.ash.org.uk). Although the state acts to deter smoking by raising taxation, printing warnings on cigarette packets and advertising the harmful effects of smoking, it still allows the tobacco trade to expand. At the time of writing, however, the British government is becoming more proactive in its health campaign against smoking. Following the Irish and New York examples, proposals to ban smoking in public places in the UK are to be put before Parliament. And yet, the rationale of the proposed legislation is not the personal risk smoking poses to individual smokers, but rather the harmful effects smoking has on others from passive smoking.

Alcohol, equally as addictive as tobacco, is closely associated with slower human reaction times, road accidents, violent crime and unsafe sex. As with tobacco, alcohol is directly linked to specific illnesses. These include stomach, throat and liver cancer, cirrhosis of the liver, and a range of other potentially lethal physical diseases (see Brookes at www. brookes.ac.uk/health).

The smoking of marijuana, which, it is argued, is of therapeutic value in some contexts, is still illegal. Even its possession is punishable in law in many western nations, including Britain. In the Netherlands, however, medical practitioners can now prescribe marijuana for some conditions. As Douglas (1992) argues, some risks appear to be culturally defined and the drinking of alcohol is one such risk.

Conclusion

In this chapter a number of health-related areas of risk have been examined. Social scientists have become preoccupied with attempts to understand how some phenomena come to be defined as risky to the health and well-being of populations while others do not. In advanced industrialised societies individuals are reliant upon the media for gaining an understanding of health risks. The media have a vitally important part in setting the agenda for health and, in the search for larger readerships, will over-dramatise and reduce events to their simplest form (Lupton, 1993; Elderidge, 1999). But the media are not solely responsible for defining risk. Government action is based upon the use of different forms of expert explanation. The state will choose to promulgate those expert opinions that are most likely to defuse a community's fearful reaction. The examples in this chapter show how MMR, BSE and SARS reflect a complex enmeshing of risks. The chapter has also shown how claims to truth about the nature of risk are based in contested forms of knowledge and expertise.

Smith (2004) uses the health field to challenge Beck's contention that risk is directly connected to developments in modernity. Definitions of risk are useful to governments since they are both ambiguous and scientific. However, in the risk society, Beck's notion of 'sub-politics' becomes important. The medical establishment is one of the most powerful social institutions. It possesses the power to define the nature of risk. Yet there is a growing and widespread cynicism as to the ability of the medical establishment and policy-makers to provide trustworthy explanations of risk. Beck questions whether medicine has improved the well-being of the world. He argues that, due to the technology of diagnosis, there has been a dramatic increase in the number of illnesses defined as chronic. There is no hope of ever treating many of these chronic illnesses. Health risks that have been technologically defined by the medical profession have now come to overshadow other particular interests, such as class, race and gender (Adam and Van Loon, 2000).

Further reading

Ratzan's editied volume, *The Mad Cow Crisis* (UCL Press, 1998), has excellent sections on the politics of health and risk, and the lessons and possibilities which have emerged from the BSE crisis. The special issue on food in the journal *Social Policy and Administration* (2000) 36(2) provides original material on risk, safety and food that is clearly related to the development of social policy. Christopher Barclay and Alex Sleator (1997) give a clear account of the BSE and CJD crises in House of Commons Research Paper 97/27. House of Commons Research Papers are designed to brief Members of Parliament in the UK and provide a freely available description of most risks which have been considered by the House of Commons. Gabe's collection, *Medicine Health and Risk* (Blackwell, 1995), although now slightly dated, uncovers some important theoretical debates relating to risk and the sociology of medicine. O'Malley's essay, 'Drugs Risk and Freedom', in Hughes, McLauglin and Muncie's, *Crime Prevention and Community Safety* (Sage, 2002), gives a critical account of public health campaigns from a postmodern perspective. Martin Smith analyses the politics of risk with reference to exchange rates policy and BSE in 'Mad Cows and Mad Money: Problems of Risk in the Making and Understanding of Policy', *British Journal of Politics and International Studies* (2004) 6: 312–32.

FIVE Professional Practices and Risk

Outline

Giddens (1990, 1998) has suggested that in the transformation from modernity to late modernity the judgements made by professionals are being constantly exposed to scrutiny. Any claim made by a professional to know what is best can be called into question as a result of clients' greater awareness of what can constitute risk. Professionals are more open to questioning from clients, can be exposed to charges of incompetence, and are required to justify their actions and present the service user with possible alternatives for action. Users of professional services are now faced with a proliferation of knowledge from various sources, which can conflict with what they are being told by professionals. As the distinction between 'lay' and 'professional' knowledge becomes blurred, solutions to minimise risk have also become unclear. Clients, managers of public services and politicians now demand that professionals justify and explain their decisions and interventions. This has also created new risks for professionals. This chapter examines the relationship between risk and professional blaming systems. It also examines some of the risks clients pose to the safety of professionals.

Risk management and professionals

Risk prediction has become a standard practice in many professional activities. Risk management intrudes into areas of work which have hitherto been regarded as professionally sacrosanct. The judiciary in Ontario, Canada, is now required to undertake risk assessments when sentencing (Hon. Judge Cole, 2000, personal communication). It is no simple matter to mark the point at which considerations of risk emerged as a central prerequisite of effective professional practice (Parsloe, 1999). The ascendancy of the concept of risk can be associated with systematic de-professionalisation. In the public sector, managers set targets for professionals which are prescribed by central government. Such managerial imperatives now appear to dominate professional considerations. Professional pre-eminence has given way to a more managed form of professionalism. Professionals are now accountable to audit appraisal and inspection, while service users have emerged from the margins to a position where they have gained a voice (Foster and Wilding, 2000).

Risk assessment is driven by a form of public service management that is committed to quantifying individualised risk and the level of danger through a process of audit. The process of listing and numerically rating risk factors is one of the elements that has contributed to the erosion of trust that individuals once had in the competence of professionals (Power, 1997). Risk is managed through new managerial relationships which operate between centres of political decision-making and front line professionals. Regulatory procedures, forms, and other bureaucratic devices are used to facilitate this new form of managerial regulation (Parton, 1998: 21). Thus, as Beck (1992: 54) argues, all the risks

> falling within the compass of knowledge production are never questions of the substance of knowledge (inquiries, hypotheses, methods, procedures, acceptable values, etc.). They are at the same time decisions on who is afflicted, the extent and type of hazard, the elements of the threat, the population concerned, delayed effects, measures to be taken, those responsible, and claims for compensation.

This narrows the parameters for scientific enquiry while the potential for managerial threat increases.

Risk, professionals and blame

Professionals are required to make risk assessments in relation to dangers posed by individuals to the 'community' and can become caught in a complex web of blame. The complexities of these situations are often exacerbated when professionals and organisations attempt to prove that another is to blame and has created the risk in the first place.

The relationship between risk and blame is exemplified by the media. For example, the negative treatment of social work by the UK media is well documented, but in countries like Australia, social work is seen in a more positive light (Aldridge, 1994). By the mid-1980s in the UK something of a watershed was reached when the media directly attributed the deaths of a number of children to the apparent inability of social workers to recognise and act upon risk. Jasmine Beckford, Tyra Henry, Charlene Scott,

Reuben Carthy (all in 1985), Kimberley Carlisle (in 1987) and Stephanie Fox (in 1990) were killed while technically in the care of social services. And in 2001 Victoria Climbie was brutally tortured and murdered. One newspaper suggested that a social worker and a police officer allowed Victoria to return to Marie Theresa Kauao and Carl Manning after medical staff had raised concerns relating to marks on Victoria's body (*Guardian*, 2001b). Kauao and Manning were sentenced to life imprisonment for Victoria's murder.

The essence of the recommendations of the enquiries into the deaths of children supposedly being cared for by social services is that social workers should be aware of the risks of violence to children and be vigilant in removing children from high-risk situations. The British media in particular have placed 'risk' at the centre of an unprecedented attack against a professional group carrying out an extremely complex and difficult task in situations of family crisis. In some cases, social workers have been castigated for failing to take action early enough, as in the case of Jasmine Beckford and Kimberley Carlisle. In other cases, they have been portrayed as being callous and manipulative agents of a 'nanny state', removing children from parents without justification. In the tragic cases in which children have been killed while in the care of social services, the media has freely apportioned blame. Although the media are right to point to professional failures, the many cases in which social workers safely remove children from risky situations receives negligible media attention.

The conduct of some individuals has also led to professional workers as a group being regarded as a risk. At the Bristol Royal Infirmary, between 1990 and 1995, the high incidence of death among children under one year, during and after surgery, shook the trust that patients had in the competence and integrity of the medical profession. The Bristol case was widely reported and eventually raised questions about more general failings within the National Health Service. It should be added that, as a result of the Bristol Royal Infirmary incidents, professional corrective action was taken, and yet other misconduct cases followed. In June 1998 James Wisheart, a cardiac surgeon, and John Roylance, a medically qualified hospital manager, were found guilty of serious professional misconduct and their names were erased from the Medical Register. At the same inquiry Janardan Dhasmana, also a heart surgeon, was found guilty of serious professional misconduct and was prevented from practising cardiac surgery for three years (Irvine, 2003). Individual criminal acts by professionals have an immense impact. The murder of over 200 elderly patients by Harold Shipman, a general practitioner in Hyde, Greater Manchester, shook public trust in the professional integrity of medical practitioners.

Since 2001 the 'success' rates of the operations of surgeons are routinely publicised in the UK, in the name of openness and transparency.

The government argues that the publication of the results gives patients the choice of joining waiting lists at their local hospitals or obtaining treatment further afield. The publication of such data enables patients to discover whether surgeons in particular areas have had specialist training (*Observer*, 2001a). But is there access to such data for all social groups? Do older people, who have the greatest need of medical care, have access to the data? Do socially excluded groups have equal access to risk-related knowledge? How can 'results' of success be satisfactorily measured and interpreted in ways which are understandable to non-professionals?

Douglas (1985) argues that cultural background provides a framework for understanding what constitutes a risk and what the likely consequences of taking a risk might be. In the risk society, every death and every accident occur as a result of the negligence of an individual, and every mishap can be used as grounds for potential litigation (Douglas, 1992). This is paradoxical given that, as Beck has acknowledged, the complexity of risks makes it difficult to establish who has ultimate responsibility (Beck, 1992).

The process of numerically rating risk factors is one of the elements that has contributed to the erosion of trust that individuals once had in professionals (Power, 1997). The accountability of professionals has increased, while their influence in the policy-making process has diminished. Layers of organisational management also serve effectively to remove the professional from sources of organisational power.

One possible problem resulting from the proliferation of technical or quasi-technical knowledge is that the service user may, due to a lack of basic technical knowledge, only be in a position to gain a partial understanding of the complexities of a particular risk. Managers also, in some cases, have a partial understanding of technical questions, and this can have disastrous results. In 1986 the US space shuttle *Challenger* exploded 73 seconds after launch. The investigation which followed indicated that the knowledge needed to prevent the accident was not only known, but was also transmitted to a team managing the launch. Engineers had warned that the 'O' ring seals in the rocket booster joints could fail at temperatures below 53° Farenheight. Even though the real temperature was predicted to fall, the management team proceeded with the launch, with catastrophic results (Green, 1997).

In other cases risks are created, allegedly, by a combination of bad communication and technical design fault, which result in dangerous professional practices. In 2001 American Airlines Flight 587 crashed, killing 265 people including five people on the ground. American Airlines and the aircraft manufacturer blamed each other for the accident. The stress on the tail fin and rudder exceeded the ultimate load prescribed by the Federal Aviation Authority. The airline blamed the lightweight tail design of the airbus. The manufacturer of the aeroplane, Airbus Industrie, argued that an American Airlines training programme contributed to the accident. In some circumstances pilots were encouraged to use the rudder to perform necessary corrections in extreme turbulence. Flight 587 had encountered severe wake turbulence created by another plane which had taken off immediately ahead of the stricken aircraft. Airbus Industrie argued that the rudder should never have been used for correctional purposes in such circumstances. The airline countered by claiming that Airbus Industrie had knowledge, following a previous incident, of the possible risks involved in attempting to correct the aeroplane with the rudder. Following the accident, air safety regulators worldwide have issued instructions and warnings about the risks involved in using the rudder to deal with wake turbulence. This is an example of a battle to avoid blame for a tragic accident, and a recognition of two factors which could have contributed to the crash (British Broadcasting Corporation, 2003c). The organisational response to this disaster emphasised the self-interest of the various professionals involved, and the complexities of risk perception.

Professionals, risk and self-interest

The creation of client professional relations based upon managerial accountability increases the potential for conflict. Only recently have risks posed by service users begun to attract media attention. How far professional avoidance behaviour with regard to blame is attributable to a greater fear of media involvement in the event of professional negligence or incompetence is important. There is now, according to Lowe (1993), an acceptance of the argument that the behaviour of public officials and professionals could be better understood if it is assumed they are largely motivated by self-interest. Although this judgement may seem slightly harsh, there is, as Le Grand (1997) suggests, a widespread belief on the part of service users that professionals are preoccupied with budget management and workload, rather than the need to provide good quality service in the public interest. It is the focus on the application of managerially defined goals to various forms of professional practices that has kept, over the last decade, the potentially harmful consequences of risks at the forefront of infractions between professionals and their managers.

Risks to professionals

There have been many examples of incidents in which professionals going about their duties have been injured or killed while working among their clients/pupils/patients. In 1996 Thomas Hamilton massacred 16 children and a teacher in a primary school in Dunblane, Scotland. Eighteen people were killed in a school in Erfurt, Germany, in April 2002, when a recently expelled pupil fired on former teachers and pupils. Two months previously, in Freising near Munich, a 22-year-old German who had lost his job killed two former bosses and a head teacher. In Gary, Indiana, in 2001, and in Colubine, Colorado, in 1999, students killed staff and other students in schools.

In the UK a focal point of media attention has been the prevalence of attacks perpetrated against social care staff that have resulted in death or serious injury. Isabel Swartz in 1984, Norma Harris in 1985, Francis Betteridge in 1986 and Audrey Johnson in 1998 were all killed while carrying out their duties as social workers. Kate Sullivan was murdered in 1992, Jonathan Newby was killed in 1993 by a psychotic patient in a South London hostel, and in 1998 social worker Jerry Morrison was stabbed to death while she was visiting a client with a psychiatric history (National Institute of Social Work, 1999). The murder of Rev. Christopher Gray, an Anglican priest, at his presbytery in 1996, powerfully illustrates the risks to professionals from clients and service users.

In the risk society, attention seems to be more frequently focussed upon the risk created by professional activity to clients, and little to the risks that professionals face from those with whom they work. Media coverage in the mid-1990s temporarily swung from creating 'moral panics' about the alleged incompetence of professionals, an activity which had become prevalent in the media during the 1980s, to recognising the risks posed by service users to professionals.

In a UK study of violence against professionals in the community, Gabe et al. (2002) found that some general practitioners saw some level of personal risk as being acceptable and an occupational hazard. Professionals working in the community had different views of what constitutes violence. Professionals saw violence as a transgressive act which disrupted normative expectations of professional relationships. The most common form of violence was verbal. The notion of the 'risk society' did not capture the complexities of the risk management strategies adopted by professionals. Probation officers, who are government employees, were the most risk-conscious of the three professions examined, and would use risk assessment procedures proactively. General practitioners and Anglican clergy used risk assessments in a more haphazard and reactive manner. General practitioners in particular distinguished between predictable and unpredictable violence. The fluidity and elusive nature of risk also suggests that the notion of an all-embracing 'risk society' oversimplifies the occupational and professional attempts to respond to risk (Gabe et al., 2002; Denney and O'Beirne, 2003).

The notion of predictable, understandable and rational violence presents an explanation of violence based upon the individual professional. It constitutes what O'Malley (2000) calls the criminology of 'us'. The context of the violent outburst enables the professional to identify with the particular form of violent or threatening behaviour. Driven by extreme circumstances, the professional, or any 'normally rational' individual, may also act in the same way. This contrasts with the criminology of the 'other'. Here the spectre is of the 'image' of evil or madness, which could not possibly be 'us' or related to 'us', and is beyond the rationally acceptable and the predictable (O'Malley, 2000).

The recognition of the risks posed by service users towards professionals in childcare work has become evident. The figure for assaults is particularly high for social care staff working with people with learning difficulties or mental health problems. Pahl (1999) found that social care workers in England and Wales who are supporting either of these two groups were twice as likely to be attacked than those working with other client groups.

Despite the many challenges to child protection practices made by the media, little, if any, research in Britain addresses the possible impact of violence on professional decision-making. However, according to research undertaken by Stanley and Goddard (2002), there may be an association between the trauma and isolation experienced by child protection workers and the re-abuse of children known to the protective services. Elements that are closely associated with the development of 'hostage-like behaviour' include ongoing trauma involving threats and fear, and isolation from support. The 'hostage's' perception of reality becomes distorted in this situation. Stanley and Goddard (2002), drawing on a systematic examination of victims who were held in a Stockholm bank vault for four days in 1974, found that the victims displayed behaviour that did not seem congruent with being a victim. They negotiated on behalf of their captors, attempting to protect them from the police. They also refused to testify against their captors in the courts. The term 'Stockholm Syndrome' is now used to describe a situation in which victims, due to severe trauma, attempt to understand and co-operate with those who violate them.

Following interviews with 50 child protection workers and an examination of 50 files drawn at random from the current caseloads of the social workers who were interviewed, Stanley and Goddard (2002: 146) reached the conclusion that: 'Child protection workers, who experience the most intimidation and violence and receive the least support, sometimes demonstrated hostage-like behaviour. This behaviour, in turn, may contribute to a failure to protect some children who may be harmed'.

Conclusion

Beck argues that experts who define acceptable levels of risk are engaging in a 'phoney con trick' (Beck, 1992: 64). Yet risk has affected both the status and manner in which professionals are able to operate. In a society in which the idea of 'risk' and risk assessment is dominant, it becomes difficult for professionals to present themselves as the guardians of expert knowledge. No professional authority can stand simply on the traditional basis of position and status. This change has had a greater impact on professionals who have a higher status, for example doctors, than on others such as nurses and social workers, whose status as professionals has been contested. Users of professional services are now more likely to demand that risks are understood and, whenever possible, quantified, so that they can make their own decisions based upon evidence provided by the professional. As litigation against professionals proliferates, clients and patients are more confident in their own capacity to tackle the problems they face, and are mistrustful of the abilities of professionals and experts to act in their interests.

The impact of the notion of a risk society places professionals in a double jeopardy. First, the general public and the media blame professionals when a calculated risk results in damage to a vulnerable person. This is the case, for instance, when offenders released on parole continue to commit offences. Second, professionals are blamed by management for failing to carry out procedures which are thought to be virtually infallible if applied with enough precision and enthusiasm. Both service users and professionals are at risk from each other, while both groups can also be seen as a threat to the collective community. Other service users pose a risk of self-harm, particularly in the field of mental health. Beck's contention that those who use professional services are socially reflexive, in that they are able to filter information relevant to their life situations and routinely act on this process with confidence, is useful in understanding the context of some of the situations within the community which are potentially harmful to professionals (Beck, 1992).

Further reading

Friedson's *Professionalism Reborn* (Polity Press, 1994) examines the reduction of autonomy of individual professionals, while Foster and Wilding's 'Whither Welfare Professionalism?', in *Social Policy and Administration* (2000) 34(2): 143–60, puts the changing position of professionals into the context of a developing risk society. Elston et al. describe how violence against doctors has emerged within the British National Health Service in 'Violence Against Doctors: a medicalised problem? The Case of National Health Service General Practitioners', *Sociology of Health and Illness* (2002) 24(5): 575–98. Donald Irvine's *The Doctor's Tale* (Radcliffe Medical Press, 2003) documents the rise and fall of professionalism and public trust in the medical profession.

SIX Communicating Risk Through the Media

Outline

Beck (1992) claims that the media has created 'standardisation and isolation' which has become a feature of the risk society. The mass media are central to the creation and maintenance of a society in which fear of risks dominates consciousness. This chapter seeks to address critically how risk-related topics are constructed by the media and become part of popular consciousness. The chapter will examine the manner in which ideas relating to risk are communicated in print media, television and film. Competing forms of discourse will be compared, and attention will be focused on the differences between the portrayal of individualised risk and the prediction of risk made by experts. Research has often concentrated on the complex ways in which ideas about risk are shaped by the media and the manner in which professionals are presented by the media as the cause rather than the controllers of risk. The nature of media discourses will also be discussed in relation to specific examples of risk reporting.

The media and perceptions of risk

Understanding how the media present risks in society is an under-researched area (Slovic, 1986). Some work indicates that the media ignore risks like road accidents, while exaggerating more dramatic incidents which may make readers feel that they are at risk (Sumerai et al., 1992).

In the mid-1980s HIV/AIDs was transformed into a moral panic by the media. According to Elderidge (1999), there were two reasons for this. First, the seriousness of the illnesses associated with HIV/AIDs and, secondly, the association of the disease with forms of sexual behaviour. HIV/AIDs was turned into a gay plague and was accompanied by vindictive representations of possible solutions to the problem. The *Daily Star*, in its editorial on 2 December 1988, which was also International AIDS Day, reported that 'experts' had suggested the creation of offshore island colonies for those infected with HIV. For Elderidge, this suggestion was the language of panic (Elderidge, 1999).

Other work (Phillips, 2000; Pidgeon, 1999) has shown how difficult it is to make any simple link between possible political orientation and the presentation of risk. From a Marxist perspective, it can be argued that parts of the media, as supporters of global capitalism, minimise risks from the potentially dangerous products of capitalism. On the other hand, it can also be argued that an arm of the media that is more critical of the status quo can over-emphasise risk, for political purposes. No such simple correlation appears to exist, if the evidence relating to portrayals of risk and the media are examined. Fiske (1994) counters any suggestion that the mass media merely reproduce messages meant for mass consumption by a dominant capitalist class. Capitalism produces messages which convey different meanings to people. Fiske also rejects the idea that individuals are passive recipients of messages constructed by a mass media industry which merely reflects the interests of a dominant capitalist class. Fiske and others (Petts et al., 2001) have argued that individuals receive texts in a way which reflects varying forms of resistance. For Fiske, a text is a 'site of struggle' between those who produce and consume cultural commodities. He rejects the idea that any text conveys the same message to all people (Fiske, 1994). The media produce differentiated messages reflecting struggles as to the nature and definition of risk in society. Competiton in the field of risk communications is centred on four processes.

- Control – over the timing and visibility of the risk message.
- Legitimacy – having the risk story treated as credible and authoritative.
- Trust – maintaining and enhancing public trust in the message.
- Precedence – establishing the dominant definition of the situation and structuring the agenda for debate (Petts et al., 2001).

The media seem to be heavily reliant upon definitions of risk created by experts, while at the same time appearing to be moderately 'pro-technology' (Freudenburg et al., 1996). Although media content is influenced by risks, as calculated and defined by experts, there is considerable randomness in what is defined as constituting newsworthiness. The possible dangers to the ozone layer posed by spray cans, for instance, was not immediately covered by such newspapers as the *New York Times* since it was thought by editors to contain 'doomsday' reporting. The population of Europe in the mid-1980s was profoundly affected by the Chernobyl accident, in which a nuclear power station located in the then Soviet Union 'melted down', emitting radiocesium over large areas. Here, a combination of weather reports on wind direction added to the risk of radiation contamination in Europe (Moores, 2000). However, media reports on the Chernobyl disaster were not sensationalistic, but were described by some commentators as 'low key' (Wahlberg and Sjoberg, 2000).

One model that has been proposed to explain the creation of risk in mass media messages is the social amplification of the risk framework. This framework attempts to integrate individualistic and culturalist perspectives to account for how some phenomena come to be defined as risks and others are not (Kasperson et al., 1992). Some hazards, which present quite low statistical risks, for example CJD in the UK, become amplified into a cause for political concern. Other potentially serious risks, for instance exposure to Radon gas, receive comparatively little media attention. The term risk amplification is used to describe the impact of an event beyond its initial effect. Although the media can be regarded as the primary definers of risk, other agents including independent experts, government agencies and pressure groups respond to the imagery and signs which have been communicated through various forms of media discourse. In some cases a loss of trust in an organisation or industry can result. Communities and products can also be stigmatised. Ultimately an event can have a political impact if new regulation legislation or some form of immediate government action is required (Petts et al., 2001). Risk amplification is used to explain why some events have both a primary, secondary and in some cases tertiary impact. The hazardous event moves through a series of stages of amplification. Although the media are regarded as the primary definers of risk in this model, other agents, including experts, government agencies and pressure groups, respond to the imagery and signs which have been communicated through various forms of media discourse. The initial signal can transform the risk message itself, while the amount of information made available for mass consumption can regulate the impact of these messages, though ripples can be felt through local communities and industry.

Although the social amplification of the risk framework can explain the exaggeration and, in other cases, the attenuation of risk-related events, there are a number of problems with the model. First, attempts to test this model have proved to be inconclusive (Pidgeon, 1999). Secondly a considerable body of research has failed to establish a link between media messages and public understandings of risk (Wahlberg and Sjoberg, 2000).

Studies of the coverage of risk by the print media and television have been made in France, Norway, Sweden, and Britain. Scandinavia has had particularly high levels of risk reporting. Generally, the media tend to combine alarmism and the creation of fear with reassurance. International comparisons suggest that it is therefore difficult to make the allegation that the media are obsessed with the reporting of rare, dramatic events. There is a tendency for the media to concentrate on apportioning blame in the event of risk warnings being unheeded, and there is some evidence of the construction of conspiracy theories with respect to the apportioning of blame (Frewer et al., 1997).

The language of risk

Although Beck (1992) acknowledges the importance of the mass media in identifying and defining risks, he does not engage with the complexities of the construction of risk through language, or to what some writers have described as the 'language of risk' (Eldridge, 1999). Linguistic theory can assist in understanding the ways in which meanings ascribed to the term 'risk' have been constructed in the media. Structuralist theorists, who predate postmodernism, have attempted to analyse the different levels of meaning that reside both within words used, and beyond them. The basic premise of structuralism's analysis of language is that words are not symbols which correspond to referents, since there is an arbitrariness which lies at the heart of language. It is the systematic relationship between words which enable them to communicate the relationships between words and objects. Language is not an instrument for reflecting a pre-existent reality, because subjects are produced by linguistic structures. There is no reason why, for instance, the word 'cat' should denote a feline quadruped. The English language would work equally well if 'cat' were to change places with 'dog' (Lodge, 1981).

Structural linguists like Saussure make an important distinction in the literature between '*langue*' and '*parole*'. *Langue* is the linguistic system that we learn from a language. An example of this would be the basic rules governing the conjugation of verbs in any language. *Parole* denotes the way in which speech is used in everyday life, the innumerable utterances spoken in language that may not always adhere to the basic rules of language. An analysis of *parole* produces a diversity and complexity of meanings in relation to risk. The *parole* of risk can best be described as the examination of the 'signification' of risk. Saussure defined the verbal sign or word as the union of the signifier, that is, the sound or written symbolisation of a sound, and the signified, which is the concept (Saussure, 1974).

Some writers have used the example of traffic lights to further illustrate the point. Red denotes stop, therefore connoting risk, amber means caution and green means proceed. Red, amber and green lights work as a system which is devoid of meaning unless the lights are used together, and in a particular sequence (Selden, 1989; Carter et al., 1997). Thus, signification is part of a linguistic system which can be understood. Analysis of the *parole* of risk enables the deconstruction of innumerable utterances, both spoken and written.

In writing about risk, Kemshall (2002) has argued that the notion of discourse facilitates an understanding of the social world while simultaneously limiting our understanding of social institutions and culture. 'Discourse' is a term often used in linguistics to describe the rules and conventions underlying the use of language. Differentiated forms of competing risk discourses permeate presentations of risk in the media. The analysis of different forms of discourse throws light on how power is mediated through varying forms of risk discourses. 'Discourse' can be regarded as that which mediates between the sentence and meaning. It facilitates an exploration of the numerous contradictions and complexities which are inherent in attempting to understand language. Crucially, discourse analysis can reflect complex power relationships and the manner in which competing discourses of risk can become dominant at a particulate point in time.

While discourse makes the world intelligible, heuristic devices are 'mechanisms' utilised by individuals for the 'framing' of information in relevant, accessible forms. 'Frames' make the world 'knowable', and help interpret the cues that we receive about the world (Edelman, 1993). The utilisation of such heuristics can lead to significant discrepancies between the objective calculation of risk probabilities by experts and the subjective perceptions of individuals (Kemshall, 1997: 249).

The framing of events represents an attempt to impose order on a disordered and confused world. One of the major problems which journalists experience in attempting to create a frame is when there is disagreement among official expert sources. Durham (1998) shows how the framing of the crash of TWA Flight 800 in 1996 constituted an ideological narrative that was accomplished through the creation and repetition of frames. Durham analysed coverage of the crash between 18 July 1996, the day after the crash, and 31 July 1997. He found that competing frames emerged to explain the crash. There was, in the case of Flight 800, a disjuncture between narrative journalistic forms of discourse and the official discourse of the expert. The journalists relied upon speculative historical frames and comparisons with previous air crashes. In their presentation of the possible causes of the crash, they explored the possibility of a bomb or missile attack, or mechanical failure. The experts used the 'rational' language of logic and empiricism to conclude that the cause of the crash must lie in the 5 per cent of plane debris which lay at the bottom of the sea. This crash represented an untraceable story, because there was insufficient empirical specialist opinion to frame a social meaning. Although such inconclusiveness satisfied the scientific method of forensics, such disorganisation defied and frustrated the journalists' ideology to organise the evident facts into a coherent frame (Durham, 1998: 113).

Sassure (1974) recognised that the signified and the signifier constituted two systems, but that they, having conceptualised language as a system independent of physical reality, retained the coherence of the sign. Postmodern theorists such as Selden (1989: 109) have attempted to 'prise apart' the two halves of the 'sign' in order to understand the changing nature of the 'signifier': 'Structuralist critics set out to master the text and to open out its secrets. Poststructuralists believe that the desire is vain, because there are unconscious, or linguistic, or historical forces which cannot be mastered'.

The competing nature of risk discourses determines what is possible and impossible to say in respect of a risky situation. In attempting to understand discourses of risk, we should be aware of what Foucault has described as 'systems of dispersion'. Foucault (1972) describes such systems in terms of a series of interplays of differences, distances and substitutions. The reader of accounts of risk is confronted with 'concepts that differ in structure and in the rules governing their use, which ignore or exclude one another, and which cannot enter the logical architecture' (Foucault, 1972: 37). Basing their work on Foucault, writers have described how risk discourse is dominated by a complex and ever-increasing number of social practices, institutions and individuals (Stenson and Watt, 1999). The image in the advertisement 'Head of Risk Management' (Box 6.1) illustrates the presentation of a risk signifier. The first line of the text accompanying the image emphasises the hidden and all-pervasive nature of risk: Risk is part of everyday life. You never quite know what's round the corner or what could happen the next minute – but there's still a great deal that can be done to keep risk to a minimum.

The post-holder is required to:

Manage a new Risk Management Group which will have responsibility for emergency planning, corporate health and safety, service continuity and risk management.

Box 6.1   Head of Risk Management Group

Risk is a part of everyday life. You never quite know what's round the next corner or what could happen in the next minute – but there's still a great deal that can be done to keep risk to a minimum. A forward-thinking council serving a fast-changing county, our aim is to make Bedfordshire a healthier and safer place in which to grow up, live and work.

As Head of Risk Management, your brief will be to manage a new Risk Management Group which will have responsibility for emergency planning, corporate health and safety, service continuity and risk management. Moreover, as the Council's principal advisor on all risk management matters, you will ensure there is a proactive approach to risk management across all of the Council's activities. In addition, you will champion the work of the new Group internally and externally with key stakeholders.

A dynamic, highly visible leader who can earn the respect of people both within and outside the Council, you will have a broad understanding of the increasingly important role of risk management as part of the corporate governance role of the Council. You will therefore require substantial experience of working in either emergency planning or risk management, along with a recognised qualification or equivalent experience.

These will be supported by an in-depth knowledge of Local Government and proven and highly developed management skills.

Finally, you will need to have the personal drive to help us achieve our objectives and be prepared to live within 20 miles of County Hall.

Source: The Guardian, 20 November 2002. Reproduced by kind permission of Bedfordshire County Council.

The warning board portrayed in the advertisment is more usually associated with slippery floors and danger. One possible connotation that could be connected with this image is the risk of an infection waiting to harm the unsuspecting victim. While proactive risk management can protect, individuals must always be mindful of potential danger.

Risk can also be signified through a legalistic form of discourse. The *Management of Health and Safety at Work Regulations, 1999* require:

Every employer to make a suitable and sufficient assessment of–

1 The risks to the health and safety of employees to which they are exposed whilst they are at work; and
2 The risks to the health and safety of persons not in his [sic] employment arising out of, or in connection with, the conduct of his undertaking.

This assessment is supposedly designed for the purpose of identifying the measures an employer needs to take in order to comply with the requirements and prohibitions imposed upon her/him by, or under, the relevant statutory provisions. Apart from the apparent assertion that employers are male, the discourse is couched in such wide terms so as to render it almost meaningless. It is not difficult to imagine the endless battles arising out of what is meant to constitute an employer's 'undertaking'. Also, the words 'suitable' and 'sufficient assessment' appear to give great breadth to the employer in deciding what forms of risk assessment are necessary. In this case the discourse appears to give linguistic legitimacy to minimal safety procedures, and have seemingly little relevance to safety.

Print media

Brindle (1999) has argued that there are a number of 'media triggers' which will determine whether a particular story is newsworthy. If a known risk exists, and an incident related to that risk occurs, usually an individual has to be publicly blamed. If a civil aircraft crashes, an individual or number of individuals, such as the pilot and aircraft engineer are sought and blamed. If a child is murdered while under the care of social services, an incompetent social worker or group of social workers are identified as being blameworthy. Within these dramas there must be recognisable heroes, victims, dupes and incompetents. The incompetent is often the professional individual who has the responsibility of recognising and acting upon the risk, but failed to do so, with tragic consequences. It is also possible to be portrayed as an incompetent consumer who is aware of risk but unwilling to take the necessary steps to avoid it (Brindle, 1999).

Media and the signification of risk

One possible outcome of the presentation of risk in the media is that there is an attempt to create and feed upon anxiety. The creation of anxiety by the media is a contested area, according to reviews of international empirical studies (Wahlberg and Sjoberg, 2000). However, many of the messages that are given through the various forms of media appear to be directed at anxiety-provoking themes. One particular theme is the identification of risk in mundane and everyday activities. The media justify this as providing a public service which draws attention to dangers which would otherwise remain unknown.

On Friday 28 June 2002 the *Daily Mail* reported that chips and crisps may cause cancer (see Box 6.2). This warning had the backing of 'science' and constituted a 'cancer alert', after scientists discovered acrylamide at 'alarming' levels in crisps and chips (*Daily Mail*, 2002a: 6). Some 25 experts from universities and food authorities had held talks on the topic for three days. Their deliberations had led them to the conclusion that 30–40 per cent of diet-related cancers might be caused by acrylamide, which was found not only in chips, but also in breakfast cereals and crispbread. Exposure to acrylamide produced by baking or frying was also associated with nerve damage. Although a clear link is made between particular kinds of popular food and the onset of major and fatal disease, two major caveats are included. First, despite the deleterious effects of acrylamide, towards the end of the article the actual health risks appeared to be less immediate: 'On the basis of animal experiments, acrylamide is considered a "probable" human carcinogen.' Secondly, scientific opinion does not suggest that there is an immediate risk of developing cancer after consuming acrylamide. The risk is associated with constant consumption over time.

Box 6.2 'Chips may cause cancer' and 'Alert as GM pollen spreads' (*Daily Mail*, 28 June 2002)

Chips may cause cancer, warns top food expert

By **James Chapman**, Science Correspondent

CHIPS and crisps were at the centre of a cancer alert last night.

After scientists found the two favourite potato snacks can contain high levels of a chemical linked to cancer, the world's senior food safety expert warned people to cut back on eating fried products.

Dr Jorgen Schlundt said there is 'major concern' over the detection of acrylamide at alarming levels in staple foods enjoyed by millions every day.

Dr Schlundt, the World Health Organisation's head of food safety, said after an emergency meeting in Geneva that teams of scientists in Britain, Sweden, Norway, Germany and Switzerland had confirmed the findings.

They have detected acrylamide in foods such as fried potatoes, crisps, crispbreads and breakfast cereals: Levels appear to be highest in foods that have been cooked at high temperatures for long periods.

The substance has long been linked to many different forms of cancer, nerve damage and infertility. But until April this year, experts had no idea that it could be produced by cooking.

The 25 experts from universities and food safety authorities around the world who gathered for the three-day talks said further tests on different types of food were now urgently needed.

Scientists, manufacturers and food safety bodies have to co-operate to find ways of lowering acrylamide levels.

'It is likely that this is causing cancer in the human population,' said Dr Schlundt. 'It is a genotoxic substance, which means it goes into the genes and changes something, and causes cancer. This is something that people will get in their food all the time, over the whole of their lives'.

Dr Schlundt added that he believes a 'significant' proportion of the 30 to 40 per cent of all cancer cases thought to be linked to diet might be caused by acrylamide.

'You should not have a picture that if you eat something once that has acrylamide then you will get cancer tomorrow,' he said. 'The longer you eat it, the greater the risk.'

Dieter Arnold, a scientist with Germany's Federal Institute of Health Protection for Consumers, who chaired the WHO meeting, said: 'We need to do research quite urgently to be able to reduce the levels of acrylamide in food.'

He said that at this stage, there are no plans to single out specific brands of food which should be avoided. 'People should eat a balanced and varied diet which includes plenty of fruit and vegetables and they should moderate consumption of fried and fatty foods.'

Acrylamide in food appears to be produced naturally as a result of baking or frying. It is also likely to be produced by grilling and roasting.

Early experiments suggest that boiling does not increase levels of the chemical.

In industry, it is used in the production of gels called polyacrylamides. These are used in water treatment and in manufacturing paper. Other uses include as a soil conditioning agent, and as a grouting agent in the construction of dams, tunnels and sewers.

On the basis of animal experiments, acrylamide is considered a 'probable' human carcinogen. Exposure to the chemical in the work-place is also known to cause nerve damage. In studies on male animals, it has also been shown to impair fertility.

The Food Standards Agency in Britain was prompted to investigate levels of acrylamide after Swedish scientists claimed in April to have discovered that frying and baking created potentially dangerous amounts.

There are strict European rules on the amount of acrylamide allowed in food packaging – no more than ten parts per billion.

But the FSA study found 310 parts per billion of acrylamide in potatoes after they were chipped and fried.

Alert as GM pollen spreads

POLLEN from genetically modified plants can contaminate other crops within a two-mile radius, scientists warn today.

(Continued)

(Continued)

The Australian researchers discovered that a third of conventional oilseed rape plants growing near GM fields showed signs of contamination.

Their study, the first on gene flow from commercial GM crops, found that GM material will inevitably escape into the environment.

The alert comes as another report warns that farmers in the U.S. may have to use damaging pesticides to kill stubborn weeds growing among GM plants. Iowa plant scientist Michael Owen said some weeds did not respond to pesticides used for GM crops, and could require stronger chemicals known to damage wildlife and humans.

Both revelations will heighten concerns about GM crop trials in Britain.

The Australian scientists, from the University of Adelaide, collected seeds from 63 conventional oilseed rape fields growing near GM oilseed rape fields in south-east Australia.

After testing more than 48 million plants, they found that one third showed signs of GM contamination. The furthest field affected was about two miles from the nearest GM field.

The scientists believe the contamination could give some plants an advantage that would allow them to crowd out other varieties.

They warn that their findings, published in the journal Science, show that small-scale laboratory experiments cannot accurately predict what will happen when GM crops are grown on a large scale.

Of the GM crops tested in the United Kingdom, oilseed rape and beet have wild relatives with which they could cross-pollinate.

On the same page as this article was another which drew attention to the hidden dangers of GM crops. In this article readers were warned of an 'Alert as GM Pollen Spreads': 'Pollen from genetically modified plants can contaminate other crops within a two-mile radius, scientists warned today' (*Daily Mail*, 2002b: 6) (see Box 6.2). Australian researchers had discovered that one-third of all conventional oilseed rape plants growing near fields with (GM) crops showed signs of contamination. GM food crops would 'inevitably' escape into the environment. This could result in GM crops 'crowding out' other varieties. Cross-pollination with other plants was another possible risk. A further risk could be located in the use of the 'damaging' pesticides which were needed to kill stubborn weeds growing among GM plants. Yet the scientists also warned against over-reacting to the findings: 'They warn that their findings, published in the journal *Science*, show that small-scale laboratory experiments cannot accurately predict what will happen when GM crops are grown on a large scale' (*Daily Mail*, 2002b: 6).

These articles have a number of common characteristics, which illustrate the way in which risk is conceptualised in the print media:

- Risk stories constitute a warning to the population.
- The risk to public health is based in science.
- Stories contain a shock to the reader.
- A sense of crisis is created in that the scientific discussions are recent and reveal a hitherto unknown risk.
- Risk stories resonate with existing public concerns. The coverage of GM foods, for example, draws on pre-existing public anxieties (see Elderidge, 1999).
- Risk stories provide an orientation to the unfolding risk-related events.
- The consequences of the risk interrupt the normal flow of events.
- News stories often examine the immediate consequences for everyday life in households and families.
- Risk stories contain elements of controversy.
- The scale of the potential risk is qualified.

In summary, there are a number of elements, that are necessary to a good risk story, and they can be seen in both of these *Daily Mail* articles (see Box 6.3).

Box 6.3   Thematic progression in the representations of risk

- *Identification of risk* (Acrylamide/GM pollen)
- *Link between risk and everyday living* (Frying, baking or eating crisps and chips/GM crops kill off other varieties or cross-pollinate)
- *Scientific validation for alert*
- *Risk assessment* (e.g. small quantities of chips constitute low risk)
- *Risk management* (eat chips in moderation/concerns about GM crop trials in UK)

Petts et al. (2001) have also emphasised the importance of local news in circulating local risk knowledge and responding to the grounded experience of individuals. In their research in the UK, 89 per cent of their participants read local newspapers, a large proportion of which were free, while 25 per cent did not read a daily paper. The piece in Box 6.4 is taken from a local paper and illustrates how numerous levels of risk discourse operate in competing and often contradictory ways. Here, the discourses of risk are integrated into a wider matrix of community safety. The focus of the risk is not on the individual, but on aggregate populations. This 'hybrid discourse' identifies the problem both as a limited number of individuals and entire sections of the population (Matthews and Pitts, 2001).

Box 6.4 Ethnic groups at risk

Ignorance and fear about health problems such as depression, diabetes and heart disease are putting many people in Merton's 30,000 ethnic minority population at risk.

Merton Council has raised concerns about access to health services in the borough in its three-year race equality plan. Some sections of the borough's total population enjoy very good health and access to health care, while other communities are experiencing multiple levels of deprivation, including high rates of teenage pregnancy, death and avoidable illness. (*Wimbledon, Mitcham and Morden Guardian*, Thursday 11 July 2002: 6)

Another theme which runs concurrently with the fear of risks within mundane everyday activities is the risk of an omnipresent and oppressive state, which uses the threat of risk to coerce the population. The introduction of technology into the control of crime has been accompanied by some press derision. Mair (2001) has described the reaction of two broadsheet newspapers to the use of the Offender Group Reconviction Scale (OGRS) 'risk of conviction scale,' the measure taken by the British government to quantify the risk of conviction. *The Independent* described it as a 'magic formula' which was meant to distinguish the 'incorrigible' from the 'redeemable'. However, *The Guardian* Editorial observed that 'Postcode sentencing cannot deliver justice'. *The Guardian* presented the use of computerised risk assessments as constituting the spectre of a '1984 world', in which judgements which should be made by human beings are dominated by technology. Such a practice, it is suggested, could threaten the delivery of justice.

Magazines

Boyne (2003) has commented that the language of risk within the media is not rigorous and does not form a basis upon which to form judgements. This is particularly the case with coverage of risk stories in some magazines, yet the fields of health and surgery provide numerous examples of complex risk assessments made by individuals. Some forms of surgery involve risks that are taken voluntarily, cosmetic surgery being an obvious example. In an article entitled 'Cosmetic Surgery – Before and After', *She* magazine (2000) asks the question 'Which ops are the riskiest?'. The magazine reports that there is no law to stop insufficiently qualified surgeons from performing delicate and sometimes irreversible procedures. The magazine warns its readers that one in five operations are performed to correct previous post-operative complications. However, *She* magazine reports that the number of cosmetic procedures carried out in the UK has risen by 50 per cent in the past five years and that 4.6 million cosmetic procedures are carried out in the USA annually. Beck (1992: 205) comments: 'Anything and everything is "sick" or can actually make you sick – quite independently of how one feels'. According to Beck, cosmetic surgery is being carried out for questionable reasons, the effects of which can make one sick. The *She* article, like many other presentations of risk in the media, presents manufactured and impossible dilemmas. Technology offers the possibility of looking more attractive. How does the individual balance this against potential risk of personal physical damage? The context for this dilemma is also constructed within the scenario of a growing disillusionment with the skill of the expert. Increasing awareness of risk is centred on risk choices made on the understanding that experts and professionals frequently make mistakes and, in some instances, can create risks by their activities.

Television

Beck is vitriolic in his comments on the impact of television within the 'risk society'. Television, he argues, 'removes people from traditionally shaped and bounded contexts of conversation, experience and life. At the same time, however, everyone is in a similar position. They all consume institutionally produced television programmes, from Honolulu to Moscow, to Singapore' (Beck, 1992: 132).

The power of television to create and define what constitutes risk has taken on a new significance, as it has become the leading form of news media. Biernatzki (2002) claims that there is a strong link between emotional reaction and authenticity in television accounts of news. If the emotion an individual feels as a result of watching a television news story is real, then the story must also be real. Television thrives on the idea that it is only what is visible that deserves to be regarded as news. Events which produce strong emotional responses go to the top of the hierarchy of news, even if, in absolute terms, they are not of great significance (Biernatzki, 2002).

Risks, and the fixation with danger, are represented not only in the presentation of news but also in drama and documentary programmes. Films such as *Independence Day* (1996) and *Men in Black* (1997) and television shows such as the *X Files* are dominated by themes connected to risk. Vail (1999: 2) argues:

In the *X Files* the paranoid imagination has come completely unglued. The world is controlled by chain-smoking men in dark suits who run the media, the military and the government: our political leaders, whose 'official versions' of the truth can no longer be trusted, have entered into Faustian bargain's with mysterious outsiders: the cult of secrecy and the art of the cover-up, exemplified by the supposed crash of a UFO at a site in Roswell, New Mexico.

Television is the medium which disembeds and displaces social relationships. Developments in the medium have stretched communication globally; distant happenings permeate the lives of private consumers (Giddens, 1990). The medium provides global coverage of events, while social relations are lifted from an immediate interactional setting and stretched over global time and space.

Moores (2000) has shown how the time–space disassociation can give rise to new connections between globalised scenarios and local life. Such linkages can be presented in ways that provoke anxiety. On 11 September 2001 footage of two civil aircraft being deliberately flown into a building was flashed across the globe. The event came to represent a globalised risk to all air travellers. During the invasion of Iraq by American and British troops in 2003, events unfolded on the screen as they happened. However, television reporting of risk, in the form of news or drama, is characterised by its brevity, often leaving the viewer with a limited perception of what is happening. Complex events are often condensed into small 'vision bites' in news slots, while complex issues are dealt with in a way designed to create the most immediate dramatic impact.

Television and soap opera

The mass popularity of soap operas globally has made this form of drama a significant part of television entertainment. The power of television soaps to influence perceptions of risk has yet to be fully researched, even though many of the topics within which the drama is located deal with risk. In June 2001, according to *The Guardian*, 'cancer charities' expressed reservations about the portrayal of cervical cancer in the British soap opera *Coronation Street*. Alma Hallowell, a character in the long-running British series, despite having had negative smear tests, was suddenly diagnosed as having terminal-stage cancer. Granada Television claimed that after the relevant episodes a Manchester hospital had reported to them that smear tests had increased from 2,000 a week to 1,000 a day. Granada Television claimed that this was a positive result of the portrayal of this type of cancer (*Guardian*, 2001a).

Yet some reports suggest that television dramas are putting lives at risk with misleading advice. A report by the British Broadcasting Standards Commission found that viewers were convinced of the accuracy of drama programmes, and used them to make critical judgements. One ambulance driver described a situation he faced when attending an emergency situation:

> This guy had obviously seen something on television or film that you put something in epilepsy sufferers' mouths to stop them biting their tongues. So he pulled out a 50p piece. Not only am I dealing with this guy fitting, he is now semi-choking on a 50p piece. It was just chaos. (Burrel, 2003: 8)

Television tends to represent the world as a violent and threatening place, de-emphasising any sense of existing order or security. Over-exposure to television images encourage viewers to adopt the images as their own view of the world (Gerbner and Gross, 1976).

Drama documentary

A more recent innovation within the presentation of risk has been the creation of a particular kind of drama documentary which creates disastrous situations based upon the combination of particular hypothetical circumstances occurring in a specific sequence. In Britain, this has been combined with the simulation of a terrorist chemical weapons attack in the centre of London, as occurred on 6 September 2003.

The events portrayed in drama documentaries are purely fictional, but supposedly are presented within a context of possible combinations of events. Actors play the parts of those involved in the drama, and provide retrospective views of the incident. Mock archive footage is used to increase the sense of reality further.

In 2002, the British Broadcasting Corporation broadcast a drama documentary which explored the consequences of a biochemical attack in the UK. The programme, *The Day Britain Stopped,* followed this in May 2003. It presented a scenario which, according to the story, occurred on 19 December 2003. In this combination of events, Britain was brought to a standstill by a variety of disastrous factors (British Broadcasting Corporation, 2003d). A chain reaction was created by a national rail strike, poor weather conditions, weight of traffic, and accidents occurring at key points on motorways. Air traffic controllers were unable to reach their work and exhausted air traffic controllers were left to direct aviation movements in the air lanes over London. Two planes collide after one aircraft is told to abort its landing. The narrative dramatically drew attention to the failure of government policy to address the problem of overcrowded roads, under investment in transport, the pressure on air traffic controllers, and the weakness of specific procedures when aircraft miss their approach.

This form of broadcasting is, according to the BBC, a legitimate journalistic attempt to draw attention to the lack of capacity in the air and on the roads of the UK, which creates a potentially catastrophic risk to public safety. The potential risk that is inherent within a normal flying manoeuvre is also intended to compound the impact of the programme. Although this approach probably makes for good entertainment, it pushes the notion of legitimate journalistic enquiry to its limit. The catastrophe that unfolds in the drama documentary is dependent on the convergence of a number of separate complex and seemingly unconnected incidents. The likelihood of these events occurring in such a sequence stretches credulity. In its apparent concern to warn the population of the risks of neglecting transport policy, fear and mass insecurities are fed.

Representations of risk and crime in the media

Individual perceptions of risk are linked to information which is most readily available and easily recalled. Thus Kemshall's assessment of the portrayal of the risks associated with crime can be applied more generally to the way in which the media presents risks: 'Perceptions of crime risks may be prone to error and exaggeration, and "public anxieties and fears" may be "inflated"' (Kemshall, 1997: 256).

A recent study of media coverage of crime found that one of the most significant changes has been the prominence given to the victims of crime. Details of the traumas created by crime have come to dominate newspaper, television and cinematic coverage of crime. The proportion of newspaper stories devoted to crime has increased over time, while the rise in the number of police protagonists in film is related to the all-pervasive crime risk (Reiner in Stenson and Sullivan, 2001).

Sparks (1992) concentrates on the metaphorical and figurative dimensions of crime. Fear of crime is neither irrational nor a static variable which can be measured. People's fear of crime is based upon intuition and a grounded theory of life. Fear of crime, for Sparks, does not take sufficient consideration of the diffuse and complex anxieties that individuals have about their own position in the world. Sparks offers a direct challenge to the idea that the 'stimulus response effect' of the media structures mass understandings of crime risk. Lupton and Tulloch's research on the fear of crime has positioned viewers as 'reflexive subjects who experience and respond to crime via communal, aesthetic and shared symbolic meanings' (Lupton and Tulloch, 2000: 515). Their work draws on postmodern assumptions that notions of subjectivity are often contradictory and fragmentary, and concludes that rationality and emotion are constituted through 'the discourses of a number of subcultures or social collectivities, of which individuals are members, as well as through personal experience' (Lupton and Tulloch, 2000: 516).

Lupton and Tulloch describe the experiences of Mae, a 68-year-old widow who has little contact with the police and lives a private life behind multi-locked doors in New South Wales. For some years, although reasonably fit and well, Mae lives in fear of the risky world outside her doors. Her fears, according to Lupton and Tulloch, were created by the death of her husband. Mae no longer watches any programmes relating to crime on the television, whereas before his death she would have happily done so with her husband. Fear of crime should not be couched simply in terms of questions which relate to rational or irrational fears. Neither should Mae's perceptions of crime and the risk from crime be seen as the product of an unquestioning acceptance of anxiety-provoking and specially selected coverage of particular events in the media. Mae's fears result from a circuit of experiences, including, principally, the death of her husband. These construct her knowledge of insecurity, danger and crime. Lupton and Tulloch argue that individuals are not simply drip-fed fearful messages by the media to form an overestimation of risk. Drawing on the work of Douglas (1992), they see risk as a cultural, symbolic product of the community. Understandings of fear represent an interplay of perception and cultural reality, together with a personal psychodynamic aspect of response to crime. The approach taken by Lupton and Tulloch draws attention to the complexity of the 'macro' and 'micro' circuitry of understandings which form the basis for perceptions of risk (Lupton and Tulloch, 2000: 516).

Media presentation, risk and 'moral panic'

Sociologists have documented the manner in which some risks have been transformed into moral panics over a long period of time. In his classic study of moral panics, Cohen (1972) examined disturbances on bank holidays in the UK between two rival groups of young people – mods and rockers. Cohen provided a detailed analysis of the way in which the media constructed mods and rockers as representing a risk of moral disintegration. In this analysis the media are seen as orchestrating moral indignation and moral panic with respect to particular social groups and thereby amplifying deviance (Cohen, 1972). A decade later, Hall and his colleagues provided an analysis which also sought to demonstrate how the media amplify 'mugging' and construct the phenomenon as symbolising black crime (Hall et al., 1978).

Much of what has been written above with respect to media presentations of risk suggest that some parts of the media actively engage in 'panic creation'. There has been considerable theoretical interest in the relationship between risk and moral panics. Goode and Ben Yahuda (1994) list five crucial elements 'which constitute a moral panic': concern, hostility, consensus, disproportionality and volatility. Although risk contains a moral imperative, it is distinct from a 'moral panic'. In his classic study, Cohen (1972: 9) defined a 'moral panic' as a 'condition or episode, person or group of persons who are defined as a threat to societal values and interests. Its nature is presented in a stylised and stereotypical fashion by the mass media'.

Ungar (2001) argues that moral panics and conceptions of risk are distinguishable. 'Moral panics' appear to take the form of a top-down approach. As Cohen points out, bishops, politicians and right-thinking people man the moral barricades. For Ungar, however, risk society issues do not filter down from the top. Responses to risk appear to be 'prototypical' in that a catalytically real event is given credence by interest groups and is carried forward by groups within the population who are well informed. Political authorities can often be the target of such protest. While moral panics have conventionally focused upon social control, risk society issues focus upon sometimes intractable scientific claims. Moral panics are, according to Ungar, largely conducted in the context of a search for safety. Deviants can be identified by the powerful and then subjected to various forms of social control. Such a 'safety discourse' ruptures in the context of a 'risk society'. Risks, as Beck (1992) has argued, can become invisible, unpredictable and diffuse. The British government, as Ungar (2001) points out, could have had no idea that, as a result of announcing the possibility of a link between CJD and BSE, a political storm would erupt (see Chapter Four). Thus, in the risk society the idea that institutions can control safety is severely challenged.

Risk and the creation of controversy

The controversy surrounding risk is an important factor in the way in which particular situations are presented by the media. Existing risks are drawn to mass attention, not by available 'expertise' or 'science', but by a story's capacity to gain the interest of large numbers of people. The story therefore requires room for disagreement and controversy (Luhmann, 2000). The notion of risk lends itself to such media treatment especially well because it is often easy to create a 'for' and 'against' argument that is both intelligible and engaging. One such story, which ran for a number of months, related to the risks created to world peace by a pre-emptive attack against Iraq. Other examples include the risk of eating beef, which ran during the BSE crisis, and the risks involved with the production of GM crops.

When there are no immediate reactive risk stories available, the media will resurrect more long-term, endogenous risk debates and controversies. Should individuals have a right to smoke in public? How safe is security at international airports or in secure establishments like prisons? Devices are used to create good risk stories, which will grasp the imagination of the risk-conscious public. An undercover journalist with a fake gun boards an aircraft without being challenged, or enters a prison and manages to take a picture of a notorious criminal unnoticed. The story which follows relates the global risks of lax security at international airports and prisons to the reader's personal safety.

The media therefore require both positive and negative reactions to risk stories, and the creation of a debate, which will be current for a short time, only to be extinguished by the next *cause célèbre*. Such a rapid and insatiable need for risk stories that engage the public are far removed from any 'rational' discourse on risk (Boyne, 2003). This approach to discussion about risk feeds and lays bare what Beck (2000) referred to as the 'cosmopolitan significance of fear'.

Conclusion

This chapter has explored the language of risk. The main concern has been with the ways in which messages about risk are constructed, transmitted and received. All arms of the media are concerned with risk, and the presentation of risk is a potentially profitable form of activity for the media. Risk is intrinsically newsworthy. Publicity about a particular risk does not depend on any political intervention or bias. Neither does it simply reflect the positions held by those who control the media. Risk is not simply a political tool which can be manipulated by politicians or their supporters in the media. The chapter has shown that the presentation of risk is more complex than that. Studies of newspapers and television have failed to establish a consistent or significant link between media messages and public perceptions of risk. The media draw their explanations of risk from a variety of sources, although the dominant source is science. Explanations of risk are dependent upon the role of experts, although it is not the case that the media drip-feed fear and risk into a simple, gullible, unsuspecting public. Media organisations increasingly regard people as consumers with rights to personal safety and well-being. Knowledge of risk and personal biography are important factors in determining how an individual responds to reports of risk. Whenever possible the media attempt to generate controversy in the presentation of risk. The creation of dichotomous viewpoints encourages and fosters public interest in a particular risk scenario. The media tend to amplify risk if such amplification resonates with an existing public mood. There is a tendency to personalise explanations of risk events, and to look to individuals as a cause. The media will also use powerful images to focus on the consequences of risk (Petts et al., 2001).

Beck's analysis, according to Elderidge, does not help us to understand what happens when experts disagree, or when differences between the legitimacy of lay knowledge and professional knowledge emerge. A responsible media has to distinguish accurately between real knowledge about risks and propaganda that may mislead the public (Elderidge, 1999).

Further reading

For general coverage of the relationship between the medias message and the generation of meaning, see John Fiske's *Reading the Popular,* (Routledge, 1994). Slovic's work has been influential in understanding the way in which risk is communicated through the media. See, for instance, Slovic's important contribution 'Informing and Educating the Public about Risk' in *Risk Analysis* (1986) 6: 403–15. Wahlberg and Sjoberg's 'Risk Perception and the Media' (in *Journal of Risk Research* (2000) 3(1): 31–50) provides a comprehensive guide to research in the area. Sparks' *Television and Drama of Crime* (Open University Press, 1992) is still an important contribution which challenges over-simplistic ideas about the media's power to inculcate fearful responses in the public. Reiner, Livingstone and Allen examine media representations of the risk of crime in their chapter 'Casino Culture: Media and Crime in a Winner–loser Society' in Stenson and Sullivan's edited collection *Crime Risk and Justice* (Willan, 2001). Elderidge provides useful coverage of the media presentation of BSE, AIDS and contaminated eggs in *Risk, Society and the Media* (Longman, 1999).

SEVEN   Risk and Social Welfare

Outline

Over the last decade, the notion of risk has become the basis upon which state social care is predicated. Discussions relating to risk that have taken place hitherto in the social care literature have often been too narrowly focused upon the failure of social workers to comprehend and act upon the threat of risk to services users. The relationship between risk and blame is thrown into stark relief in the provision of social welfare. A number of key features mark out a qualitative change in the way that risk is now understood and acted upon by practitioners in the welfare field. This chapter considers social welfare with respect to child protection, old age and mental health.

Social welfare and the risk society

Although Beck does not make any direct reference to social welfare, much of his work is applicable to current debates concerning the state and the provision of welfare. For Beck (2002b), calculating risk is part of the master narrative of 'first' modernity. In Europe this culminated in the welfare state, which based its legitimacy on a capacity to protect citizens against dangers through the provision of state-funded assistance. First-order risks can best be described as the physical hazards which are destructive to life. These would include pollutants and disease. Second-order risks refer to social and cultural insecurities like unemployment, lack of education, family breakdown (Boyne, 2003). The idea of the welfare state developed in a world in which risks were definable, first-order risks. Second-order risks, for Beck, are less tangible and more uncontrollable. The parameters for scientific enquiry become narrower as the perceived potential for risk increases. 'Risk assessment' is a way of working which is managerially focussed and driven by a form of public service management that is committed to the quantification of future potential danger through a process of audit. For Beck, the 'sub-field of risk communication' is procedural, constituting a defence against awkward questions which might be asked by service users. From this position risk procedures can be seen as dis-empowering and de-professionalising, because public sector employees are required to apply risk assessment procedurally, without any reference to their own skill or knowledge. Risks, and their possible causes, become pre-defined and subsumed in a structure which covers managerial requirements. Protocol and procedures come to dominate working practices.

The changing nature of security provided by the state

In the British case, Beveridge identified the risks to living a healthy and fulfilled life in 1945 as being idleness, ignorance, squalor, want and disease (Beveridge, 1945). The British welfare state, which was created in the post-Second World War period, created state-funded systems to cushion the impact of such risks by implementing the principle of social insurance. Citizens made contributions which were supplemented by the state. The risk of suffering as a result of one of the factors listed above while they were in employment was thus ameliorated by a combination of individual contribution and state intervention.

States such as Britain, which during the postwar period fostered various forms of state welfare to guard against risk to its citizens, have now modified their commitment to service provision into a complex service partnership between the private and the public sectors. This change in policy is predicated on the assertion that economic growth and prosperity in western democracies have reduced the need for welfare provision funded entirely by the state (Giddens, 2000). As the perceived need for welfare has increased, there has been a concomitant growth of regulatory systems within welfare provision. This has led to the political demand for greater accountability within the public sector. The new climate of regulation is manifested most clearly in audit systems. Throughout the 1990s, emphasis was placed upon value for money, accountability and efficiency within public services (Power, 1997; Denney, 1998). The new global orthodoxy marked a break with earlier ideas, giving a higher priority to self-responsibility than was the case under the postwar settlements. The fastest growth of social services took place in the UK during the 1970s, and in Scandinavia in the 1980s. Even in Scandinavia, where taxation levels have been traditionally high in order to pay for high-quality collectively funded provision, services are now becoming individualist and dependent upon the private sector (Jordan, 1998).

Lane (2000) has noted that rich countries such as the USA, Japan and Australia have small public sectors, even though they form so-called 'welfare societies'. A form of service brokerage has replaced collectivism, where governments become reliant on the private sector to create market or market-like conditions in order to facilitate the delivery of services. This system of brokerage has also become globalised. The British government, for instance, now purchases bed and operation capacity in French hospitals, in order to reduce National Health Service waiting lists.

Risks which are currently preoccupying the 'international community' are not divisible into neat compartments or equally distributed. Globilisation is seen by some as representing the possibility of eradicating disease, increasing access to markets, utilising productive technology and modern management methods for the benefit of all. What is less frequently mentioned are the risks which are inherent in the process of globalisation, which go beyond the immediate set of ecological risks. Claire Short, the then Secretary of State for Overseas Development, argued that '[t]here is a real danger that some countries could become marginalised from the world economy, and that this would cause inequality within nations, unless we manage the process of globalisation in a way which ensures that its fruits are equitably distributed' (Short, 1998).

Other risks are associated with the more sophisticated development of economic market forces. Subsistence farmers may be poor, but when they enter any formal market they become more vulnerable to debt or risky investments (Spicker, 1998). The development of economic globalisation is dependent upon the emergence of recently industrialised economies, the breakdown of trade barriers, the entry of former Soviet Block countries into the world market, and the expansion of international speculative capital (Taylor-Gooby et al., 1999).

Risk and social work

It was in the early 1980s that Brearley, in his path-breaking work, offered an analysis of risk in social work (Brearley, 1982). Unlike Beck, and more in keeping with the views of Giddens, Brearley argued that risk is not simply about 'bads', but that it can have potentially positive consequences if used appropriately. Brearley conceptualised risk in terms of relative variations in possible loss outcomes. With hindsight, Brearley's work has been described as 'slippery', and of little assistance to practitioners requiring help in making decisions in complex areas (MacDonald and MacDonald, 1999). His book drew heavily upon approaches used in the insurance industry. In the area of social welfare it did mark an important milestone in the development of ideas relating to risk, and it also served to signify the centrality of the risk within social work practice.

The publication of Brearley's work coincided with the point at which the notion of state-funded social work itself was subject to attack from a number of directions. The polemics of authors such as Brewer and Lait in 1980 attempted to demonstrate that, while social workers failed to make any measurable difference to the lives of those whom they were professionally charged to assist, they could themselves be a danger, thereby creating serious risks for clients. These risks emanated from a lack of training and an undue emphasis on socialist politics and ideology. Thus, social work posed an ideological risk. There seems little doubt that the case made by Brewer and Lait was not lost upon conservative politicians, although the 'moral panic', which was created in relation to social work practice, did not appear to have any immediate impact on wider government policy (Brewer and Lait, 1980). As Glennester (1995: 178) argues, the first Thatcher administration 'returned to principles established in the 1940s containing public spending, shifting the finance of services away from direct taxation, targeting social security, enforcing tenants rights to buy council houses. Structural change came later, not least because spending proved so difficult to check'.

By the late 1980s risk was becoming a more institutionalised concept, which was also structured into the training of social work practitioners. Pragmatised practice, in which social work educators ticked boxes which ostensibly denoted the successful accomplishment of particular competencies, laid the foundation for the ticking of boxes in relation to risk assessment. Competencies could be easily translated into tasks which needed to be completed in order to avoid risk. Thus, lack of competence could, in itself, constitute a risk.

The differentiated impact of risk

The majority of those who are poor are not ranked among the excluded. Exclusion contrasts with being poor, deprived or on low income in several ways. It is not a matter of having fewer resources, but of not sharing in the opportunities possessed by the majority.

In attempting to assist people in long-term poverty, Giddens (2000) thinks that more questions should be asked about the 'why' rather than the 'who'. Drawing on the German research of Leisering and Leibfried (1999) he identifies different modes of dependency. A limited number of people are victims and feel trapped in poverty by unemployment. 'Pragmatic copers' treat social assistance as a means to a wider end. 'Biographical copers' will change their attitudes and strategies to pursue other goals. 'Strategic users' of welfare are purely instrumental in that they use state assistance and other sources of income, some illegal, to achieve a particular style of life (Giddens, 2000).

Giddens' description fails to make sense of a world in which the actions of every person are open to scrutiny and subjected to managerial and procedural constraint. In a society dominated by the idea of risk, an essential part of the welfare function is to enable those who are unable or unwilling to take advantage of current opportunities which exist for all citizens. Social workers are also expected to protect the vulnerable, in many cases by law. Giddens presents a voluntaristic view of rights and responsibilities, in that individuals can choose whether to seize their opportunities or not. Individuals have a right to opportunity and a responsibility to reach the predefined outcomes that will reward social inclusion. Giddens argues in favour of an investment in human capital, on the basis that most people in a state of poverty actively seek independence. While acknowledging that specific help is needed for particularly vulnerable groups, such as children, the disabled, the sick, or the elderly, assistance must be provided by means of a partnership between the state and the private sectors. It is when Giddens talks about those who have no chance of getting from a state of welfare dependency into work, that he becomes less clear.

Although Giddens (2000: 109) argues that policy should reflect an attempt to 'action potential and reduce dependency', no specific suggestions are given as to how those who cannot, or will not, 'take part in the game' can be assisted, or what incentives there are for the private sector to enter into partnership with the state to unlock potential. Even when people have taken a more questioning stance, in keeping with the idea of the development of a post-traditional society, this does not necessarily lead to a distrust of the welfare state to provide services. Furthermore, the impact of risk associated with such activity as flexible working patterns and the maintenance of family life has a disproportionate knock-on effect on the lives of working-class people (Taylor-Gooby, 2000). Qualitative evidence has also suggested that many people feel ambivalent about the experience of risk and uncertainty. They are often unable to differentiate between the progress that they experience in living standards and the pressures that they feel in other areas of social life.

Risk society is this complex, and is not experienced in the same way by all its members. In particular, those at most risk from social change may be more inclined to see greater flexibility in terms of threats rather than opportunities (Taylor-Gooby, 2000: 10).

Risks and human rights

In the risk society there is, for Beck (1992), a profound change in political culture, resulting in a loss of political power by centralised political systems.

This is partly created by the tension between the institutionalisation of human rights and the enduring nature of political power in the hands of individuals. The more effectively human rights are structured into government activity, the more the political system is called into question. Beck argues that it is naïve to believe that it is possible to enforce the democratic rights of citizens on the one hand and preserve hierarchical political relationships on the other. The monopolisation of democratically constituted power is contingent upon the idea of what Beck refers to as a 'democratic monarchy' (1992: 194). Once in office, the dictator develops authoritarian qualities and enforces decisions accordingly. Those affected by these decisions, Beck argues, target their rights and become democratic subjects. Clearly defined regions and co-operative politics develop in a manner which is partially autonomous from the state. Heads of political systems are then confronted by rights which have been fought for and are legislatively protected. 'Forms of a new political culture, in which heterogeneous centres of sub-politics have an effect on the process of politically forming and enforcing decisions, on the basis of constitutional rights, are becoming reality' (Beck, 1992: 194).

The complexity and reflexivity of risk is nowhere more evident than in the imposition of human rights legislation. The right to welfare provision, and some security from risk, is fundamental. On first inspection, the imposition of human rights by government would appear to have the potential of reducing risk by protecting the vulnerable. Human rights legislation can have unintended consequences, producing potentially litigious risk for welfare workers. Parents who lose touch with their children as a result of childcare proceedings have a right to claim damages for the loss of relationship, where it can be shown that a social worker mishandled a case. The Human Rights Act, which came into force on 2 October 2000, incorporates the European Convention on Human Rights into British law, and allows British courts to award damages for the 'loss of relationship'. There have been a number of cases in the Strasbourg Court of Human Rights where parents of children have complained that procedures have violated their right to a fair hearing (Article Six of the European Convention of Human Rights) or respect for family life. This adds another risk to an area of social welfare work which is already highly contentious.

The nature of risk management

Risk management, like risk assessment, is linked to improving decision-making, minimising harm, maximising benefit to the service user and diminishing the possibility of danger. Risk management then seeks to predict outcome and the potential for harm (Alaszewski et al., 1998;

Manthorpe, 2000). Risk assessment constitutes a way of working that is focused and managerially controllable.

Sargent (1999), describing a more uncertain approach to risk assessment, describes a combination of 'science', usually comprising a series of checklists of predictive factors, and the more elusive 'art' as a means of assessment. The latter includes the shared opinions of practitioners.

As considerations of risk have come to dominate practice, the concept itself has become narrower and is defined in a more quantifiable form. In Sargent's terms, the 'science' is coming to dominate the 'art'. This is most clearly reflected in the attempts that have been made to predict risk.

Regulation risk and the contract culture in social welfare

Risks are addressed by service providers which are publicly financed and controlled by central and local government. In a post-traditional society, users of social services are more likely to be vulnerable to the often-unintended consequences of decisions made within social institutions.

In the UK, by the 1990s, individualised therapeutic services based upon casework skills were being superseded by the internal market within social welfare. Part of the assessment process involved an assessment of risk. The 1990 NHS and Community Care Act created the backdrop for the materialistic approach to social work which now resonates within all forms of risk prediction (Denney, 1998). The notion of quantified, tailor-made packages of care, supplied by providers who had successfully bid for contracts with local authorities after a tendering process, tied aspects of risk to cost and effectiveness. Thus, risks to service users were prioritised on the basis of an actuarialised form of individual risk assessment. Within this process, risks became linked to cost. More resources would need to be directed towards service users assessed as being at high risk.

'Needs' now have to be included within the discourse of risk. The 1990 NHS and Community Care Act introduced the idea of needs-led assessments. Over the last decade such needs assessments have become risk assessments. Thus, as Matthews and Pitts (2001: 20) argue, '[n]eeds assessment becomes a variant of risk assessment and serves as a regulatory mechanism'.

In accounting for the surge of interest in evidence-based practice, which has come to characterise social work practice since the late 1990s, Amann (2000) points to such factors as the availability of knowledge and research, the decline in deference to government, and the demand for greater accountability. One could add to this list the growing dominance of risk as a concept. The central idea of predictability is based upon the collation of evidence relating to the likelihood of the development of specific, potentially dangerous situations. Social workers, when making predictions of harm, look back to previous evidence in order to make judgements about the future. Social services departments and welfare organisations are becoming part of a 'risk regulation regime'. The concern of social welfare organisations with the management of risk has become dominant in organisations which are preoccupied with the management of individualised blame (Hood et al., 2001). Risk management is the context in which this form of regulation occurs.

Risk and child protection

It is in the area of childcare that the emergence of risk as a central concept can be most graphically demonstrated. The effects of professional negligence in childcare are the best documented and the most emotive aspects of risk management in social care. They also attract considerable media attention (Aldridge, 1994). Risk has come to dominate childcare policy and practice in Britain. Individuals and organisations are held morally and organisationally culpable if they fail to report their concerns about suspected abuse to an investigating agency. It was events directly connected with child protection practice in the mid-1980s which called into question the ability to predict risk and placed social work on the political agenda.

Suggestions that social workers were unable to appreciate risks to vulnerable service users are not new. The death in 1945 of Dennis O'Neill while in foster care as a result of neglect and ill treatment does not appear to have prompted any particular attention being given to the notion of risk. In 1971, when Maria Colwell, a child under the care of social services, died, the warnings of neighbours were ignored by social workers and other professionals. The public enquiry into Maria's death resulted in the creation of new sets of regulations and procedures designed to assist in the recognition of high-risk situations (Hendrick, 1994).

Non-tabloid newspaper analyses of child protection practices reveal a number of shortcomings, which in some cases, it has been argued, constitute avoidable errors in state child protection practices. These include:

1 The misinterpretation and selective interpretation of valuable evidence when making assessments.
2 Treating information discretely, so that no overall pattern emerges.
3 The dominant and all-pervasive belief systems that dominate practice. An example of this would be the desirability of keeping children in the care of birth parents.
4 The creation of concrete solutions to situations at the expense of complex analysis.

Claims have also been made that child protection workers can be professionally intransigent, listening more seriously to other professionals rather than, for example, to relatives, neighbours and friends, who are more directly involved in the case (Dingwall et al., 1983; Reder et al., 1993; Munro, 1996).

Older people

The number of older people has increased rapidly since the turn of the century. In the UK in 1901, 7.5 per cent of the population were over 60 years old. In 1997 this had increased to 20.4 per cent. The number of people in the UK of state pensionable age will reach 15 million by 2031. The numbers of people aged 85 and over are projected to grow from 1.1 million in 2000 to 4 million in 2051. It is this latter group who are most likely to need long-term residential care (GAD, 2004). In the European Union (EU) there has been a general fall in birth rates, accompanied by an increase in life expectancy. Significant increases in the numbers of people aged 65 and 80+ are forecast within the next 30 years (Akers and Dwyer, 2002). The risk of needing assistance at home or in residential care is also set to increase. Greater uncertainty about the future of care for the elderly is created by a number of factors which include:

- The increase in the number of people over 85.
- Family size.
- Levels of intergenerational dependency.
- The development of internal markets of care.
- A greater emphasis on individual responsibility for the costs for care in old age.

Baldock has argued that it is possible to over estimate the immediacy of the crisis and the concomitant risks faced by older people. Although the number requiring intensive social care is growing, the increase according to Baldock does not pose an immediate problem (Baldock, 1997). However, later research suggests that in the longer term any reduction in the number of long stay beds in the National Health Service could significantly threaten the well being of older people. Spending on residential care will have to rise by 315 per cent in real terms between 2000 and 2051 in order to meet demographic pressures and rising costs. This level of spending also assumes that dependency rates, patterns of care and current funding arrangements remain the same' (Wittenberg, R., Comas-Herra, A., Pickard, L., Hancock, R. (2004).

One of the great risks for older people is that they will have little or no support from younger generations. Older people, while aware that they live in a risk society, seem to draw a distinction between personal and overall risk. Individuals have a tendency to assess their own risks as being lower than that of the population as a whole (Taylor-Gooby et al., 1999: 187). This underestimation of risk is fed by exhortations from the government to become more independent in old age.

Although old age can bring many benefits, most notably leisure time, there are risks associated with increased age. These include health deterioration, although the relationship between the risks of poor physical or mental health can be exaggerated. Some 9 per cent of people over age 65 have difficulty in negotiating stairs, 2 per cent have problems getting in and out of bed, and only 8 per cent have difficulty bathing. Those over the age of 75 may experience a slightly higher risk of experiencing difficulty. Research indicates that 13 per cent of the over 75s have problems with bathing, with a similar number experiencing difficulty climbing stairs. Senile dementia affects one in five over the age of 80 (Twigg, 1999). A high proportion of the elderly population are able to manage their own personal care.

What does increase with age is the risk of major bereavement and the fear of extreme old age. Old age creates a feeling of greater vulnerability. It is the risk of social exclusion, created by a lack of work, accommodation, adequate income and a full social life, which is most likely to impair the lives of older people (Heywood et al., 2002).

Abuse can be a risk faced by older people. As is the case with the abuse of vulnerable children, there can be difficulties in establishing what constitutes abuse. This is especially the case in relation to emotional abuse and neglect. Whereas in law, relatives have a duty of care to children, it is not the case with older people. There is no requirement, as is the custom in some eastern traditions, for 'filial piety' with respect to the care of parents. The combination of respect and duty does not pertain in western societies.

Risk of inadequate income is another factor that can create a sense of insecurity. It is in the area of pensions that Ring (2003) has linked the work of Beck to risks associated with old age. Drawing on Beck, Ring argues that the traditional frameworks upon which the idea of state pensions were based no longer exist. As the postwar settlement exemplified in the Beveridge Report begins to dissolve, it is no longer possible for the state to shelter older individuals from risk. Giddens's positive view of potential risks is reflected in the Green Paper *Partnership in Pensions* (Department of Social Security, 1998), in which the UK government made it clear that individual citizens were expected to secure their own financial security in old age.

Mental health and risk

In *Risk Society* (1992), Beck argues that the 'driving force in the class society can be summarised in the phrase: I am hungry! The movement set in motion by the risk society, on the other hand, is expressed in the statement: I am afraid! The commonality of anxiety takes the place of the commonality of need' (1992: 49). This almost existential statement expresses a condition of fear and accumulative insecurity. The desire to be safe in an individualised and isolating society increases as instant global communication facilitates detailed knowledge of terrible events. It is now possible to create instant communication 24 hours a day. The global nature of instantaneous electronic communication also results in pressure, which can be constant and intrusive, obfuscating the difference between work and leisure.

Ontological insecurity has created a number of complexities and a multiplicity of systems, each making separate and simultaneous demands. A diverse and technicised group of specialists is now part of a diagnostic system, which exists to support those who feel distress or are unable to function within the risk society. This, Beck argues, is particularly evident with respect to psychiatric medicine. There are a number of risks associated with being a mental health patient. First, there are the risks posed by those diagnosed with mental health disorders living in the community. Secondly, there are risks associated with being a voluntary or a sectioned psychiatric patient. Thirdly, there are long-term risks connected with compulsory admission to psychiatric units. Once a patient has been compulsorily admitted to a unit, the likelihood of further admissions increases because the service user's 'support networks' can collapse. Social and legal status is significantly reduced, while the admission itself may be therapeutically ineffective (Fisher et al., 1984).

Risk assessment and psychiatric surveillance

The public demand for more risk assessment has been reflected within the mental health field. Increased surveillance and attempts to predict dangerous and violent behaviour in the mentally ill is now an essential requirement of the mental health system. Failure to respond to risk results in the apportioning of blame. Traditionally, as Foucault observed, the therapeutic gaze was a prerequisite to disciplinary techniques of intervention (Foucault, 1965, 1977). What appears to have been created in mental health is what Castel (1991) has referred to as the new space of risk. Here, a risk does not arise from a concrete danger, but from the effect of a number of factors which render the possibility of an undesirable mode of behaviour or consequence a reality. Preventative 'outreach' policies constitute 'systematic pre-detection'. Such policies have the specific aim of anticipating and preventing the emergence of an undesirable consequence and require the physical presence of the watcher, over the watched (Castel, 1991).

The 'risk society' comprises a dangerous combination of insecurity, fear, exhaustion and technologically driven competitiveness. Research suggests that one of the consequences of this is a rise in the incidence of mental instability, which is being experienced at an ever-earlier age. In research carried out by the Mental Health Foundation (Kay, 1999), it was suggested that 20 per cent of children suffer from some form of mental health problem. The Director of the Mental Health Foundation, June McKerrow, claimed: 'The problems are getting worse. We are obsessed by material rewards, economic pressures and physical safety which all influence our mental health' (British Broadcasting Corporation, 1999: 2).

Following revelations of ill treatment in Ely Hospital in the late 1960s, media coverage of mental hospitals has associated particular risks with mental illness. Media interest in mentally ill people in the community has also been generated by some dramatic individual cases which emphasise the risks that mentally ill people pose to themselves and others. Ben Silcock, a user of mental health services in 1992, was severely mauled after climbing into the lions' enclosure at London Zoo. This led to the Department of Health reviewing its procedures for the care of mentally ill people in the community. New measures were introduced as a result. These emphasised the control of risk, including the tightening up of arrangements for the discharge of mentally ill people who are considered to be a danger to themselves and others (Sharkey, 1995).

In the UK, the outline of risk assessment management and audit systems are intended to ensure that public safety is at the forefront of policies with respect to mental health. The 'Assertive Outreach Programme' is meant to provide mentally ill people in the community with management that is intensive enough to match their needs and levels of risk (Kemshall, 2002).

From another position, mental health has emerged as a criterion which defines eligibility for services (Kemshall, 1997). Many individuals with mental health problems are left in the community to fend for themselves with support from relatives provided at no cost to the state. It is not until the risk posed by mental illness becomes critical that action is taken by the state.

The usefulness of risk assessment in cases of homicide by people with mental illness has recently been called into question. Risk assessment in the area of mental health usually involves estimating the probability of risk from an individualist position. The probability that an individual patient poses a risk to the public is like an escalator of dangerousness, up and down which a patient might move at different moments in his or her life. Patients are not divided into the categories 'dangerous' or 'non-dangerous'. When a homicide is considered predictable by an enquiry panel, this suggests that the likelihood of violence at a certain point is high enough to warrant professional preventative intervention.

Munro and Rumgay (2000) have examined all 40 reports of enquiries into homicides perpetrated by people with mental illness between 1988 and 1997. The researchers note that there has been a sharp increase in the number of reports published since 1994, which reflects an increased governmental interest in risk and a natural desire to prevent homicide by dangerous patients. Twenty-six cases, some 65 per cent of the homicides, were considered to have been preventable. Munro and Rumgay suggest that one way of reducing the risk is to identify high-risk patients and target resources on them. Improvements in assessing risk have, they argue, limited value. Existing risk assessment tools have low accuracy rates, while their findings indicate that only 27.5 per cent of homicides could have been predicted.

There are a number of problems inherent in mental health risk assessment. There are often inadequate cues to forecast violence and an inability to determine the extent of violence. Munro and Rumgay also argue that research designed to relate risk factors to mental health risk have been unco-ordinated. The fallibility of risk assessment in the area of mental health can have worrying consequences. A false positive may lead to a non-violent patient being detained, whereas a false negative may deprive someone of much-needed help (Munro and Rumgay, 2000: 118). An over reaction to public pressure for more risk assessment can mean that patients who are not dangerous are at risk of being detained. Munro and Rumgay reach the conclusion that there are serious obstacles to increasing the safety of the public through risk assessment. The public would be better served by having a good standard of care for all patients.

Risk and schizophrenia

One of the most contested and highly publicised forms of mental illness is schizophrenia. To use a psychiatric diagnosis such as schizophrenia, doctors must estimate the patient's unpredictability and the danger he/she poses in the community. Castel (1991) argues that medicine bases it interventions on prudence, but when in doubt in the psychiatric field, doctors will usually act. Failure to do so exposes the psychiatrist to blame. Such was the risk thought to be posed by schizophrenics that 50 years ago patients would often have been detained compulsorily on a long-term basis in a psychiatric hospital.

Scott (1998) has classified the 'types' of risk that are most likely to be encountered by patients diagnosed as schizophrenic. Most risks, including that of labelling, the loss of civil rights and the side-effects of medication, mean that the patient experiences economic exclusion, homelessness and exploitation by others. Other risks, including long-term emotional volatility and family stress, are more likely to be experienced only by the patient and relatives. Professionals can be at risk from litigation. The patients' professional helpers and relatives are most likely to be at risk from violence, verbal abuse and aggression (Scott, 1998).

Schizophrenia occurs in all countries, cultures and societies. The risk of developing this condition has been calculated in many ways but, globally, epidemiologists suggest that an individual has a one in one hundred chance of developing the disorder (Scott, 1998). Although there is no consensus on recurrence figures, there is some indication that patients diagnosed with schizophrenia fare significantly better in developing, rather than developed, countries. In developed countries, only 15.5 per cent of those experiencing a first acute episode of schizophrenia have no relapse. Some 26 per cent experience multiple episodes, while 20 per cent suffer continuing and severe long-term disability. In developing countries, the figures are 37 per cent, 12.8 per cent and 12 per cent respectively (Scott, 1998).

There is a long line of research suggesting that some groups within society are more at risk of being diagnosed as schizophrenic than others. Huxley (1997) has argued that although female rates of mental illness exceed male rates, when drug dependency and various forms of anti-social personality are taken into consideration, a greater parity between the sexes is found. In Britain, young Caribbean men are at a high risk of being diagnosed as suffering from schizophrenia and compulsorily admitted to hospital. After admission to hospital, they are more likely to be detained in locked wards and have high doses of medication (Fernando, 1995). Black people are over-represented in involuntary mental hospital admissions, although the over-representation of black people is diminished if other factors like unemployment, social class and life events are taken into consideration. Six million psychiatric diagnoses are made in the UK by general practitioners every year, while 71 million days are lost annually as a result of mental illness (Huxley, 1997).

It is the continued power of professionals to predict the risks posed by those whom they have defined as mentally ill that illustrates the dominance of risk. Fears of governmental blameworthiness provide an impetus for more risk assessment.

Risk, mental health and 'dangerousness'

While the incidence of mental illness has increased, homicides by mentally ill people have not. Individuals are at far more risk of being attacked by the sane, than by the mentally ill (Wadham, 2002). Although risk has been primarily connected with danger to service users, risk assessment has become an integral part of professional practice. In reviewing the research into risk and work with mentally ill people, Langan (1999) reaches the conclusion that people diagnosed as having mental health problems are more likely to commit suicide than the population at large. The picture, when considering the risk posed to others by people defined as mentally ill, is less clear. There is a 'modest link' between mental illness and 'dangerousness'. Diagnoses of severe mental illness such as schizophrenia may have little, if any, predictive power. Pilgrim and Rogers (1993) have emphasised how the risk of dangerousness, particularly with regard to mental illness, can be exaggerated. The overwhelming majority of people designated as mad are 'perplexing', but they are harmless and docile, not constituting a threat to anyone around them. However, the unpredictability of those deemed to break social expectations without intelligible reasons 'fuels fantasies of threat to others' (Pilgrim and Rogers, 1993: 190).

Conclusion

Parsloe (1999: 8) suggests that what is now being called 'risk management' is little different from what welfare workers have always done: 'Much social and probation work has always consisted of working out with users ways in which they could improve the quality of their life, and in effect, reduce the risk of negative outcomes such as reconviction, ill health, eviction and mental health illness, to name only a few'.

Risk-based social work does constitute a paradigmatic shift in the way in which social care and social work is conceptualised and practised. It reflects wider tensions within society, and also a shift in power from individual practitioner towards more centralised managerial structures. A cluster of factors is associated with the emergence of risk and marks out the characteristics of risk-oriented practice. Risk is defined in terms of the likelihood of the perpetration of harm to others. This is particularly true in relation to mental health interventions. There is a significant and widespread cynicism about the ability of policy-makers and professionals to provide trustworthy advice in relation to risks posed by mental illness. One important consequence of a risk-based professional practice is that, while the accountability increases, their influence in the policy-making process has diminished, and becomes structured by managerially defined criteria. This has served to curtail professional authority (Harris, 1998).

Further reading

Hazel Kemshall's *Risk Social Policy and Welfare* (Open University Press, 2002) contains well-researched chapters on health promotion, rationing, child protection, older people and mental health. Peter Taylor-Gooby's excellent *Risk Trust and Welfare* (Macmillan, 2000) successfully and clearly combines theoretical discussion related to risk in welfare with consideration of empirical evidence. Pilgrim and Rogers' *A Sociology of Mental Health and Illness* (Open University Press, 1993) is still a useful text in critically analysing risks associated with mental illness. Parsloe's edited volume *Risk Assessment in Social Care and Social Work* (Jessica Kingsley, 1999) brings together discussions of risk in the management of offenders in the community, mental health, child protection and older people.

EIGHT   Risk Management and Crime

Outline

As in the case of social service provision described in the previous chapter, it will be argued that risk management constitutes a new paradigm within criminal justice. In Europe, the USA, Canada, Australia and New Zealand, risk management has come to be associated with more sophisticated forms of prediction to 'improve' the allocation of offenders to appropriate supervision. The chapter will show how risk management is linked to pragmatism in the criminal justice system. Offenders are now routinely profiled in order to ascertain whether they are high or low risk. Policing and community interventions are inextricably linked to the increased desire for security. Risk, it will be argued, has come to dominate both the theory and practice of law enforcement. The chapter will consider the argument that risk is replacing concerns related to justice and the due process of the law. Much of the work which has examined risk in the area of crime draws upon the theoretical groundwork of postmodern writers. The chapter includes sections on governance, globalisation and localisation.

Theoretical approaches to crime and the 'risk society'

Although Beck (1992) does not specifically consider law and order, criminologists have given themselves a wide latitude in interpreting how the risk society thesis can be utilised (Reiner et al., 2001). It is also worth reflecting at this stage that the work of Douglas (1992) demonstrates how the perceiver of risks is part of a social and cultural system in which the understanding of risks is constructed. Risk, according to Douglas, has become a 'forensic' concept, serving sometimes to exaggerate and create insecurity and danger. The creation of an increased sense of insecurity gives rise to an unquestioning belief in the legitimacy of established law and order policies to provide protection from the ever-increasing, insidious pervasiveness of global crime risk. The forensic nature of risk enables future criminal harm to become more tangible, through the quantification of risk factors, while simultaneously providing a framework for investigations into what crime has occurred, and how 'things have gone wrong' (Douglas, 1992).

The critique of the risk society thesis is most highly developed within criminological accounts of risk representing the so-called 'governmentality' school, which in turn is strongly influenced by the ideas of Foucault (1972, 1977). As Garland (2001: 177) argues:

> Matching input to risk is the new gatekeeping role which offers intensive supervision only to those offenders who score highly on the scale of risk and on the scale of responsivity. The management of risks and resources has displaced rehabilitation as the central organisational aim of the criminal justice system.

Risk assessment is becoming a far more integral part of the criminal justice system at a number of stages, from pre-sentence to community sentence and within custodial regimes. The risk of re-offending and harming the public is now a crucial determinant in the treatment of offenders and to some degree replaces rehabilitative goals.

Security and governance

Both security and governance are contested concepts. 'Security' is a problematic concept since it appears to have different meanings in different contexts. Crawford (2002b: 6) has argued that:

> Security connects with ideals of happiness and order. It is bound up with people's hopes and fantasies as well as their fears and anxieties, it informs people's sense of self, their notions of collective and personal identity, their grasp of and relation to the world around them. It is imagined and re-imagined, damaged and reconstituted.

Some criminologists have identified the emergence of new forms of 'governance', 'changing nature form and location of responses to crime insecurity in terms of the way in which these are governed regulated and ordered' (Crawford, 2002b: 2). According to Crawford, there has been a shift from state-centred government to a form of 'networked governance'. Although this movement is seen most clearly in the European Union (EU), it is also evident in other parts of the western world. The 'hollowing out' of state activity has occurred co-terminously with 'joined up' governmental thinking, a situation which is relatively autonomous from the state. Part of this process has been linked to the development of internal markets and the contracting out of services within the criminal justice system to companies within the private sector. The use of private security companies to transport prisoners and the development of private prisons are examples of this process. Within this situation, intergovernmental organisations develop interdependencies and trust (Rhodes, 1997).

In the area of crime, there is a global emphasis upon networked forms of policing in drug enforcement, cyber-crime and the control of asylum seekers. The relationship between security and the re-orientation of powers across and between states can also clearly be seen in the global efforts being made to combat terrorism. It is the all-pervasive nature of the notion of security which has provided a justification for a form of governance which combines the efforts of criminal justice agencies, government and other social services such as education and child protection. The link between security and governance blurs distinctions between internal and external security, civil and military policing, and the regulation of the private and public sectors (Crawford, 2002a).

Globalisation and the risk of crime

The fear of crime at international, national and local levels lies at the centre of many individual perceptions of risk. Internationally, governments identify crime as a major social problem which needs to be managed. A new politics of insecurity has arisen around the risks created by local, national and international crime. This involves a preoccupation with personal security, and an attempted engagement with the possibility of addressing future risks. Technology has generated new forms of crime which can have a global impact. The Internet can enhance fraud and the trading of sexually explicit material. Cyber-crime can be directed towards individuals, as is the case with cyber-stalking. Terrorist groups can also use the Net. The mass insecurity created by crime is further fed by the development of global communication systems, which can instantly stretch all social relations across time and space (Crawford, 2002c).

The risk of crime is presented as a form of social malignancy by governments globally, which, if not checked, will spread, eating away at the core of social order. Drawing on a medical analogy, risks posed by crime have to be treated swiftly and at the site where most damage can be caused. Although the figures for recorded crime might be falling, the public have their own view of risks related to crime. Everyday perceptions of the increasing risk of crime are fed by common-sense assumptions about the availability of drugs in schools, unsolicited begging and harassment on the streets. The almost predictable incidence of car crime, burglary and pick-pocketing is for many far more of a risk to personal safety than is suggested by any government-produced data. The failure of the 'welfare lobby' within the criminal justice system to acknowledge the significance of these perceptions of risk has not assisted in making the case for a less punitive form of rehabilitation. Fears about crime continue to gain public momentum, while at the same time well-publicised rhetoric seeks to persuade us that crime is under control.

Some have seen the phenomenon of globalisation as increasing the risk of crime. According to Hogg (2002: 196): 'The convergence of regional and political conflicts, weakening states and economic and technological global-isation is fuelling new patterns of transnational crime, and blurring the boundaries between politics and crime, political and criminal violence.' Global communications have been necessary for the development of more co-ordinated international terrorist attacks and forms of crime. Ethnic, religious and other conflicts are intermingled with drug trafficking, people smuggling and other forms of organised crime. The risk of crime varies globally. Rates of burglary, for example, when broken down internationally, show marked variations in degrees of risk. Burglary rates in Africa and Latin America are high, but they are significantly lower in western Europe and Asia (Zveric, 1998). Much empirical research in criminology internationally is government-sponsored and is used to target problem populations.

Individualised risk factors

Risk factors associated with the family include poor parental supervision, family size and low parental involvement with children, parental conflict and physical punishment within the family. Andrews has claimed that there is a psychology of criminal conduct, which can be applied to the delivery of effective service. This is based upon identifiable and tested 'risk factors'. These include anti-social values, criminal associations, a history of anti-social behaviour and family factors, including poor parenting, criminality and a lack of affection. Low levels of personal achievement and education are also high risk factors (Andrews, 1995).

Beaumont (1999) has argued that statistical prediction in criminal justice cannot provide a 'quick fix' to the risks posed by offenders. Despite considerable research activity in the field, re-conviction devices are at best able to offer between 70 and 80 per cent accuracy. Prediction devices are least useful with regard to serious offences, where there is only a 50 per cent accuracy rate (Beaumont, 1999).

Risk prediction, which is used in sentencing and in the implementation of community sentences can be seen in two forms. 'Static' risk factors refer to the characteristics of the person and the nature of the offence, for example age, sex and criminal record. They cannot be affected by intervention. 'Dynamic' risk factors refer to the risk of offending, and can therefore be potentially changed. These include education, employment, family, attitudes and beliefs (Mair, 2001). The agreed goals and plans for interventions with offenders are now firmly embedded in the idea of risk assessment. Objectives, and the means to achieve the goals, are coded and measured against risk by law enforcement agencies.

Community safety and the risk of crime

Risk is no longer confined to individuals. The notion of community is central to the delineation of geographical spaces, which are designated high risk by experts. One of the problems with using the notion of 'community' is that it is a word which carries a variety of meanings which relate to history and culture. Despite the complexities encountered in attempting to define 'community', it is a concept which has been associated with risk by politicians. The need for protection against risks which are present within communities has now come to represent a complex set of overlapping and contradictory political agendas. A 'hybrid discourse' of community safety has emerged, in which it is claimed that the perpetration of crime is seen as being limited to a number of individuals, and yet, simultaneously, sections of the population in specific geographical areas are targeted as being responsible for the 'problem' of crime and the consequent risk to the property and safety of citizens (Matthews and Pitts, 2001).

Wiles and Pease (2001: 234) have argued that in some of the least crime-prone areas, residents limit crime by 'installing protections to their homes, ferrying their children to places rather than entrusting them to public transport, mobilising policing effort by persuasive articulation of their concerns, backed by political influence'.

In the name of community safety and development, 'high-risk' neighbourhoods and populations have been targeted for increased surveillance and control. Thus, 'community safety', to use Beck's terminology, becomes a 'systematic' way of dealing with the 'hazards' and 'insecurities' induced by late modernity (Beck, 1992). Citizens expect governments to control and manage the risks connected with crime in their communities. Systematised and efficient identification and management of risk populations has also become a key political imperative. At the same time, individuals assume that they are responsible for finding solutions to their own problems (Edwards and Glover, 2001).

Community and the territoriality of risk

The principal distinction between crime prevention and community safety is, according to Van Swaaningen (2002), that the former aims to reduce crime levels while the latter is designed to increase public feelings of safety.

Crime-related policies have incorporated an assumption that the state can intervene in 'the social'. This assumption asserts that areas where there are high risks from crime should be targeted in order that more desirable forms of social behaviour are encouraged. Such policies, it is claimed, would strengthen local communities and families and improve the quality of life. The notion of 'community' has played a role in national debates relating to crime prevention. Armies of experts using market research social audits advise on how communities can be governed in terms of their own values (Rose, 1999a, 1999b).

Stenson, in a study of community safety in middle England, argues that 'policy strategies are not just responses to external social problems. Rather, the "problems" they address are given shape and recognition by the emerging policy discourses in which academic theories and research can play a critical role' (2002: 120). One such policy discourse relates to the desirability of various social agencies working together in a co-ordinated way to provide integrated services. The pitfalls of this approach to risk are now well documented. Agencies tend to become self-protective, while multi-agency work is often characterised by inadequate resources and infighting, with some agencies having dominance over others. Bradley and Walters (2002) have argued that this strategy has paralysed the ability of local agencies to deliver crime prevention measures, and has a potential to alienate and divide groups. The possibility of a seamless and co-ordinated system of community safety in response to the risk of crime would therefore appear to exist only in the imaginations of politicians.

Risk management and crime

Risk management constitutes a new paradigm in criminal justice practice. Globally, risk management has come to be associated with sophisticated forms of prediction targeted at 'improving' the allocation of offenders to appropriate supervision. Offenders are profiled by probation officers and others in the criminal justice system in order to ascertain whether they are high or low risk. Rehabilitative probation practice in the UK was dominated by personal counselling and a befriending model until the late

1970s. This has been replaced by structured programmes that address the possible risks to the public. Re-conviction rates are used as a measure of success and the probation service in the UK was merged with the prison service in 2004.

Garland (2001) argues that a number of underlying forces have shaped the development of crime control arrangements since the 1980s. The distinctive social organisation of late modernity and the free market have generated a form of socially conservative politics. Ideas about rehabilitation have changed since the 1970s. The rehabilitative model which is operating in the new millennium focuses more upon issues of crime control than upon the welfare of the individual. Interventions are now more 'offence-focused' than 'client-centred'.

Policing the risk society

Problem-solving policing strategies have accompanied the rise of community safety strategies. This approach to policing is meant to extend beyond individual responses to specific incidents, which in turn are conceptualised as being symptomatic of other more deeply embedded problems within the local community.

In the USA, other experiments that concentrate on tackling the physical environment and clearing up rubbish and graffiti could have a major positive impact on the control of crime in local neighbourhoods. The New York Police Department were given clear local goals in tackling local crime. This included 'the removal of beggars, "shakedown artists", unlicensed street peddlers, squeegee pests, graffiti and other so-called incivilities' (Wright, 2002: 113). This approach to eliminating potential local crime risk became known as 'zero tolerance'. Although a number of chief constables in Britain regarded this approach as too aggressive, and as having only short-term impacts, a number of attempts have been made at zero-tolerance policing in Britain.

Ericson and Haggerty (1997) have described how the police developed a role in risk communication. Here the police co-operate with other publicly funded professionals to provide risk management and security throughout society. The police thus become important disseminators of risk knowledge, providing a service to public agencies like schools and the insurance and security industries. Although the police have traditionally gathered knowledge for purposes of social control, the emphasis is now on the creation of security. Police now work with a host of other agencies to communicate knowledge. Risk communication police work provides an example of the governance of risk through the combined efforts of social agencies, including social services and education.

Controlling risk through surveillance

The use of surveillance and the use of closed-circuit television (CCTV) has been one of the major forms of social control in the policing of public space. It has been claimed that individuals moving around a city in Britain will, on average, be caught on CCTV cameras 300 times per day (Mair, 2001). CCTV cameras are now normally visible in shopping malls, schools, universities, gated communities and cemeteries. Over 600 town and city centres are now 'wired up' with CCTV, and the use of CCTV constitutes the fifth utility. 'Closed-circuit television has become the key technology in contemporary strategies for the management of risk' (Newburn and Hayman, 2002: 18). The aim of CCTV surveillance, according to Rose (1999a), is to pre-emptively act in areas where a high risk of crime and disorder are either recorded or projected. Such action is meant to prevent the occurrence of undesirable events.

Some explanations for the rise of private policing are also clearly linked to the work of Giddens, Beck and the rise of the 'risk society'. The heightened concern about the risk of crime has had a direct impact upon the development of private security. Many organisations of various types and sizes now have sophisticated risk identification procedures, which lead to the deployment of particular risk strategies. The British Post Office has a number of complex risk models for use in its post offices in connection with burglary and robbery prevention. Data relating to the proximity of post offices to major roads and motorways, and the number of previous attacks, are now connected to risk analysis models. Risk assessments are routinely taken into consideration when large organisations are planning the development of security measures (Button, 2002).

With inadequate numbers of police officers in many towns, the night-time economy is under the control of door supervisors often referred to as bouncers. Acts of violence now occur during the night and are controlled by unofficial police employed by the entertainment industry (Hobbs et al., 2000). Evidence is mounting to suggest that the violence handed out by door attendants at places of entertainment can be severe, and occasionally result in serious injury or death (British Entertainment and Discothèque Association, 1995). Demands for private security appear to increase exponentially, in parallel with a preoccupation with the concept of risk (Loader, 1997).

Risk and community penalties

Community penalties have been described as 'sentences other than fines for dealing with convicted prisoners outside prison' (Nellis, 2001: 17).

Sentences now served in the community are based upon individualist notions of risk assessment. Subjective risk assessment has always taken place within the pre-sentence reports that probation officers write as part of the court social enquiry process. Evidence suggests that the subjective licence afforded to probation officers in making assessments of the risk of crime leads to a service which at times can be discriminatory (Denney, 1992). The likelihood of re-offending is calculated on the basis of a subjective analysis of an individual's history of offending and subsequent rates of offending. Meta-analysis of the risk of re-conviction has used international data from large samples. This research has linked individual risk factors to the probability of further offending (McGuire, 1995). Mair (2001) describes the mid-1980s as being the point at which the probation service attempted to make risk assessment more sophisticated. By the mid-1990s a computerised risk assessment scale (OGRS) had been introduced into Britain.

Little, if any, research was conducted to establish the reliability of such techniques, or how such a risk assessment tool can be used effectively in practice. OGRS can be better explained as a political expedient, at a time when the probation service was out of favour with the Conservative government of the day (Mair, 2001). The system in Britain has now been abandoned in favour of a more user-friendly system of risk assessment, which attempts to combine risk factors with the individual characteristics of the offender. At the time of writing, the system known as OAsys (Offender Assessment System) is used nationally by the probation service, and forms the basis of a risk-based approach to the community-based treatment of offenders.

Community-based penalties, which have traditionally involved the probation officer in a befriending and advisory role, are being superseded by more coercive surveillance techniques. Electronic monitoring has been used in the USA through the 1980s and 1990s. In New York, booths were introduced, where those serving sentences in the community would report at regular intervals. The techniques for risk management in the community that are currently envisaged by the Home Office include 24-hours-a-day surveillance, voice verification, electronic monitoring, and the tracking of offenders (Mair, 2002). Electronic tagging is an integral part of the Home Detention Curfew for prisoners on early release, and will possibly be used for persistent petty offenders, such as fine defaulters, and for offenders aged between the ages of 10 and 15 (Mair, 2001). If offenders who are at risk of re-offending are monitored, then it is argued that they are less able to do damage to public safety.

Risk, justice and punishment

Hudson (2001) has argued that the notion of 'justice' in popular discourse has become synonymous with punishment. The breakdown of the rule of law in response to a perceived risk can be seen at both a national and an international level.

In England, for example, the new millennium has been marked by the emergence of groups of citizens administering summary justice which is community-based. The victims of such punishment are defined as constituting a risk to the safety of children. The risk posed by paedophiles has prompted a huge public reaction, the results of which indicate a breakdown in the rule of law. In December 2001, a suspected sex offender on the Kirkholt estate in Rochdale in the north of England was murdered. George Crawford was due to face ten charges of child sexual abuse. The victim's brother and local police believed that the murder was connected to the charges brought against Crawford. Following the murder and sexual assault of a small child, Sarah Payne, in West Sussex, the media campaign to name and shame paedophiles was launched by several tabloid newspapers. In July and August, 2000 names, residential details, and in some cases pictures of sex offenders were published. One of those named, having received 50 letters accusing him of child sexual abuse, required police protection following the publication of the story. The organisation responsible for this claimed that they were providing a service to the local community.

The most drastic example of this form of community involvement in the administration of justice occurred on the Paulsgrove Estate in Portsmouth in 2000. For five nights, hundreds of residents rioted in protest against a named paedophile. A car belonging to the victim's sister was ransacked, and the victim's home was besieged and attacked. Local police were also attacked when they attempted to protect the suspect. The editor of the *News of the World* claimed that the newspaper had a public duty to monitor the activities of paedophiles within the community (Edwards and Hughes, 2002).

These developments reflect a failure on the part of democratically elected governments to control vigilante actions and uphold the rule of law. Such examples also reflect the power of 'risk talk' to create a form of anarchy. Although the relationship between the creation of a 'moral panic' in connection with risk is complex, it is clear that the media, in embarking on a course of action which led to the breakdown of the rule of law, knew that they had strong public support.

The longer-term danger is that social divisions could be created within communities, on the basis of supposed but unsubstantiated risks posed by targeted individuals. At worst, as Hudson (2001) has argued, societies come to resemble the 'rival communities' of Northern Ireland or the former Yugoslavia. The culture of rights is essentially inclusive, where no one is outside the constituency of justice, while an over-emphasis on risk can serve to fracture society and stigmatise particular groups who are framed as a threat or danger (Hudson, 2001). Justice and due process appear less important than 'risk' in that the politics of 'safety' have overwhelmed considerations of 'justice'. If someone, or some category of persons, is categorised as a risk to public safety, there seems to remain scarcely any sense that they are nevertheless owed justice. The vocabulary of justice is almost entirely absent from current debates about sexual offending, safety in public places and mass surveillance techniques (Hudson, 2000).

Feeley and Smith (1992) have drawn attention to the possibility that increased surveillance might well be determined by membership of a particular high-risk group, rather than the seriousness of the offence committed. Others have been concerned that risk assessments applied to women and ethnic minority service users are derived from data gathered on white male offenders. This can lead to an over-prediction of risk and the inclusion of factors which are of marginal relevance (Raynor, 2001).

Wright (2002) has shown how it is possible to over-emphasise the importance of risk and crime, consequently reifying risk and concomitantly underplaying its ambivalence and complexity. Risk assessment fails to take cognisance of some of the complex arguments put forward from a cultural perspective by Douglas (1992), who emphasises the link between crime and cultural bias in risk definition. Although risk is important, it is not the sole factor in defining the tasks of the police (Wright, 2002).

Conclusion

A critical appreciation of ideas relating to risk, governance and security has, over the last five years, come to preoccupy criminologists and law enforcement agencies (Stenson and Sullivan, 2001). In the risk society, internal and external security appears to have been merged under the all-pervasive fear of global risk (Crawford, 2002a). The nature of policing has been transformed in a way which incorporates technology and the increasing use of public and private surveillance methods. The distinction between state surveillance, private surveillance and policing has also become blurred. Concerns with security have combined with a form of governance that has facilitated the development of community safety. Such governance incorporates the private and public, obfuscating any distinction between social and criminal policies. Crime has thus become designated as a social problem that poses a risk to the well-being of the law-abiding majority.

The language of partnership to combat the risk of crime is used to emphasise the need for a collective struggle against crime in geographical areas of high risk, while local groups respond to perceived risks through vigilante activity. Risk assessment has become ever more sophisticated, drawing on complex monitoring technology and anti-risk procedures. The psychometry of the individualised risk assessment model is based upon a form of pragmatism which is inextricably linked to the much wider question as to 'what works'. In the area of criminal justice in Britain and USA, the 'what works' movement predominates. Effectiveness research suggests that 'higher risk offenders should be targeted for more intensive services since the effects of treatment typically are found to be greater among higher risk cases than among lower risk cases' (Underdown and Ellis, 1998: 72). A corollary of this in the area of public policy is that government funding can only be expended on projects that can be empirically demonstrated to work. One of the problems which this creates is the creation of what McLauglin (2002: 48) has referred to as a 'non-descript, uninflected narrative devoid of complexity, tensions and contradictions'.

Another important feature of risk assessment is its tendency to treat populations as being undifferentiated. Risk assessment characteristically treats race, class and gender as controllable variables. Populations are not random, but are stratified (Brown, 1995). Racism, homophobia and sexism are harmful and pose specific risks, which at one end of the continuum can be described as harassment, and at the other murder (Cooper, 2002). The pragmatism of the 'what works movement' in the area of community and custodial interventions is also predicated on a supposed consensus that the risk of crime removes the need to ask any further questions. Seemingly unmentionable questions relating to the legitimacy of different approaches to risk, and whether new approaches to risk control are subject to democratic accountability, are not asked (Matthews and Pitts, 2001). Despite fears about the development of the Net and predicted criminal disasters waiting to happen, the global use of the Internet has remained remarkably orderly considering the scale of its use (Wall, 2002). The actuarial and exaggerated approach to the all-pervasive relationship between risk and crime is caricatured by Beaumont, when he argues:

> Take no chances; join the ranks of the punitive pessimists. There are no prizes for taking risks, only penalties. There are no political penalties if you err on the side of caution and estimate risks as higher than they are (offenders will suffer, but who cares if the criminal justice social work services doesn't). (1999: 142)

Although it has potential for producing clear evidence of crime in public places, the potential for an Orwellian nightmare of constant surveillance justified by the risk of crime has yet to be fully debated.

Further reading

Adam Crawford's edited collection *Crime and Insecurity* (Willan, 2002b) contains important chapters on CCTV, the policing of cyberspace, organised crime and immigration. Stenson and Sullivan's edited volume *Crime Risk and Justice* (Willan, 2001) offers a postmodern critical account of the risk society with respect to crime. Jock Young's *The Exclusive Society* (Sage, 1999) is an important text which puts risk and crime in a wider perspective of increasing social divisions based upon mass feelings of insecurity. Ericson and Haggerty have produced an important contribution to debates about risk and policing in *Policing the Risk Society* (Clarendon Press, 1997). Edwards and Hughes' edited collection, *Crime Control and Community* (Willan, 2002), analyses the idea of crime control in the community as a response to risk. Tim Hope offers a useful analysis of the relationship between victimisation and risk in 'Crime Victimisation and Inequality in the Risk Society' in Matthews and Pitts' collection *Crime Disorder and Community Safety* (Routledge, 2001).

Part III International and Global Risk

NINE   Risk and the New Terrorism

Outline

Following the attacks on the World Trade Center and other strategic targets on 11 September 2001, a new dimension of insecurity and global risk powerfully overshadows concerns about more mundane risks. This chapter examines the contention that a new form of terrorism poses an all-pervasive risk post-11 September. Human rights and ideology will also be discussed in the light of international responses to organised global terrorism.

Conceptualising terrorism

What constitutes terrorism has formed the basis of a continuous debate among social scientists (Biernatzki, 2002). Official definitions of terrorism emphasise the 'unlawful use of force or violence against persons or property, to intimidate or coerce a government, the civilian population, or any segment thereof, in the furtherance of political or social objectives' (Terrorism Research Centre, cited in Biernatzki, 2002). This definition can be applied to various forms of terrorism perpetrated against citizens by the state. Historically, members of militant groups who use violence have regarded themselves as freedom fighters, although they are often defined by governments as terrorists. Nelson Mandella, imprisoned as a terrorist, was elected head of the South African state which had imprisoned him soon after his release from prison.

Terrorism also has a psychological impact. Drake (1998: 54) has defined terrorism as 'the recurrent use or threatened use of politically motivated and clandestinely organised violence, by a group whose aim is to affect one or more psychological targets in order to make them behave in a way in which terrorists desire'.

Terrorism can be regarded as the indiscriminate use of violence against specific targets, and the concomitant creation of a belief that the population is at continual risk of attack without warning. It is the longer-term risk of violent attack on civil society that is examined in this chapter.

The global risk of terrorism

Following 11 September 2001, the risk of terrorism has accelerated an endless search for global safety, which has now become a major preoccupation of governments and social agencies, both public and private. 11 September demonstrated how a mundane act, in this case air travel, was open to attack from a well-organised global terrorist group. Terrorist attacks involving civil aircraft are not new. Bader Meinhoff and other groups attacked aircraft during the 1970s and the 1980s. In 1994 a plan to crash an airliner into the Eiffel Tower in Paris by an Algerian group with close ties to Bin Laden failed because none of the terrorists knew how to fly. An accidental bomb explosion in the Philippines the following year prevented a known terrorist who had learned to fly from carrying out his plan of crashing a aeroplane into the CIA Headquarters.

Although much has been written following the attacks of 11 September 2001, there are a number of pointers which should be emphasised as underlining the long-term impact of this act. There was widespread international incredulity that the USA had failed to recognise the risks to national security that had been building up over a long period of time, despite the existence of one of the largest intelligence networks in the world. Once fundamentalist Islamic groups had been established in the country, the American intelligence services failed to keep tracks on their whereabouts. For example, documents found in the flat of a Muslim extremist who had assassinated a Jewish cleric in 1990 in New York were not translated from Arabic until after the first, less serious World Trade Center bombing in 1993 (Wright, 2002). The attacks reflected a failure in the co-operative activities of western intelligence services. Al-Queda was a well financed, technologically driven, global organisation, which had been developing since 1996. In 1998, Bin Laden enforced a *fatwa*, urging his followers to 'kill Americans – including civilians – anywhere in the world' (Schultz and Vogt, 2002: 384). The apparent laxness in security gave substance to the view that the events of 11 September must never happen again. This provided a licence to take unprecedented aggressive action against suspected terrorists.

The events of 11 September were even more dramatic since they exposed the fragility of the intelligence services designed to protect a world superpower. Explanations given by the security forces as to why they were unaware or unable to respond to the possibility of attack appeared to be non-existent. The ease with which 19 suicide bombers were able to attack key targets in the USA, revealed some major structural failings in international intelligence.

Speculation as to how this failure occurred can be seen on a number of levels. There were failures to read previous signs. Although there is an element of chance in the effective implementation of intelligence, the ability of the terrorist organisation to penetrate the USA on 11 September reflected an unco-ordinated and privatised approach to international security. Some attempts were made by the Clinton administration to rectify this, but these were often overshadowed by other events, such as the war in the Balkans and the scandal emanating from the personal relationship between President Clinton and Monica Lewinsky. Thus the American intelligence agencies did not establish good co-operation with overseas intelligence agencies, and this hampered their ability to deal with the terrorist groups that were emerging during the 1990s. The attacks of 11 September also exposed a number of fundamental tactical errors on the part of the USA. For example, they failed to keep Bin Laden in Sudan, where it would have been much easier to keep him under surveillance, and allowed him to escape to Afghanistan where the rugged terrain made it impossible to keep track of him. All this pointed to a risk which should have been managed more effectively in order to increase security for civilians.

The emergence of the new terrorism

The lapses mentioned above left the USA and other nation states vulnerable to risks from a new form of terrorism. In the preface to a text on terrorism and counter-terrorism, Howard (2002: xv) describes a 'new terrorism', which has a number of recognisable features:

> The haunting image of New York's falling twin towers defined the reality of the 'new terrorism' for the United States. Americans have faced terrorism before September 11; however, in its previous incarnations, it was not as organised, deadly, or personal as the attacks inflicted that day on New York city and Washington, D.C.

The new terrorism is also inextricably linked to globalisation. In an interview in 1997, Bin Laden described Al-Queda as a product of globalisation and a response to it (Schultz and Voght, 2002). This interpretation of events following 11 September 2001 can be conceptualised within the idea of the risk society. It is driven by technology and globalisation, defined by experts and de-emphasises class, racial divisions and inequalities existing within the social structure. See Box 9.1 for some of the risks posed by new terrorism.

Box 9.1   Risks posed by new terrorism

- New terrorism triggers more aggressive forms of international risk management.
- It poses greater risks to symbolic targets.
- The systematic and planned nature of new terrorism increases risk.
- The suicide bombings that are a feature of new terrorism have created selective and targeted risks.
- New terrorism's use of global technology increases risk.
- Its aim to create maximum and indiscriminate loss of civilian lives poses new risks.

Terrorism risk and vulnerability

A major theme in the work of Beck is the invisibility and all-pervasiveness of risk (Beck, 1992). The attacks of 11 September, which were immediately followed by the discovery of anthrax spores in the American postal service, did appear to point to the vulnerability of western institutions that had hitherto seemed indomitable. Since Palestinian suicide attacks have often been directed at buses, and the 11 September attack on the Twin Towers in New York involved the aviation system, public transport security has been a particular focus of political interest. The use of germ warfare in the wake of the World Trade Center attack presents another risk, creating further mass insecurity. The apparent ease with which basic services and utilities like air travel and postal services could be infiltrated with weapons of potentially terrifying destruction rocked the American and British establishments, and even threatened the very continuity of the American way of life. The effectiveness of the attack of 11 September exposed the risks created by a well-resourced global organisation, operating at times in a sophisticated manner, and harnessing modern technology. Al-Queda functioned through email, websites and global communications. Operatives carrying out the attack were trained to fly sophisticated civil aircraft. The organisation used CD-ROM disks to store and disseminate information with respect to bomb-making, recruitment and operations. Satellite cell phones were also used to co-ordinate operations (Schultz and Vogt, 2002).

It is also possible that technology was used to create counter-intelligence that was deliberately designed to divert attention from the real risk. Threats were intercepted by American intelligence agencies relating to imminent attacks on the European Parliament, the US embassy in Paris and elsewhere.

The scale of risk – real and imagined

One of the themes which runs through both empirical and theoretical accounts of risk is a collective propensity to overestimate some risks and underestimate others (Kemshall, 1997). However dramatic the events of 11 September were, it is imperative to attempt to understand the scale of the risks involved in terrorism. In the year of the attacks on the Twin Towers, terrorist attacks globally had fallen to 350 incidents, from a high of almost 700 in 1988 (Howard and Sawyer, 2003).

Much effort has been expended on making a link between risk and terrorism. In a report published by the World Markets Research Centre, risk assessments were carried out on 186 sovereign states and a 'Top Ten' list of terrorist targets was produced (see Box 9.2). Such statements, although intended to warn of the potential capability of Al-Queda to conduct synchronised attacks against symbolic targets in the West, fail to take sufficient account of the possible impact of anti-terrorist policies and the high levels of international anti-terrorist co-operation since 11 September 2001.

Box 9.2 Top ten terrorist targets

1. Columbia
2. Israel
3. Pakistan
4. USA
5. Philippines
6. Afghanistan
7. Indonesia
8. Iraq
9. India
10. UK
11. Sri Lanka } (UK and Sri Lanka designated as being at equal risk)

Source: bbc.co.uk/uk10thonterrortargetlist/ accessed 19 August 2003 citing World Markets Research Centre

---

During the 1990s, much global governmental effort was centred around imagining new 'worst-case' scenarios. These 'asymmetrical global risks' included the spreading of both biological and computer viruses, the poisoning of water systems, the collapse of the banking system through Internet corruption, and the disruption of air traffic and power supplies. The principal asymmetrical risk, which prompted action in Iraq in 2003, was encapsulated in the idea of the 'rogue state' sponsoring terrorism and acquiring long-range missiles.

At the time of writing, terrorists have seldom used weapons of mass destruction and have never detonated a nuclear device. However, many constellations of potential risk could be envisaged. Iran, North Korea, Syria and other states could produce and use chemical and biological weapons. Pathogens could also be used as biological weapons. These include common food poisons, such as salmonella, shigella and staphylococcus. Information for the production of potentially deadly chemicals is globally available on the Internet. Chemical or biological agents could be used to poison water supplies, although it should also be remembered that many water surfaces in the USA and Europe are so vast that any poisonous substance would be diluted. Well systems, however, make easier targets (Cohen, 1997).

The most successful chemical and biological terrorist attack was carried out by the Aum Shirikiyo cult in Japan. In June 1994 residents of the Matsumoto noticed a fog, which eventually killed seven people and made 600 people ill. Sarin gas, a chemical agent which acts upon the nerves, was traced in the victims. In March 1995 the cult again used sarin, filling polyethylene pouches and releasing the chemical on five Tokyo subway stations. In this attack, 12 people died and over 500 were injured. Another case involving the use of biological agents occurred in September 1984 when the Rajneeshpuram cult in Oregon poisoned salad bars with salmonella typhimurium (Stern, 1999).

Risk and responses to terrorism

While acknowledging the reality of risks posed by terrorists and the impact of the terrible events of 11 September 2001, the international reaction reflected a concern for increased security and vigilance. Given the existence of allegedly unheeded warnings of risk given to the FBI and CIA prior to 11 September, the US Department of Home Security was created by President Bush to co-ordinate anti-terrorist activity after the attacks. Much of the work carried out by the Department is directly connected with the threat posed by Al-Queda. However, neither the FBI nor the CIA was included within the new Department.

Following 11 September, the world has been divided into two groups by America, Britain, and their allies against terrorism. These can best be described as 'insiders' and 'outsiders'. Designation into either group is defined by nationality and religion. The events of 11 September served to legitimate the arrest of individuals merely on the assumption that as 'outsiders' they were a potential risk to national security. Such is the priority given to the risk of terrorism that 'outsiders' are routinely investigated and held without trial. Some nation states, like America and Britain, licensed themselves to carry out unprecedented levels of surveillance and racial profiling based upon subjective judgements: 'In the immediate aftermath of 11 September up to 5,000 men aged between 18 and 33 from middle eastern countries were rounded up in what critics see as a dragnet based upon ethnic profiling, and not evidence' (*Guardian*, 2002c: 57).

The partial suspension of the rule of law creates a situation in which punishment appears routinely to supplant justice. In the UK, those suspected of terrorism can be held without charge indefinitely. At the time of writing, those suspected of belonging to Al-Queda and the Taliban fighters captured in Afghanistan are being held at 'Camp X-Ray' in Guantanamo Bay, Cuba, and will be tried secretly by military tribunal, without traditional legal safeguards. Although the failure to be vigilant to dangers is not only characterised by the media as an act of supreme incompetence, it is also presented by the American and British establishments as immoral and unpatriotic weakness.

In March 2003 the 'Human Rights Watch' groups argued that there was no legal basis for holding suspected terrorists without trial at Guantanamo Bay. Attempts to provide legal representation had proved unsuccessful. Under the Geneva Convention, the USA should release Taliban soldiers unless they were being charged with war crimes or other similar offences (*Guardian*, 2003a). Such is the emphasis on the risks posed by terrorists, that the US authorities are able to argue that they were holding prisoners who can provide useful intelligence, while releasing others.

The passing of the US Patriot Act in 2001 reflected the perceived urgency of the risk that was posed by the 11 September attack. The legislation was introduced on 2 October and became law on 26 October 2001. Debate was restricted by the timetable. As President George W. Bush argued: 'In order to win the war, we must make sure that the law enforcement men and women have got the tools necessary, within the Constitution to defeat the enemy. ... We're at war. ... A war we are going to win' (cited in Thomas, 2002: 95). The US Patriot Act has introduced sweeping powers that are ostensibly designed to reduce the risk of further terrorist attack. The Act enables the Secretary of State to designate any group, foreign or domestic, a terrorist. Powers of detention and surveillance are given to the executive and law enforcement agencies, and the courts are prevented from offering any significant judicial oversight. The Act also creates a new crime, that of 'domestic terrorism', which includes activities deemed by the executive and law enforcement agencies to coerce or intimidate the civilian population, or affect the conduct of government by mass destruction. Section 412 of the legislation permits the indefinite detention of immigrants and other non-nationals. (Thomas, 2002).

Less attention has been paid to the treatment of British Muslims arrested in the wake of the 11 September attack. An unknown number of prisoners were held at Belmarsh Prison in Britain under the provisions of the Anti-terrorism, Crime and Security Act, which was passed by Parliament with amazing speed and despite opposition in the House of Lords at the end of 2001. Under this Act, 'foreign nationals' who are 'reasonably suspected of terrorist activities' and who cannot be immediately returned to their country of origin can be detained indefinitely without charge. In order to pass this legislation the then UK Home Secretary David Blunkett was forced to suspend Britain from the terms of the European Convention of Human Rights. The Terrorism Act of 2000 creates new offences and extends the powers of the police to investigate, arrest and detain suspects, as is the case with the Patriot Act in the USA. British detainees took their case to the House of Lords. The case was heard by nine Law Lords rather than the usual five due to the constitutional importance of the case. On 17 December 2004 the Lords ruled that indefinite detention without trial for foreign subjects suspected of terrorism contravened the European Convention of Human Rights. They ruled that it discriminated on the basis of nationality and immigration status. They further ruled that current legislation was disproportionate and discriminatory. On 26 January 2005, four UK citizens accused by the US of being Terrorists were released from Guantanomo Bay. They had been detained for three years. After being questioned by the UK Police they were released without charge. The Home Secretary Charles Clarke was compelled to change the position adopted in Section IV of the 2001 Anti Terrorism, Crime and Security Act. On the 26 January the Home Secretary announced his intention to extend his executive powers by imposing 'control orders' which could include curfew tagging and being placed under indefinite house arrest. These orders could be imposed on British or foreign nationals (*Guardian*, 2005).

Reflexivity and the terrorist risk

Beck, as was noted earlier, conceptualises risk as being a form of reflexive modernisation: 'In reflexive modernity the social production of wealth is systematically accompanied by the social production of risks. Wealth and power are defining concepts of classical modernity, but the signature concepts of reflexive modernity are risks and uncertainty' (Boyne, 2003: 100). In the risk society, technological innovation also possesses downsides which create new kinds of risk. The Internet, although creating many benefits, can also facilitate the objectives of terrorist organisations. Thus, technology and science reflexively and simultaneously solve problems and produce new ones. Beck makes a clear distinction between the 'already destructive consequences' and the 'potential element' of risk. Since 11 September 2001, potential risk has been a powerful driving force in international and domestic politics. Before 11 September, judgements could have been affected by an over-emphasis on the potential risk, at the same time as real global risk was synthesising. It is easy to make such an observation with hindsight since in the 'risk society' fear generated by terrorism often lies in the future world of the 'unreal' (Beck, 1992: 33). The destruction of the Twin Towers, as people were attempting to live their lives on the streets of Manhattan, was bizarre and surreal. Yet on 11 September, for the individuals trapped or killed in the building, the catastrophe was real, and the intelligence services, over a long period, failed to act upon the threat of what turned out to be a real risk of attack. Previously, military action to avert such an attack was deemed to be diplomatically too risky. In this case events appeared to culminate making what was an almost implausible set of probabilities become reality.

The ramifications of the events of 11 September also included a reflexive response among other nation states. On 12 September 2001, Russian President Valdimir Putin suggested that Al-Queda was connected to Chechnyan terrorism. On 13 September the Australian Prime Minister John Howard used 11 September to justify his government's efforts to prevent asylum seekers entering his country (Glasius and Kaldor, 2001).

The 11 September attacks on four passenger aircraft, and the attempt by Richard Reid to blow up a civil aircraft over the Atlantic with explosives hidden in his shoes soon after, adds a further dimension of risk to flying. Some airlines have responded to the risk of terrorism by suggesting that armed guards should be placed on flights. The Israeli national carrier El Al has used armed guards on flights for many years, and Australian airlines have trained teams of guards with low velocity fire arms which can kill without penetrating the fuselage of the aircraft. This is in addition to searching procedures for staff and passengers at airports, baggage handling security measures, and increasing the number of prohibited articles that are allowed on board the aircraft.

The use of so-called 'sky marshals' presents a number of examples of reflexive risk. Sky marshals would carry weapons on to an aircraft which

143

could lead to the possibility of a shoot out in a confined space. This could pose a greater risk to the passengers if caught in cross-fire and if the fuselage of the aircraft was damaged. Some British airlines, at the time of writing, prefer the idea of preventing potential terrorists from boarding an aircraft. Vetting procedures could be enhanced through the development of advanced identification techniques such as a computerised biometric examination of the iris of the eye and passenger profiling databases.

International law and human rights

The events of 11 September 2001 presented a global risk which has served to accelerate and intensify coercive state action against those who are defined as posing a risk to national security. 11 September emphasised the relationship between danger, risk and human rights. Some writers have drawn attention to the American contravention of the Geneva Convention on the basis that some terrorist suspects not charged with war crimes have been held indefinitely without legal representation (Smiljanic, 2002). What has emerged is the beginning of an enduring military offensive which, in itself, could pose a risk to stability in politically volatile areas.

In discussing future risks, politicians are dealing with complex causes and future unpredictability. The events of 11 September marked the point at which an almost implausible risk became a horrifying reality. The control of the terrorist risk took a central place within international relations.

Beck, in his analysis, changes the basis upon which human rights can be viewed in the context of the risk posed by globally organised terrorism. Writing in the year before the attacks occurred, he centres his arguments, in what he has referred to as the second age of modernism, on the complex relationship between international law and human rights (Beck, 2000b). Within the first age of modernity, the interconnectedness of separate states (which came into being with the Treaty of Westphalia in 1648) dominated international relations. Beck (2000: 109) states: 'The principle that international law precedes human rights which were held during the (nation state) first age of modernity is being replaced by the principle of the (world society) second age of modernity, that human rights precede international law'. The risky results of such a paradigm shift have not been sufficiently considered by governments because it blurs the distinction between war and peace, foreign and domestic policy, upon which the old order was based. The resulting 'cosmopolitan' society degrades the importance of international law, while also ignoring nations and states creating a 'legally binding world society of individuals' (Beck, 2000b: 111).

Beck suggests that it is unclear which poses the greatest risk of world war, the disappearing world of international law, or a self-appointed hegemonic power defending human rights. The major problem with the emerging paradigm is that global superpowers have the power to select which countries can be defined as being human dictatorships constituting global risk. This strategy favours the American way of life and increases the cleavages between rich and poor (Glasius and Kaldor, 2001).

One of the major risks associated with this approach to international relations is that the 'humanism of the west is founded on an un-interrogated world monopoly of power and morality that, especially in the course of the transition to the second age of modernity has become extremely questionable' (Beck, 2002a: 112). The dangers inherent in the situation are unknown. When Beck wrote this article, the attack on the World Trade Center and the resulting American-led invasion of Afghanistan had not occurred. Beck's position was vindicated by the unilateral decision of the USA to invade Iraq without the support of the UN Security Council, a position which means that the international legality of the action is still debated. Such unilateral American action could pose a major local and global security risk.

Terrorism and world risk society

Beck has argued that the events of 11 September 2001 reflect the *World Risk Society* (Beck, 1999). There are three forms of interrelated risk to be considered. The first is ecological destruction, the second is global financial crises, and the third is the threat of global terror. These three forms of risk, according to Beck, interact. Dangers from terrorism increase exponentially with technical progress and global capital transactions are used to finance terrorist operations. Advances in global communication technology made global terrorism possible in the first place. Every advance in technology opens a Pandora's box that can be utilised by terrorists (Beck, 2002a).

Beck regards the attacks of 11 September as being the Chernobyl of globalisation. As the Russian disaster undermined faith in nuclear energy, the events of 11 September exposed the vulnerability of western civilisation. Beck considers that the perceived risk of global terrorism has had the opposite effect to that intended by the terrorists. It marked a point at which a new phase of globalisation, which moulded new transnational co-operative networks, occurred. Terrorist resistance to globalisation has only accelerated this transnational co-operation. The events of 11 September have produced alliances which preserve internal and not external security. Borders which divide domestic from international relations have disintegrated. Foreign and domestic policy, and international security, have now become intertwined.

The link between international terrorism and aviation has created a perception of danger which is globally pervasive. The use of civil aircraft carrying civilian passengers to destroy key American targets was an event of iconoclastic significance, and has destroyed the distinction between dangers posed by internal and external agencies. The relative ease with which it was possible for terrorists to carry out four independent attacks using civil aircraft simultaneously has increased the all-encompassing perceived risk of international terrorism that can strike anywhere in the world at any time.

Regimes of truth

The struggle for truth is about making public and private institutions accountable for their definitions, policies, strategies and actions. It is about challenging what Foucault called 'regimes of truth' through the critique of power relations' (Scraton, 2002: 231). Such a combination of beliefs has justified intervention and the licensing of external, military pre-emptive action, using patriotism and risk to neutralise opposition and disqualify knowledge. Macey (2002) also argued that large numbers of Muslims live in materially deprived, overcrowded conditions of poverty and ill-health. These factors are not emphasised by 'risk society' theorists, and some would argue that they are important omissions from 'risk society' analysis (Taylor-Gooby, 2000).

Howard (2003) claims that the new terrorism is not ideological in any political sense and is inspired by religious fundamentalism. From this position, religious ideas appear to be separated from the political. New terrorists, according to Howard, do not answer to any government operating across national boundaries. At the same time they have access to funding and new technology. This new form of terrorism, he claims, has a disregard for the number of civilian casualties and does not respond to diplomatic or military deterrence (Howard, 2003).

Ideas about the nature of the west are central to the religious fundamentalism which underpinned the attacks of 11 September. Ideas have also been central to the creation of 'constellations of risk' which have been used to construct a global response to the events of 11 September.

Al-Queda can be regarded as a collection of ideas around which a disparate number of groups operate rather than a single organisation. Drake (1998) has emphasised how ideology plays a critical role in the selection of terrorist targets. Ideology provides terrorists with an initial motive for action, and a 'prism' through which terrorists view the actions of other people. Some ideologies, as Drake has pointed out, incorporate not only political identity, but also politicised religious beliefs which might contain elements of the historical, semi-mythical and the supernatural (Drake, 1998). The buildings that were selected on 11 September were not chosen at random, but reflected, for the attackers, ideas about central commercial and governmental institutions.

Conclusion

The new global risks represented by the events of 11 September 2001 add a number of complex dimensions to the way in which terrorism has been conceptualised. The risk to the USA and its allies has been less well defined than has been the case with other groups who have attacked America. Global terrorism appears to present dangers which are simultaneously external, internal and unknowable. The construction of the terrorist as a global, and possibly national and cultural, risk makes it extremely difficult to identity the enemy. Action against particular nation states like Iraq, Afghanistan and possibly Syria and Iran, serve to create more tangible legitimate targets and are defined as part of a collective, yet highly differentiated enemy.

The precautionary principle appears to have dominated the response of the USA and states such as the UK and Australia to post-11 September terrorism. Within this framework of understanding, prevention and state security take precedence over the need to gather evidence as to the nature of the risk posed by terrorism. This approach to terrorism stands in stark contrast to that taken with regard to environmental risks, where the precautionary principle has not been applied (see Chapter Eleven). In the longer term the risks posed by global warming and pollution may well be greater than those associated with international terrorism.

In a situation in which global risk prevention dominates, it becomes possible to construct the terrorist enemy in ways which are politically significant. President George W. Bush made constant reference to his proven ability to protect the American population from international terror in his successful presidential election campaign in 2004. Democratic candidate John Kerry, on the other hand, was presented by the Republican Party as an individual who gave inconsistent messages on vital questions of homeland security.

Greater defensiveness and exclusivity has accompanied the ascendancy of the precautionary principle in US foreign policy. Risk has been a vitally important backcloth to the reaction to 11 September, while a greater sense of exclusiveness and a need to identify aliens has turned out to be a vote winner in the USA. Risks from the 'outside' are reduced to simplistic certainties based upon an exclusivist ideology. Draconian measures to deal with risk are attractive to the risk-conscious and ontologically insecure. In what Young (1999) has referred to as the 'exclusive society', insiders are more distinguishable from outsiders, whereas good and evil are reduced to simple juxtaposition. The events following 11 September contain all the elements of the exclusive society. As the role of the United Nations (UN) diminishes and gaps between the European and American worldview widen, a new international security doctrine matures, which has at its foundation self-protection and proactive action against those who are themselves, or might be associated with, terrorists. How far the new exclusivity, risk-based doctrine increases the possibility of terrorist attacks on civilian targets remains to be seen. Given the endless number of possible terrorist targets, which can never be adequately protected, it is difficult to see how the risk to life through reprisal attacks has been diminished.

Further reading

Howard and Sawyer's *Terrorism and Counter-Terrorism* (McGraw-Hill/ Dushkin, 2003) is an edited collection of readings and interpretations of events following 11 September 2001. Several chapters are relevant to risk, including considerations of 'new terrorism', weapons of mass destruction and strategies for combating terrorism. A readable and incisive account of global society before and after 11 September can be found in Glasius, Kaldor and Anheier's edited volume *Global Civil Society* (Oxford University Press, 2001). Scraton has edited a collection entitled *Beyond September 11th: An Anthology of Dissent* (Pluto Press, 2002), which critically examines some of the reactions to the events of 11 September. Marie Macey explores the motivation of young Muslim men in crime in her chapter, 'Interpreting Islam: Young Muslim Men's Involvement in Criminal Activity in Bradford' in Spalek's edited volume *Islam, Crime and Criminal Justice* (Willan, 2002). Ulrich Beck's 'The Terrorist Threat: World Risk Society Revisited' (2002a) and Douglas Kellner's 'September 11th: Social Theory and Democratic Politics' (2002) deal with the relationship between risk and the post-11 September world in a special issue of *Theory, Culture and Society* (2002) 19(4).

TEN   The Management and Regulation of Risk

Outline

Beck (1992) has argued that the by-products of new technological developments have increased the demand for the management of risk. Managing risk is not confined to the work of professional risk analysts and managers. It has now become an operational imperative for individual professionals, organisations and governments. Risk assessment and management constitutes a way of seeing the social world, which appears to be focused and managerially controllable as risks become more elusive and complex. Consumers of services expect risks to be identified and eliminated. This chapter examines some of the implications of the ascendancy of risk management and regulation.

Regulation and risk management

One of the biggest difficulties facing policy-makers with respect to risk and the environment is how to deal with the uncertainty that limits any understanding of risk. The precautionary principle, which has been enshrined in international treaties and domestic law in a number of states, appears to guide organisations and governments. Much of the regulatory enterprise is concerned with attempting to identify hazards before they occur, and taking appropriate precautions to ensure the minimisation of harm. Risk assessors apply conservative assessments in order to create margins of safety.

One of the central questions concerns what constitutes reasonable levels of precaution. A basic requirement of administrative law in the USA is that regulators must base their decisions on intelligible principles. Marchant (2001) has argued that the precautionary principle fails to provide consistency, accuracy, predictability or accountability, which renders regulation unintelligible. The regulatory approach taken by the countries of the European Union, for instance, is far more restrictive than the position taken by the USA, yet both claim to rely upon the precautionary principle. A 'precautionary' approach for one nation appears to be 'paranoia' for another. Even in countries that are adjacent to each other, wide variations in the regulatory approach exist. In 1991 regulatory systems in the USA and neighbouring Canada contrasted with respect to the use of cyclamates and saccharin, both artificial sweetening agents. Both substances were banned in Canada although they were permitted in the USA. Following a campsite tragedy in Spain in 1996, in which 86 tourists died in a flash flood, the variations in the regulations governing the safety of campsites across Europe became apparent. Some countries had regulations bordering on the draconian, while other countries were relatively lax in their approach (Hood et al., 2001).

Trade wars can also result in differences in risk regulation between states. In the case of food, regulation differences emerged between France and Britain as the BSE crisis progressed. France, for a considerable period, was unprepared for their citizens to eat British beef, while regulations in Britain reflected the belief that British beef was completely safe and constituted no risk whatsoever to health (see Chapter Four).

The regulatory state

An accompaniment to the risk society has been the development of the 'regulatory state'. The 'regulatory state' is based upon the idea that a new institutional and policy style has emerged, enhancing the role of government as a regulator of risk. Simultaneously, a government's role as a direct employer declines. The increase in sub-contracting essential services by the state marks a shift from the collectivised centralised state, which, as we have seen in Chapter Seven, was evident within the field of welfare. The tendency towards privatised forms of welfare and public services have fostered the further development of inconsistent regulatory regimes. Given that public services are now provided by private companies, it may well be that risks are created in attempts to cut costs in order to maximise profit. The sub-contracting of services may also lead to less stringent control and the creation of risks in essential public services.

In the UK, investigations into the Potters Bar rail crash, which occurred in May 2002, and the earlier Hatfield train disaster on 17 October 2000 suggested that points and rails were in a state of disrepair, a factor which could have contributed to the crash (CNN, 2002). The contractor with responsibility for track maintenance claimed that sabotage to the track was the most likely explanation. In the Potters Bar crash seven people lost their lives and 70 were injured, some seriously.

Green (1997) has cogently argued that the 'risk society' has created a mythological belief that accidents should not happen. However, risk management cannot predict individual misfortune, but can link risk factors to the possible likelihood of risk within the general population. This is illustrated with regard to maritime accidents. The design of roll-on roll-off ferries has been a source of risk. Investigations into ferry accidents have concentrated on the immediate cause of accidents, always in an attempt to apportion blame. If there has been a miscalculation in the risk assessment, then someone should be held responsible. In 1987 the *Herald of Free Enterprise* sank near Zeebrugge with the loss of 193 lives. In 1994 the *Estonia* sank in the Baltic with a loss of 823 lives. At the time of the accidents the ferry companies were enjoying good profits. In both accidents attention was focused on the doors and the open design of the car decks. The practice of allowing cars to roll on and roll off quickly has obvious economic advantages, keeping turn-around times to a minimum. Naval engineers are agreed on the need for 'transverse bulkheads', which would be positioned across the car deck, but the introduction of bulkheads would not only reduce space for vehicles, but would also delay loading and unloading times, thus making the mode of transport uncompetitive. The economics of space therefore bore a direct influence on the assessment and presentation of risk with this particular ferry design (*Guardian*, 1994a).

In the immediate aftermath of the disasters, experts and regulatory authorities were blamed for the accident. In the case of the *Estonia*, Swedish safety inspectors found defective seals on the car deck doors, although after the accident they claimed that only minor faults were found. In both cases, allegations were made that the doors had not been properly closed.

The tragedy of accidents in transportation such as the *Herald of Free Enterprise* and *Estonia* disasters is the immediacy and scale of the loss of life and injury. The *Estonia* sank in an hour. Yet if the levels of risk associated with ferry travel are compared with population rates, the risk seems miniscule. The British Chamber of Shipping has compared mode of transport with the number of people killed per 100 million hours of travelling (see Table 10.1). With the exception of trains and buses, ferries are the safest form of transport. How such expert statistics impinge on an individual's sense of well-being on boarding a ferry, particularly following an accident, is unclear.

Although governments in advanced capitalist social formations would not normally intervene to regulate markets, one possible explanation for the development of such regulatory regimes is 'market failure'. Regulation occurs in situations where market mechanisms and processes have not adequately or safely provided a service. For example, as residential care

Table 10.1 Fatalities per 100 million hours of travelling

Mode of transport	Deaths per 100 million hours of travelling
Motorcycles	660
Aircraft	240
Bicycles	96
Cars	57
Ferries	7
Trains	5
Buses	3

Source: Adapted from *The Guardian* (1994b)

for the elderly has become privatised and is not provided by the state, a system of regulation for the inspection and registration of private homes has been established. In a perfect market, risk will be factored into product prices or be dealt with by insurance companies. Any control system must contain three components:

1. There must be standard setting in order to facilitate more or less preferred states of the system.
2. There must be a system for gathering or monitoring information in order to produce knowledge about the current or changing states of the system.
3. There must be the capacity to modify behaviour in the light of the information gathered.

If any of these components is absent, then the system is out of control. Risk regulation systems are not static. After every major failing of a system, new items are added to the list of checks and precautionary procedures. Thus, in the health field, for example, regimes include the attempt to control risks for doctors and other health care professionals, dangerous drugs, and medical equipment. Other sources of risks can include power failure and infections in hospitals. These latter sources of risk can, according to Hood, Rothstein and Baldwin (2001), be regarded as 'sub-sets'. In this case, regulatory emphasis is placed on the more immediate threat from dangerous doctors on the 'sum of all controls over health care' (Hood et al., 1999).

Risk society and increased control of corporate management

Robert Maxwell improperly used an estimated £400 million pounds of pension funds in the UK during the 1980s, before his financial empire collapsed. In this case the conduct of several major financial institutions fell short of good practice in their direct dealings with Maxwell. A number of non-executive directors were also criticised for not asking questions about Maxwell's business. In 2001 Enron, the bankrupt American energy company, reported huge profits, while at the same time generating relatively small amounts of cash. In these examples, risks were created for shareholders and pensioners who are reliant upon corporate activities for their long-term security.

Given the global complexity and speed of corporate transactions, the potential for malpractice and the siphoning off of funds is increased. In the 'risk society', states respond to risk by investing in greater systems of control in the running of large companies. This has been evident in the field of corporate operations following catastrophic failures and dishonesty within management. After prominent financial or corporate scandals and collapses, formal systems of audit have been introduced as a risk control. The regulation of business and corporate risk management are inextricably linked. Different forms of regulatory activity aim at controlling specific risks. These include state regulation (through the imposition of the law) and enforced self-regulation, which combines state and corporate regulation (Power, 1997).

In the UK in 1992, the Committee on the Financial Aspects of Corporate Governance, chaired by Sir Adrian Cadbury, recommended that the Executive Boards of all listed companies in the UK should declare whether they comply with the Code of Best Practice. The Code of Best Practice recommended openness, integrity and accountability on the part of corporate management. This applied particularly with respect to the disclosure of information. The Committee's report declared that Boards of Directors should provide shareholders with good quality information on all aspects of company activities. Failure to do so, it was envisaged in the report, would result in increased regulation of corporate activities (London Stock Exchange, 1992). Transparent integrity and openness would create the trust needed to restore faith in the management of major business corporations. Although compliance with the Code is still voluntary, Sir Andrew Hugh Smith, when Chairman of the London Stock Exchange, indicated that a refusal to publish a compliance statement is more likely to result in censure rather than the de-listing of a company.

In 1999 The Institute of Chartered Accountants in England and Wales offered guidance to Company Directors on the implementation of the Code of Best Practice in a report produced by Nigel Turnbull (Turnbull, 1999). The Turnbull Report combined the principles of risk management with these enunciated in the Code of Best Practice. It was recommended that companies should have sound systems of internal control in order to reduce risks. The systems of internal control should aim to minimise actuarial misjudgements, investment risks and company insolvency. Other more indirect risks can result in potentially catastrophic consequences for companies. Turbulent weather conditions, for instance, can affect insurance companies, while the impact of the 11 September attacks were felt globally across the civil aviation, travel and tourism industries. The Turnbull Report recommended that companies should examine the nature and extent of potential risk, assess the likelihood of those risks materialising. Companies, according to the Turnbull Report, should also review their ability to reduce and respond to the incidence and impact of risk (Turnbull, 1999). In April 2003 Evers reported that half of Britain's largest companies were not complying with the regulations recommended by the Turnbull Report (Evers, 2003).

The intention of the Cadbury Committee and the Turnbull Report was to provide a reference point for shareholders who wished to raise concerns relating to the governance of a company, thus encouraging shareholders to exercise their rights and responsibilities. Both reports emphasised the collective responsibility for governance of company Boards of Directors.

One of the main safeguards against the concentration of power in the hands of a few Board members is to increase the role of the non-executive directors. In the past, non executive members have remained conspicuously silent during the build-up to financial collapse, as was the case with Enron. Company Boards in Britain now need a minimum of three non-executive directors, the majority of whom must be independent of the company. In addition to this, it is recommended that the role of the Company Secretary should be enhanced in order to ensure that procedures are followed and regularly reviewed.

One of the major problems with these new practices is that it is essentially the responsibility of the shareholders to take control of the code of regulatory enforcement. It may well be that self-interest at some point in the life of a company encourages shareholders to speak out. However, the major interest of the shareholder is in profit and dividends. Interest in raising problems related to the good governance of the company may decline if profits are increasing. Such procedures are meant to create greater trust, although how transparent such procedures are to innocent shareholders, whose pensions and mortgages are dependent upon the activities of global corporations, seems questionable.

Regulatory systems within the public sector

Risk management within the public sector incorporates aspects of managerial science. Professionals in both the private and public sectors are now accountable to audit, appraisal and inspection, while service users have gained a voice and emerged from a place of virtual social exclusion (Foster and Wilding, 2000). Risk is rendered manageable by a new relationship between political decision-makers and a variety of new regulatory systems, procedures and routines. Such systematised risk management systems are now normal practice within many public organisations (Parton, 1998: 21). Public sector working practices have become dominated by the business orientation of operational management. Scrupulous managerial attention is now paid to gate-keeping and formal risk avoidance procedures. Fewer activities are designated by managers as falling within the confines of professional decision-making, while more demands are placed on professionals to justify and explain their decisions and interventions. As Beck (1992: 54) argues:

> All decisions on the risks and hazards of civilization falling within the compass of knowledge production are never just questions of the substance of knowledge (inquiries, hypotheses, methods, procedures, acceptable values, etc.). They are, at the same time, decisions on who is afflicted, the extent and type of hazard, the elements of the threat, the population concerned, delayed effects, measures to be taken, those responsible, and claims for compensation.

Here risk assessment has been transformed into a form of defensiveness which is particularly evident in the public sphere. Luhmann (1991) has provided an example of the possible impact of such risk consciousness. In Sweden, it was thought politically opportune to evacuate large numbers of Lapps from their homeland so that missile testing could take place there. They were evacuated by helicopter. However, the risk of the helicopter crashing was greater than the possibility of a single person being struck by falling debris from the missile testing (Luhmann, 1991). In this case, politicians made the riskier choice, for fear of being held responsible for the death of even one single Lapp. The government was seen to be working to avert danger and minimise risk (Beaumont, 1999).

Conclusion

In a global society which is more risk-conscious, the identification of technological, contractual, physical, financial, personal and environmental risks are a major governmental preoccupation. Governments interpret their role as being the protection of the public at large, of vulnerable individuals and groups, and of the environment. Against this they balance the need to retain personal freedom, choice and the control of business costs. Governments often refer to the considerable scientific uncertainty involved in risk assessment. Government departments have now either published or are publishing frameworks or procedures for reaching decisions on risks (Cabinet Office, 2004).

How far regulatory mechanisms can be seen as providing a means whereby management can be protected from allegations of incompetence and corruption is debatable. Risk management is in many respects contrary to the essence of capitalist accumulation, which intrinsically encompasses risk-taking. Risk management and risk regulation can be seen as ways of diverting attention from system weaknesses and reducing the status of regulatory activities to little more than 'blaming mechanisms'. The over-emphasis on regulation and risk management can make regulatory systems unwieldy and ultimately self-defeating.

Further reading

Hood, Rothstein and Baldwin give a clear account of variations in risk regulation in The Government of Risk (Oxford University Press, 2001). This book explores the dynamics of risk regulation regimes and the implications for policy development. Deirdre Boden analyses risk and trading across a global landscape in 'Worlds in Action: Information, Instantaneity and Global Futures Trading' in Adam, Beck and Van Loon's edited collection *The Risk Society and Beyond* (Sage, 2000a).

ELEVEN   Risk and the Environment

Outline

Chapter Four examined some aspects of the relationship between risk and the environment with respect to health. In this chapter the relationship between risk and the global environment will be discussed. One of the most important recurring themes in the literature on the perception of risk is that individuals do not always use the available information in forming opinions about risk. Even in instances in which people have had facts about risk made available, it is not always the case that they will change their opinions strongly. This would appear to be the case in relation to environmental threat.

Global destruction and the risk to the environment

Rachel Carson in her path-breaking book *Silent Spring* (1962), drew attention to the impact of chemicals on wildlife. The effects of man-made pollutants included birth defects, cancer, death, population decline, and a number of other illnesses (Carson, 1962). Strydom (2002) has charted the risk discourse with respect to the environment since the end of the Second World War. He argues that the fears which followed the development of atomic weapons in Los Alamos, Hiroshima and Nagasaki, and the atomic tests being carried out by the USA and Soviet Union, provided a background to the risk discourse in the 1950s. The dominant concern was the possible risks to public safety and the environment posed by atomic energy. There was a shift in the debate in the 1960s with a growing awareness and distrust of technology generally and this set the tone for the development of the second phase of the debate:

> The year 1965 marks the turning point when the distrust of nuclear power began to be generalised into a distrust of high technology and to be linked to the natural environment. Since then, the development of the anti-nuclear movement and the formation of new environmental groups as well as the revitalisation of traditional environmental organisations ran parallel and mutually re-enforced each other. (Strydom, 2002: 17)

The third phase of the debate, which occurred in the 1970s, was triggered by the growing criticism of new technology and its consequences. The risks posed by nuclear power came to symbolise the problems of a society based upon industry, technology and consumption. A conceptual relationship was developed between the pollution of air and water and nuclear power, which came to contextualise the anxiety and dread experienced by members of society. The last phase of the risk discourse, from the late 1970s onwards, focuses upon what Strydom refers to as a 'Breakdown of generally shared, taken-for-granted assumptions about nature, social institutions, science, technology expertise and progress' (2002: 25). This phase of protest mobilised a search for participation in decision making processes. Thus the goals of the movements concerned with environmental risks moved beyond expressions of anxiety.

In 1985 a hole in the ozone layer over Antarctica was linked to the use of chlorofluorocarbons, which were used in refrigeration and aerosols. The Chernobyl nuclear accident in 1986 sent nuclear waste over large areas of western Europe. The global risk created by this pollution became clear when, in the UK, Cumbrian sheep farmers found radioactive materials raining down on the Fells. The persistence of the contamination resulting from Chernobyl went beyond scientific prediction, leading some local farmers to believe that the continued pollution had been created by the nearby Sellafield nuclear plant. Despite scientific evidence to suggest that Sellafield contamination and that of Chernobyl were not connected, there was some ambivalence as to what should be believed (Lash and Wynne, 1992).

Many writers studying climate change, air-, water- and indoor pollution have foreseen major risks to the global environment, partly because of the way resources are consumed at an individual level. Between 1970 and 1995 global income per capita rose by one-third. Increased energy consumption and the production of all kinds of waste material have destroyed 30 per cent of the natural world. This has resulted in the depletion of forests and freshwater and marine eco-systems. People put further pressure on eco-systems through the consumption of grain, fish and wood (Cahill, 2002a).

Dramatic news stories reveal the stronger effects on environmental risk perception (Milburn and McGrail, 1992; Wahlberg and Sjoberg, 2000).

Although the effects of global change are occasionally dramatic, they are often gradual, occurring over a longer period. The burning of coal and other fuels causes atmospheric pollution, and it is predicted that the emission of carbon dioxide through the burning of fossil fuels will create temperature increases of between 1 and 3.5 degrees centigrade by 2100. This will lead to a rise in the sea level of between 15 and 95 centimetres over the same period. Especially at risk of flooding are low-lying areas, leading to the destruction of coastal plains, coral reefs and mangroves. The Maldives and the deltas of the Nile and the Ganges will also be especially vulnerable (Huby, 2001). The consequences of global pollution can be starkly presented, but long-term global pollution lacks the apparent immediacy of other risks, such as cancer or violent attacks on civil society, which are perceived as having the potential to disrupt or destroy an individual's life and at any time.

Climate change has directly caused death and illness through exposure to heat waves. Disasters such as floods, mud slides, cyclones and forest fires have also been related to changes in climate. Less directly, climate change has been associated with the spread of airborne diseases such as cholera and influenza (www.bbc.co.uk/climateimpact/humanhealth). The impairment of crop production and the effects on pests' soil and temperature can also create disease and loss of life (Barton, 2000).

The 'risk society' and the environment

Beck, in much of his work, is concerned with the environment. Like Douglas, he is interested in why some risks are widely regarded as important, while others are virtually ignored or downgraded in urgency and status. For Douglas (1992) the impending global environmental disaster is a crisis of social solidarity related to the impact of global capitalist development which makes individuals feel vulnerable. However, Beck departs from Douglas in that he believes there is something new about the risks to the environment, which are distinct from anything which may have occurred before. The weakness of Douglas's position is the failure to recognise the nature of the new risks as being a by-product of technology and an example of manufactured uncertainty (Beck, 1995). Beck believes that environmental pollution follows the poor and has the potential to emerge as a revolutionary force (Beck, 1999; Wilkinson, 2001a). Risks to the environment are described by Beck as being directly related to increasing what he refers to as 'scientisation'. According to Lash and Wynne, writing in their introduction to Beck's *Risk Society*:

> The culture of scientism has in effect imposed identity upon social actors, demanding their identification with particular social institutions and their ideologies, notably in constructions of risk, but also in the definition of sanity, proper sexual behaviour, and countless other rational frames of modern control. (Lash and Wynne, 1992: 3)

Through the use of scientistic arguments and language understandable to the 'lay' observer, researchers have examined the consequences of industrialisation on the environment. Protest groups have adopted images of looming destruction. As risks become less related to individual spillages and accidents, the centre of the protest comes to be dominated by less visible threats, detectable through science. As Beck (1992: 162) argues, these threats 'require the sensory organs of science – theories, experiments, measuring instruments – in order to become visible and interpretable as threats at all'.

Some research into the relationship between individual perception of environmental pollution and risk suggests that people are mainly concerned with the immediate possibility of danger to their daily lives. This has resulted in an increasing awareness of risk in activities which in the past would not have been considered risky. Parents are less willing to allow their children to swim in the sea or to engage in particular activities such as canoeing. Perceived risks, created by atmospheric pollution are reflected, according to Macnaughten (2000), in a reluctance to leave washing outside to dry because of a concern about risks associated with car fumes.

Sustainability and risk

The idea of sustainability has come to dominate debates about risk and the environment. Arguments about the risks posed by environmental pollution are based upon the conflict between constant economic growth and the need to protect the environment. The debate also focuses on inequalities within nation states, and between nation states. In 1987, the UN World Commission on the Environment and Development (WCED) defined sustainable development in terms of meeting the needs of the present without compromising the ability of future generations to meet their needs. The Commission's report describes the importance of equity within each generation (World Commission on the Environment and Development, 1987).

Environmental risks to health are often experienced more acutely by poor people than by those who are affluent (Cahill, 2002b). Risks and global inequality are thus inextricably linked. Science has not yet reached a position in which it can gain a full understanding of the possible impact of technology on the environment in the longer term. Economists, Cahill argues, average out risks in their calculations. Worst-case scenarios, through this method, become absorbed within an overall average. Environmentalists, on the other hand, emphasise the worst-case scenario, stressing the urgency of the situation and the absolute necessity of avoiding more dire consequences. Economists draw upon utilitarian assumptions, which can be indifferent to risk. Dresner (2002: 4), however, describes environmentalists as being more 'left wing'. Dresner's approach to sustainability helps to draw attention to the appalling global inequality which distributes risks unfairly. However, concerns about risk and the environment do not always fit into neat socio-economically-determined categories. Beck (1992) describes the naïvety of some rural populations, who cannot read, write or provide themselves with protective clothing in the face of risk. Managers and entrepreneurs can take environmental risks in the undeveloped world that would be unthinkable in more developed, risk-conscious industrial states. Beck constantly stresses the reflexive nature of environmental risk and hazard. Commenting on the Bhopal disaster, he wrote: 'In contrast to material poverty, however, the pauperisation of the third world through hazards is contagious for the wealthy. The multiplication of risks causes world society to contract into a community of danger' (Beck, 1992: 44).

Regulating the risk to the environment

There have been many attempts to regulate globally the dangers posed to the economy. In 1983 the WCED, together with Harlem Brundtland, the then Norwegian Labour Party leader and Prime Minister, reflected many of the environmentalists' concerns. Despite accepting the idea of the limitation of pollutants, however, they failed to put forward proposals that were radical enough to address the problems. Still, following the publication of their report, it was no longer possible for governments to ignore the importance of regulating against environmental risk.

The risk of global destruction through worldwide war appeared to diminish as a result of the ending of the Cold War in the late 1980s. From then on, politicians and social scientists defined environmental issues as the major threat to survival. In 1992 the UN Conference on the Environment and Development (Earth Summit 1) met in Rio de Janeiro to consider global responses to environmental problems. Its aim was to create a list of global priorities for sustainable development in the twenty-first century. The framework convention on climate change signed at Rio was based on predictions that a 60 per cent reduction in carbon dioxide was necessary to stabilise climate levels, and that this should be achieved by 2040. In the summer of 1997 the United Nations Conference on Environment and Development (Earth Summit 11) gathered in New York to discuss the progress made in Rio. Little had been achieved and it appeared that many western nations were increasing their emissions of greenhouse gases rather than reducing them.

In December 1997, following the Kyoto meeting, the industrialised countries of the world agreed to an overall reduction of 5.2 per cent in their emissions of greenhouse gases during the period 2008–12. The USA was to reduce its emissions by 7 per cent from 1990 levels, Japan by 6 per cent, and the European Union by 8 per cent. Some countries, notably Norway, Iceland and Australia, were allowed to increase their emissions by 1 per cent: 10 per cent and 8 per cent respectively. The targets which were agreed seem modest, given the need to reduce emissions by between 60 and 80 per cent in order to avoid global warming (Dresner, 2002).

At the end of March 2001 President George W. Bush unilaterally withdrew from the protocol, despite global protest. The President ordered a task force to be chaired by Vice President Dick Cheney. The report from this body recommended the development of more nuclear, oil and coal-fired energy, which implied a 30 per cent increase in American greenhouse gases. The election of President George W. Bush marked a major break with the position which had been taken by President Clinton which had been to get the easiest and most painless deal for the United States, whilst also taking cognisance of the need to reduce greenhouse gases (Dresner, 2002).

Dresner has argued that the prevailing attitude amongst governments with regard to specific environmental risks has been that no danger deserves serious consideration until it actually happens. The public have been told that there is no possibility of the GM pollen travelling more than 50 metres. In reality it emerged that pollen can travel far greater distances. No testing of the safety of GM crops was carried out since governments accepted the word of the chemical companies.

> Being bold rather than cautious really means taking risks on the bet that disasters will not occur. But if you take such risks many times you can be sure that disasters will befall you (Dresner 2002: 158).

The absence of clear scientific proof, environmentalists argue cannot be used as an excuse for inactivity on environmental issues. The WHO argued in its European Charter on Environment and Health, that new policies and technologies should be introduced with prudence and not before appropriate prior assessments of potential health risks have been made (Crombie, 1995). There are good reasons to take a cautious approach to genetically modified organisms (GMOs). Firstly, risk assessments have the capacity to mislead and confuse as well as to clarify in this area. How does one compare the risk of aflatoxin B in peanut butter, with the risk of Dainozide (alar) in apple juice?

Secondly, there is a potential for irreversible danger. The extent of potential exposure to GMOs is now widespread. In 1999 GM corn accounted for 40 per cent of the corn produced in the USA. Beachy (1999) has also shown that public concern over biotechnology is a relevant factor, but one that is not clearly understood. There are compelling arguments against an over-precautionary approach. Any harm associated with GMOs is likely to be subtle rather than severe.

Concerns have also been raised about the possibility of genetically engineered materials emitting toxins into the food supply, but these concerns are, at the time of writing, largely speculative. Other potential risks include the possibility that insecticide-repellent pests could result from exposure to GM crops. Studies linking the production of GMOs with herbicide-repellent weeds have yet to be produced. The possible detrimental impact of the use of GMOs is thus contested scientifically. Such tenuous links have to be balanced against the possible benefits of biotechnology, which could be of immense assistance to developing countries. In the case of the release of GMOs, some governments have tried to take a precautionary approach, while others have been happy to proceed with the release of GMOs despite concerns about safety. The total area cultivated with GMO crops according to Freso (2001) stands at 44.2 million hectares. Some 75 per cent of this is in the industrialised countries. Only seven developing countries cultivate GMO crops commercially. No developing country with the exception of Argentina and China have areas of GMO crop development exceeding 100,000 hectares (Fresco, 2001). There is also the possibility that an over-cautious approach to the use of GMOs could result in what Marchant has described as 'risk–risk trade offs'. Thus, crops genetically manufactured to resist pests may result in a decreased use of powerful pesticides, which could benefit the environment in the longer term (Marchant, 2001).

Water pollution

Inadequately treated, contaminated water poses a major risk to global health. The sources of such risks are numerous. The accelerated growth of algae caused by discharges of phosphorous and nitrogen has been a major source of risk. Nitrates from fertilisers and human waste are polluting ground water in many regions. High nitrate levels in drinking water decrease oxygen-carrying haemoglobin levels in the blood, which in turn can have a deleterious impact on young children. Heavy metals in groundwater occur naturally in the soil. Global production of these metals and their use by industry, agriculture and mining have released large amounts of lead and mercury into the water supply (Barton, 2000; Cahill and Fitzpatrick, 2002).

Man-made pollutants have been distributed globally by air and ocean currents, and are now found in human, animal and plant tissue. Acid rain is created by sulphuric acid and nitric compounds released from industry, motor vehicles and power plants. Acid rain currently affects some parts of Europe, North America, Latin America, India and Asia (Suzuki, 2002).

The environment and transport

The car is a major source of risk, both to the environment and to the health of the individual. The car also signifies personal freedom, wealth, style and social status. People depend on their cars to get them to work and for leisure activities. Those who are unable to use a car are excluded from many aspects of living. On the assumption that people can reach them by car, large retail centres are now located on the peripheries of large urban conurbations, a factor that has created a significant social division in access to facilities. And yet, pollutants produced by vehicle exhausts include cancer-producing benzene, 1,3 Butadiene and carbon monoxide. Car exhaust also produces sulphur dioxide, which is responsible for acid rain, and nitrogen oxides, which can cause respiratory problems. Lead emissions have been linked to blood conditions and diseases of the nervous system and kidneys (Cahill, 2002a). But people are not the only casualties of cars. For example, cars kill 47,000 badgers and 4,000 barn owls each year. Roads are more vulnerable to flooding (Elkin et al., 1991).

The impact of the car on the environment was discussed globally at the Kyoto and Rio summits on the environment. Despite this, motor transport continues to increase unceasingly. The 1998 White Paper on Transport estimated that traffic in Britain would increase by one-third within the next 20 years (Jain and Guiver, 2002). Fast, expensive cars, while making a statement about social status of the driver, also pose significantly increased risks on the road. For example, it is predicted that road accidents will cause more deaths worldwide than tuberculosis, war or HIV infection. Some 70 per cent of road accidents now occur in developing countries (Cahill, 2002a).

Not only does mass car usage damage the environment through emissions of harmful exhaust gases, but it also fuels the continued global demand for oil. The market for oil is further accelerated by the location of shops and business premises in cheaper rural or semi-rural areas. Such developments are built upon a logic of increased mobility and car use, which increases the potential for further environmental damage.

Risks to the environment created by the shipping of oil have been vividly illustrated by a catalogue of maritime disasters. In 1978 the *Amoco Cadiz* released 220,000 tonnes of crude oil on to the coast of Brittany, killing 30,000 birds and covering 130 beaches. Similar incidents occurred in the Caribbean in 1979 with the collision of two tankers near Tobago. In March 1967 the Liberian-based *Torrey Canyon* ran aground on the Cornish coast, spilling 120,000 tonnes of crude oil and contaminating 140 miles of coastline. In 1989, when the *Exxon Valdez* ran aground in Prince William Sound, 1,300 miles of coastline were contaminated. During the 1990s there were five other similar incidents, in which miles of coastline were polluted (*Guardian*, 2000). These spillages have had various outcomes and illustrate the complexity of assessing environmental risks of shipping oil around the globe. For example, some crude oil is volatile and can evaporate, while other oils are heavier and are more difficult to clear. As a result, in some cases the environment can recover from damage more easily. In the *Braer* disaster off Sunburgh Head in Scotland, which occurred in 1993, most of the 130,000 tonnes of oil that spilled from the tanker evaporated into the atmosphere. However, the *Exxon Valdez* spillage, although smaller (38,000 tonnes), occurred in freezing conditions and had more devastating results. The results of the spillage from *The Prestige*, which sank off the northwest coast of Spain in 2002, will also have a long-lasting impact because thick oil smothered shellfish populations and coastal bird life (*Guardian*, 2002a; *Observer*, 2002).

Conclusion

The three great risks facing the environment in the twenty-first century are climate change, soil degradation and the loss of species. Governments have tended to deal with these risks separately, although they are inextricably linked. Extreme weather events, such as cyclones, floods and global warming, have not created sufficiently severe threats to result in an increased momentum for the global regulation of emissions. Government action is often reactive to the perceived view of public opinion and experts often base public opinion on worst-case scenarios. Policy needs to balance expediency with the regulation of risk. One of the themes which has run through this book has been the global rise of risk consciousness and the desire for security among what Beck has referred to as 'risk communities' (Beck, 2000a). Beck acknowledged that risks in the post-traditional society have tended to become global. Such a universalisation of risk has been an almost inevitable accompaniment to industrial production. The acidic content of the air and polluted food chains move beyond national borders (Beck, 1992). The developing world in the future could pose a great risk to the environment by increasing emissions still further. Yet energy is also needed for economic growth to take place.

Further reading

Cahill's *The Environment and Social Policy* (Routledge, 2002a) provides a clearly written account of green ideas and the risks global pollution poses to the environment, health, food and work. The book also contains readable accounts of policy issues in the area. Cahill and Fitzpatrick's *Environmental Issues and Social Welfare* (Blackwell, 2002) also contains some important chapters on risks posed by consumerism. Simon Dresner's *Principles of Sustainability* (Earthscan, 2002) historically links attempts to regulate the environmental risks with ethics and economics, and Barton's edited collection *Sustainable Communities* (Earthscan, 2000) has useful chapters on community governance, energy utility and planning to combat environmental risks. Enrique Larana examines the utility of the risk society with respect to environmental sociology in 'Reflexivity, Risk and Collective Action over Waste Management: A Constructive Proposal' in *Current Sociology* (2001) 49(1): 23–48. Piet Strydom's *Risk, Environment and Society* (Open University Press, 2002) provides a useful chronological account of the development of risk discourse in relation to the environment. The book also examines the major theoretical directions which debates about risk and the environment have taken. Ulrich Beck poses some important and possibly unanswerable questions about what constitutes the environment in *World Risk Society* (Polity Press, 1999).

TWELVE Risk and Global Governance

Outline

Some of the chief justifications for more globalised forms of governance and regulation have been the avoidance of risk to vulnerable groups and the creation of a more humanitarian world through the extension of democratic processes. The ever-present war against terrorism has emphasised the need to consider the possibilities offered by global co-operation in order to avoid the risk of a catastrophe. It will be argued that new global risks, which mark a significant shift in international relations, have emerged since the end of the Cold War. The perception of risk could reduce the possibility of agreement as to how global risks can be tackled. The idea of global governance incorporates the creation of a more ordered response to social and political issues which go beyond the capacities of individual states to address. Yet definitions of global governance are contested in a world in which the basis upon which international relations have been grounded is fundamentally changing. This chapter critically examines the possibility of reducing global risks through increased global democracy. The role of non-governmental organisations and the relationship between risk and globalisation will also be considered.

Humane global governance and the reduction of risk

Although the notion of global governance is contested, an optimistic current of thought suggests that the creation of more globalised forms of government will break down rivalries between nation states, ultimately creating a more co-operative and equitable world order. This is the view of the Commission on Global Governance, whose definition of global governance incorporates 'the sum of the many ways individuals and institutions, public and private, manage their common affairs. It is a continuing process, through which conflicting or diverse interests may be accommodated and co-operative government action taken' (Commission on Global Governance, 1995: 2). This almost utopian vision of global governance links the possibility of reducing some of the risks created by technology and globalisation with the adoption of democratic, globalised government.

The evangelical zeal associated with global governance also has potential implications for the regulation of trading practices, especially in the arms trade, and global ethics. Global governance, it is argued, can act as an ultimate protection from inhumane risks such as catastrophic famine through increased democratisation. Such democratisation is also necessary if environmental risks are to be effectively tackled. The pursuit of environmental sustainability requires the creation of a global moral and political community. Such a community, some would argue, can be realised in a global world because of the growth of communication technology (Dresner, 2002). 'Earth Government', an organisation which advocates the case for global government on the world wide web, emphasises global risks. These include 'world peace, security, pollution of air water and land, the removal of the war industry, the eradication of world poverty, and the enforcement of global justice' (Earth Government, 2003: 2).

At the time of writing, the risks to many millions of people from war and famine is incalculable. In Ethiopia, for example, an estimated 15 million people face starvation without food aid. This crisis is far more serious than the famine of 1984, which affected approximately seven million people. The situation has been caused by severe drought which has destroyed crops. Ethiopia is a country which has adequate water supply but no infrastructure to deliver water to the parts of the country where it is needed. Their dependence on rain for water makes the risk of future catastrophes inevitable. In order for the risk to be diminished, the developed world must assist in building and maintaining the necessary infrastructure as well as providing emergency food aid. This will require organised global governance directed at specific forms of global risks, such as famine (British Broadcasting Corporation, 2002b).

In relation to the environment, Saward (2003) has pointed out that problems such as climate change and ozone depletion cannot be tackled by national governments in isolation. The expansion of global democratic processes will ultimately lead, so its exponents argue, to a new form of democracy that receives its impetus not from a top-down force, but from below. Global governance therefore creates an atmosphere in which international relations become more sophisticated, and like-minded states can group together for the good of all and not just the few. This form of diplomacy is expressed through the United Nations System (Cooper et al., 2002). According to Falk (1995), the 'law of humanity' is inextricably associated and framed within international law on human rights. With respect to the risks posed to the environment, it advocates global governance as the only hope for the future.

Some criticisms of world governance

Although such humanitarian motives are laudable, this approach often focuses on the future, avoiding the seemingly intractable, complex risks to public safety posed by the present. Nationalism and religious and cultural differences lie at the heart of many risky conflicts. The question of how nations can create universal peace is an insoluble problem (Kemp, 1993).

Not all aspects of global agreement are conducive to the development of humanitarian aims designed to protect the vulnerable against risk. These include the possible extension of the General Agreement on Tariffs and Trade (GATT), the coercive implementation of a nuclear non-proliferation regime, and the containment of South–North migration flows. In 1994, GATT led to western countries agreeing to lower some of their barriers to imports, such as generic drugs, in locations within the southern hemisphere. This development is considered by some econo-mists to have broadly benefited Asia and Latin America, although the measure did not assist Africa – where there is the greatest risk of mass starvation. Africa had previously gained access to northern markets as a result of earlier trading agreements (Dresner, 2002).

The concentration of the authority of the UN in its Security Council, the International Monetary Fund and the World Bank, together with reliance on the G8 summits, effectively ignores the views of 80 per cent of the world's population (Falk, 1995). Held raises a number of important chal-lenges to some of the views expounded by the advocates of world govern-ment. Territorial boundaries define who is included and excluded from political processes and participation in decisions. Any breakdown in such boundaries immediately puts the idea of consent through elections in doubt, and makes it difficult to define what constitutes a political con-stituency (Held, 1995). Saward (2003) has argued that radical visions of world governance based on democratic principles and decentralisation carry some problems with regard to risk. If it is assumed that the wishes of citizens are reflected in referenda and elections, what happens if citizens do not want green outcomes, including lower consumption of energy?

Global disorder

When considering links between risk and globalisation, it is important to recognise some of the difficulties in identifying what actually constitutes the 'global'. The term 'globalisation', like 'risk', is contested within social science, and has been used in a number of contexts. The term is most usually used to describe 'The growing integration of societies across the world. Quite simply, globalisation means that every aspect of our lives in contemporary society is now influenced by a range of processes and structures operating at a global level' (Ferguson and Johnstone, 2001: 146).

For Giddens (1998), globalisation is an ever-present reality, which is self-evidently more developed in the present than it was in the 1960s and 1970s. Levels of global trade have reached proportions that were hitherto unimaginable, with exchanges of trillions of dollars being achieved at the click of a mouse. The impact of globalisation runs far deeper than this. Giddens claims that globalisation is a progressive force with a potential to create a tolerant cosmopolitanism, which will ultimately deepen democratic processes and strengthen the rule of law. Within this global optimism, risks should be embraced positively and not fearfully (Giddens, 1998). Globalisation, like risk, affects the minutiae of everyday lives and characterises the way we live now, producing, as Beck would also argue, new risks and hazards (Giddens, 1999: 19). Globalisation is often considered as pulling power away from local communities, although for Giddens the effects of globalisation 'push downwards', to create demands for local autonomy. Following this line of argument, it can be argued that risk can be dealt with by local communities rather than through state or global organisations: 'The nation is too small to solve big problems and too large to solve the small ones' (Giddens, 1999: 13).

The optimistic position taken by Giddens in relation to both globalisation and risk has gained much credence both in academic and political circles. Although globalisation can bring many benefits which are convenient to consumers, it can also create other difficulties. It is possible for an individual with a plastic card to access cash from a machine in Singapore or Swansea. Global communication has been used by terrorists groups (see Chapter Nine) and also diversifies possible employment markets, which can in turn create feelings of risk and insecurity (see Chapter Three).

Giddens's position on globalisation has been criticised from a number of positions, in ways which are not dissimilar from some of the criticisms mounted against the work of Ulrich Beck. Giddens, according to Anthias (1999), constructs a notion of the self which diverts attention from differentials in the allocation of power, and numerous forms of social subordination. The 'globalised self' also becomes identified with western ways of being. Globalisation becomes an uneven process, which produces winners and losers, and familiar and enduring patterns of inequality.

Globalisation and the risk of poverty

It would be unfair to suggest that Giddens ignores global risks of poverty. He sees the need to direct poverty programmes towards democratic participation, although exactly how this will occur is still left to the imagination of the reader (Giddens, 1998). Those who are sceptical of globalisation, according to Giddens, tend to be caught in outmoded 'old left politics', since the existence of the 'nation state' was more likely to ensure the continuation of a collectivist form of welfare state, funded mainly through taxation.

Douglas also acknowledges the importance of globalisation in the creation of risk. Risk has acquired a prominence since all cultures need a common forensic vocabulary with which to hold persons accountable (Douglas, 1992). Globalisation has been described by one British politician in 1998 as a 'fundamental and irreversible shift of history', although she doubted whether the process had fundamentally affected the power of nation states (Short, 1998).

Giddens argues that the issues, which are now global, can be explained through reference to the notion of risk. Risk unlocks some of the basic characteristics of the social world, as it is closely connected to the concept of innovation within the global economy, and as Zey (1998) has argued, risk is the driving force behind financial and entrepreneurial success.

Beck, on the other hand, appears to take a more sombre view of the relationship between risk and globalisation. He claims that globalisation has brought about a difference in the 'style' of contemporary risk, which is based upon a universalisation of hazards. Other phenomena link technology, globalisation and risk. The content of acid rain, for instance, has global consequences. Risk displays what Beck refers to as a boomerang effect, in that the rich and powerful, although having created risks, are also subjected to them (Beck, 1992).

Those who are more pessimistic about the impact of globalisation see the potential for the creation of an unstable world in which new forms of risks proliferate. Robbins (1997) has argued that the result of uneven global developments creates increased polarisation at an economic, cultural and political level.

Regulating global risk

Globalisation has existed for many years – there were empires and a global system of exchange and production in the nineteenth century.

Such networks of interaction were relatively simple compared with the complexity of contemporary global trends. Global relations have become instant and virtually annihilate territorial boundaries as barriers to socio-economic activity and relations. Global relations create 'new political uncertainties' (Held, 1995: 101).

Some would argue that a new form of global disorder, which creates hitherto unknown levels of risk to innocent impoverished people, is emerging. The post-Cold War battle scenarios of the 1990s were fought away from the 'zones of prosperity' in the West. Most of these wars also involved irregular, rather than regular, combatants, and children were (and are) often forced to fight (Hogg, 2002).

Giddens (2000) regards economic globalisation and forms of global regulation of risk as a force for good. He argues that, despite high levels of unemployment in particular states, the absolute levels of global employment in the world have increased. The Chinese economy generated 15 million new jobs between 1980 and 1994. The development of the global economy has the potential to reduce the risk of poverty and under-development. The task for government is to transform more states into thriving, dynamic economies which can then form part of a global economy.

In order to facilitate increased global wealth, and to reduce the destabilising impact of sudden surges of capital into and out of countries, Giddens (2000) calls for the development of appropriate global regulations for the surveillance of financial transactions. A world financial authority could be formed in order to oversee this. Another advantage of a global approach to financial governance, according to Giddens, is that problems of world debt can be approached in a more organised manner. Referring to the accumulation of debts in some underdeveloped countries, Giddens (2000: 127) argues that:

> Where it is accepted that a country which gets into financial difficulty will be bailed out, investors are likely to adjust their assessment of risk accordingly, as might that country's government. Means need to be found to ensure greater risk-bearing by private investors, as well as to involve the private sector early on in the process of crisis resolution.

Globalisation, as we have seen, creates new uncertainties for individuals in their daily lives and challenges previously held feelings of security. One important example of this is the potential scale of risk related to the workings of global financial institutions, which in turn can impact on essential sources, such as personal security plans (particularly pension funds and mortgages), trade, investments and employment. Not only does globalisation and instant global communication expand the scale of potential risks, it forces individuals to place trust in dis-embedded social systems and the expertise of others who can be located on the opposite side of the globe (Crawford, 2002b).

Non-governmental organisations and risk management

One of the responses to these variations in defining risk has been an attempt by some organisations to create unanimity as to what constitutes risk, and how it should be managed. During the 1990s, an orthodoxy emerged which, although not as radical or utopian as that suggested by Earth Government (2003), supported the reduction and control of global risks that were not confined to national boundaries.

The 1990s witnessed the creation of social movements and non-governmental organisations with the brief to, bring order into the chaos. NGOs created in the 1990s seemed to be most effective when they worked in networks. Third World Network based in Malaysia, the German Non-Governmental Organisation Network on Environment and Development, and the International Campaign to Ban Landmines are all examples of effective non-governmental global networks formed around this time. These were instrumental in attempting to reduce risk to citizens in many aspects of civil life through regulatory frameworks. For example, there were agreements with respect to the environment, the regulation of finances and safety regulations governing public transport.

Glasius and Kaldor (2001) have documented the rapid growth of non-governmental organisations. The 1990s also witnessed an increased number of meetings between key global leaders. The result was the ratification of significant treaties regarding risks created by landmines, global climate change, and the extortionate pricing of medicines. Glasius and Kalder (2001) have detected a greater concern for the development of norms of rights, humanity and social discourse during this period.

Since the Second World War the United Nations has attempted to widen its brief. During the 1990s the UN and other non-governmental organisations played a key role in disentangling complex risks to peace. These organisations have delivered humanitarian relief and offered assistance, both political and social, in Bosnia, Somalia, Kosovo and East Timor. Such activities have proved challenging, given the different organisational cultures and political systems (Maley et al., 2002). With respect to the environment, the UN has been responsible for creating a more globalised approach to the risk of pollution. The UN has also been responsible for drawing up a number of fundamentally important global treaties relating to ocean pollution, water pollution, endangered species, air pollution, toxic dumping, transboundary pollution and ozone depletion (Dresner, 2002). The 1992 Rio Summit on the environment was also set up under the auspices of the UN.

173

Hogg is pessimistic about the impact of such global efforts on the risk to innocent people. In Afghanistan there are an estimated 10 million landmines, scattered throughout 80 per cent of the country, which have resulted from 20 years of conflict involving the West. Unexploded cluster bombs effectively become unexploded landmines. The use of cluster bombs in Kosovo, Afghanistan and Iraq put civilians at particular risk, since they are designed to maximise civilian casualties. Children are particularly vulnerable to this risk, mistaking these objects for humanitarian relief (Hogg, 2002).

Conclusion

The relationship between globalisation and risk is an important one, since risk is presented by social theorists as a global concept (Castels, 1991; Beck, 1992). Discourses of global risk incorporate social practices which are beyond the development of global markets. During the last decade global technologies, or what Castel (1991) has referred to as the industry of 'systematic pre-detection', have developed to identify and monitor risks to aggregate populations. World government, although appearing to promise a potential for greater harmony and concomitant diminution of global risk, has a number of inherent weaknesses and difficulties. Current arrangements for global regulations are inconsistent. 'Third Way' politicians internationally see their role not as simply protecting individuals from the greater risks created by globalisation, but as creating the 'social capital' which enables individuals to adapt to a new global age (Driver and Martel, 2002).

Globalisation has been central to the creation of new forms of risk, which in turn create different kinds of mass insecurity. Although the end of the Cold War may have diminished the risk of war between states within Europe, it is possible for those European states to be completely divided on the question of supporting or assisting the American-driven invasion of a more distant state like Iraq.

Further reading

Brysk's *Globalization and Human Rights* (University of California Press, 2002) contains chapters on citizenship, commodification, communication and co-operation and questions the risk to human rights posed by globalisation. Anthony Giddens provides a clear discussion of risks in the globalised world in *The Third Way and its Critics* (Polity Press, 2000). Van Ginkel et al.'s edited collection, in *Human Development and the Environment: Challenges for the United Nations in the New Millennium* (United Nations University Press, 2002), examines the problems, processes and actors constituting human development. It also analyses some of the major risks which affect human development in a globalised world. These include population, urbanisation, poverty, education, health, climate change, and international co-operation in biodiversity. John Clark has produced an excellent account of how globalisation affects poor people in *Worlds Apart* (Earthscan, 2003).

THIRTEEN   Risk and the New World Order

Outline

This chapter develops some of the themes which emerged in Chapter Nine. The changing role of the United Nations in relation to the risk of international conflict will be discussed. The events and arguments justifying the pre-emptive strike on Iraq will also be examined. It will be argued that the concept of risk underpinned the case for war, while the action taken to address the risk was in itself a high-risk strategy within international relations.

The role of the UN in reducing the risk of conflict

The system that structured and guided international relations until the end of the Second World War was established in 1648 by the Treaty of Westphalia. Within this system, independent sovereign states settled their differences privately. At particular conjunctures there was an international acceptance that states would engage in coercive conflict and seek to place their own interest above the interests of others. Thus, from this position, the world consisted of 'separate political powers pursuing their own interests, backed ultimately by their organisation of coercive power' (Held, 1995: 104).

Since the end of the Second World War, as was mentioned in the previous chapter, the organisation that has come closest to the ideal of global governance has been the United Nations. Although initially set up following the failure of the League of Nations, the UN's primary responsibility was to lessen the risk of international conflict. Held (1995) argued that the creation of the UN following the Second World War did not constitute a fundamental break with the logic of Westphalia, since the UN failed to generate a new principle of organisation which could deal with international conflict.

This has become abundantly clear since the Cold War period. In an effort to prevent fighting in Croatia from escalating, the UN Security Council imposed an arms embargo on all the republics of Yugoslavia in September 1991. The war in Croatia ended in 1992, with Security Council backing for a UN peacekeeping force. Beck (2000b) argues that the bombing of Kosovo by NATO western forces, led by the USA, placed a higher priority on the need to oppose the genocide against the Kosovans than on the UN Human Rights Charter, which was based on international law. For Beck, there is a dilemma between international law, on the one hand, and human rights on the other. Human rights, which are asserted in international law, stand against the sovereignty of individual states and have become a 'civil religion of modern cosmopolitanism' (Beck, 2002c). Transnational humanism can become military humanism, which is what provided the justification for the Kosovo war. It also provides western nations with a cosmopolitan mission for military crusades under the banner of human rights (Beck, 2002b).

One development that has accelerated over the last decade is the apparent sidelining of the United Nations. The UN appears to be unable to control global risks of conflict between nations. Of the 190 UN member states, it only takes one of five permanent members of the Security Council (consisting of the USA, Russia, China, France and Britain) to overthrow any decision or proposal. This results in 0.5 per cent of the membership being more powerful than the other 99.5 per cent (Earth Government, 2003: 2).

The question of the continuance of American sovereignty and superpower status had been raised by a number of commentators before the attacks of 11 September 2001.

During the build-up to the Anglo-American campaign against Iraq, the USA effectively bypassed the UN following the failure of the UN Security Council to agree a second resolution (following Resolution 1411). The passing of such a resolution in the Security Council could have led to more international support for the war against Iraq.

Risk, regime change and the New World Order

Moves towards the creation of a more secure world based upon humanitarian ideas and global governance have been significantly eroded since 2000. Although the attacks on the World Trade Center in New York and in Washington, DC are not attributable to any single event or sequence of events, the election of a right-wing American President has undoubtedly had a significant influence on the course of subsequent events. The 1990s has seen the spread of social movements and non-governmental organisations and networks that have extended beyond national boundaries. As Albrow (1996: 74) argued before the attacks of 11 September: 'Globalisation is a threat to the American idea of world order, which has to be an order of nation states. But it is also a threat to the internal cohesion of the United States'. According to Albrow, globalisation offers alternative forms of economic competition and cosmopolitanism which threaten the American identity. Despite the opportunities offered by globalisation, post-11 September there has been a marked international closure as security matters dominate international relations. It may well be that a new form of global disorder has emerged, which is predicated on assessing and acting upon perceived risks to western interests. Despite the short-term appearance of vulnerability immediately following the terrorist attacks, America has subsequently emerged as a single super-state, surrounded and supported by allies who are presented as constituting the right-thinking 'international community'.

The constant campaign

It was argued in Chapter Nine that some of the measures taken after the events of 11 September 2001 appear to have been disproportionate to the risk posed by terrorism. The argument that weapons of mass destruction are currently held by particular states which are connected with globally-organised Islamic extremist groups, most notably Al-Queda, has been a major part of the discourse of risk dominating international relations. This was particularly evident in the justification for a pre-emptive attack on Iraq, principally by the British and Americans. The solution has a chilling simplicity. Remove the risk by removing the administrations which supply the weapons of mass destruction, through unilateral military means if necessary.

For those advocating a hawkish position, the events of 11 September demonstrated the results of being too conscious of diplomatic risks during the Clinton era, when urgent coercive action needed to be taken against suspected terrorists. In 1997, during the second term of Bill Clinton's presidency, influential figures like Dick Cheney (later to become Vice President), Paul Wolfowitz (Under Secretary to President George Bush Senior), Elliot Abrams, Richard Perle, Douglas Feith and Donald Rumsfeld formed a group called 'Project for the New American Century'. Kampfner (2004) regards the ideas of these individuals, all of whom were to hold important positions in the government of George W. Bush, as combining optimistic and pessimistic elements.

Their ideology was that the world was a dangerous place, that civilisation was hanging by a thread. At the same time, the USA was endowed by providence with the power to make the world better if only it would take the risks of leadership – if only it were sufficiently 'forward-leaning'. They spoke of 'full-spectrum dominance' and of a world in which each nation's relationship with the USA would be the most important (Kampfner, 2004: 24).

The George W. Bush administration took the potential risk posed by terrorist groups far more seriously than hitherto was the case. Thus, 11 September and revelations of intelligence breakdowns are now used to enforce the view that previous administrations had failed to take effective action until it was too late, due to the risk of further destabilising the Middle East's economic and political situation. From this perspective, it can be argued that hypothetical risk-consciousness concerning a possible Arab backlash created a more serious, real risk, which ultimately killed thousands of human beings on 11 September 2001.

Risk potential has formed the driving force for a permanent campaign against an ill-defined enemy. Even though a state of global war does not formally exist, actions taken particularly by America and Britain are unprecedented in peacetime. The hidden nature and sense of constant potential risk that has been created following the events of 11 September has justified the creation of societies in which the need for greater vigilance against the ever-present risk posed by outsiders is presented as being self-evident. President George W. Bush, in announcing the creation of the Department of Home Security spoke of 'thousands of trained killers planning to attack' (British Broadcasting Corporation, 2002c).

By 29 January 2002, the need to take immediate action to combat the risk of terrorism had transformed the fortunes of a President whose popularity ratings had reached an all-time low (Scraton, 2000). Heelo (2000) has argued that governments are part of a constant battle for public approval. The permanent campaign to protect citizens from the risks created by terrorists is likely to become a longstanding feature of the political landscape, and will continue to gain widespread support. The all-pervasiveness of the campaign against the unfathomable risk of terrorism has, as previously mentioned, reached unprecedented proportions:

> The repression of terrorism spirals around as unpredictably as the terrorist act itself. No one knows where it will stop, or what turnabouts there may yet be. There is no possible distinction at the level of images and information, between the spectacular and the symbolic, no possible distinction between the 'crime' and the crackdown. (Baudrillard, 2002: 31)

Since 11 September, regime change has become a legitimate, strategic goal of the USA, although, at the time of writing, terrorists have seldom used weapons of mass destruction or detonated a nuclear device. A new, confident and undisguised American dominance, which appears to legitimate pre-emptive strikes against nations deemed by the USA as posing a risk to security, has now emerged. Nye (2002: 164) has put the position succinctly in his analysis of American power: 'Some sovereignists believe that America does not have to play by the rules that everybody else plays by because nobody can make it play by them – and besides it has set its own set of more important ones'.

To some extent America's view of its own position in the world changed after the use of atomic weapons at Hiroshima and Nagasaki during the Second World War. The invasion of the small nation of Grenada in 1983 is an example of the USA imposing regime change. The attacks of 11 September added a new international impetus to regime change and resulted in a global coalition to attack Afghanistan. Although the alliance which emerged was built upon the Cold War model, the form that military action took, however, was unilateralist. America's unilateral response to the 'asymmetrical' threat was based upon the assumption that, through the use of technology, rogue states or states harbouring terrorists could be targeted and bombed with precision, using aircraft and cruse missiles, and without incurring American casualties: 'The strikes on Afghanistan were precise and they were effective in that they created the conditions for the fall of the Taliban and the capture of many Al-Queda operatives, although not the leadership' (Glasius and Kaldor, 2001: 14).

The focus on attacking leaders who posed a risk to the interests of the USA or its allies was soon to follow. In 2002, the vision of 'peace for the Middle East' involved the American President requiring the Palestinians to elect a 'new and different' leadership from that of the late Yasser Arafat so that an independent Palestinian state could be constructed. The 1993 Oslo Accords required Israel to officially recognise the Palestinian state and abandon its territorial occupation of land outside the state of Israel, including the Gaza Strip and the West Bank. Israel also agreed to end the expansion of colonial settlements. The pronouncements by the American President did not call on Israel to immediately reverse the reoccupation of towns and villages acceded to the Palestinian people under the Oslo Accords (*Economist*, 2002). The neo-conservatives viewed the Middle East as being dominated by a group of corrupt dictators whose people would, if given an opportunity, embrace a Jeffersonian view of democracy. Israel provided what they regarded as a role model for the region (Kampfner, 2004).

In an influential analysis of current relations between the USA and Europe, Kagan (2003) has argued that Europe and America no longer share a common view of the world. He likens current conditions in Europe to Immanuel Kant's notion of perpetual peace in a self-contained world. This peace and tranquillity is contrasted with the Hobbesian view of the USA, which reflects a culture of death. In the USA we have a society in which guns are commonplace and the death penalty is used. Postmodern Europe approaches problems with more subtlety, sophistication and tolerance of failure. The USA has developed a more pragmatic approach to conducting its affairs, seeking the elimination of threats through the exertion of military supremacy. Now that conflicts which ravaged Europe have been resolved, and especially since the end of the Cold War, the USA provides Europe with security from outside. For Kagan, the root of Europe's greater tolerance today is its relative military weakness:

> A man only armed with a knife may decide that a bear prowling the forest is a tolerable danger, in as much as the alternative – hunting the bear armed only with a knife – is actually riskier than lying low and hoping the bear never attacks. The same man armed with a rifle, however, will make a rather different calculation of what constitutes tolerable risk. Why should he risk being mauled to death if he doesn't have to? (Kagan, 2003: 31)

Kagan argues that America did not change on 11 September 2001, it simply became 'more itself'. American hegemony has been developing since the nineteenth century, according to Kagan. The expansionist ambitions of the USA can be seen in its westward expansion before it became a nation. America's desire to play a major role in world events is, according to Kagan, 'deeply rooted in the American character'. Americans, before the risks posed by 11 September, were developing their military power (Kagan, 2003).

Pre-emptive action against Iraq

The elimination of Saddam Hussein and his regime in Iraq emanated from an American strategic viewpoint that takes risks with international relations. A complex and volatile approach to international relations has emerged. With respect to the conflict in Iraq, most Europeans, armed, in Kagan's view, with only a knife, took the calculated view that the risks presented by Saddam Hussein were more tolerable than that posed by removing him. The USA, on the other hand, being militarily bolder after 11 September, lowered its levels of risk tolerance. Both positions made sense from their respective standpoints. However, as far as global governance was concerned, the events leading up to the invasion of Iraq resulted in one of the most significant rifts within the UN Security Council since the ending of the Second World War. In Europe, Italy, the Netherlands and Spain supported the war, while intervention against Iraq without a UN mandate was vigorously opposed by other influential nations, including France, Germany and Belgium (Connor, 2003). Even though Iraq reluctantly complied with some of the demands made by UN weapons inspectors, the respective administrations of America and Britain thought the risk to their safety warranted invasion by massive forces. This was despite the threat of a UN veto from France, and fierce opposition from many nation states, including Russia, China, Germany, Syria and Egypt. Weapons inspectors also pleaded, in vain, for more time.

The arguments used consistently by politicians favouring military intervention appears to be built around the search for a 'secure' world in the face of the all-pervasive, unknowable and vaguely described risks. The British Prime Minister, Tony Blair, facing significant rebellions from his own MPs in the House of Commons, stayed resolutely in favour of the war, committing a high proportion of the British armed forces to the battle. His position did not change in the light of large-scale local and global protests. The risk posed by Saddam and weapons of mass destruction to the security of Britain outweighed any risks to his own political career, he constantly argued. The argument in favour of pre-emptive military intervention was built around loosely defined notions of global risk to innocent citizens. Blair, in his final speech to the House of Commons on 18 March 2003, justified his decision to take military action alongside the USA on the basis that a number of risks existed:

- The risk posed by tyrants like Saddam Hussein who had weapons of mass destruction.
- The risk that such dictators could arm terrorist groups to carry out further attacks such as occurred on 11 September 2001.
- The risk of the continued and further abuse of the Iraqi people.
- The risk that a failure to act to disarm Saddam would give credibility to the next tyrant.

Blair argued that it was in the British national interest to invade and remove Saddam since he posed a risk, albeit in the longer term, to British national security. Pre-emptive action was justified because of the threat posed by the possession of weapons of mass destruction by a tyrannical, autocratic dictator. Tony Blair, during a speech in which he accepted a US Congressional gold medal on 17 July 2003, described the risk posed by the new terrorism in apocalyptic terms. In this nightmare scenario, the destructive forces of particular states, terrorist groups and weapons of mass destruction combine to attack the west. The risk is, he said, 'that terrorist groups and states that develop weapons of mass destruction come together' (British Broadcasting Corporation, 2003f).

Arguments made by President George W. Bush were similar to those of Tony Blair. Many of the differences were in emphasis only. President

Bush also justified military action on the basis of a number of unconnected and unsubstantiated risks. He argued that Iraq could arm terrorists with weapons of mass destruction and berated the UN for their ineffectiveness in dealing with Saddam Hussein's non-compliance with UN resolutions over a 12-year period: 'The United Nations Security Council has not lived up to its responsibilities, so we will rise to ours' (Guardian, 2003b).

The invasion of Iraq was presented by President Bush as a pre-emptive act of self-defence. As was the case in the UK, the nature of the link between these risks was never made explicit and was unsupported by the work of the UN weapons inspectors. Even in the postwar Iraq there is a lack of evidence of weapons of mass destruction. Lord Butler's enquiry into the intelligence used to justify the war against Iraq was reported in July 2004 (Butler, 2004). Here it was argued that although it would be rash to say that no evidence of weapons of mass destruction will ever be found, Iraq did not have significant stocks of chemical or biological weapons in a state fit for use or had plans to use them before the war (British Broadcasting Corporation, 2004).

From November 2002 to September 2004, 1,625 US and UN weapons inspectors searched 1,700 sites. Their conclusion was that Saddam had ambitions to restart chemical and nuclear programmes once sanctions had been lifted. However, Saddam had destroyed weapons of mass destruction a decade before the invasion of Iraq, and his capacity for building new capability had dwindled (Guardian, 2004c). At the time of writing, no evidence has emerged to suggest any link between Saddam Hussein and Al-Queda.

The course and aftermath of the war

During the course of the war, there were reports of suicide bombers pouring into Iraq from Syria and Saudi Arabia. According to American military statistics, some 3,650 Iraqi combatants were killed during the war. Market bombings cost 115 civilian lives, while 14 died in an attack on a restaurant in an attempted assassination of Saddam Hussein from the air (Cornwell, 2003). At the time of writing, the postwar situation in Iraq is chaotic and violent. Regular attacks against civilian, military and government targets are carried out by different groups resistant to US policy in Iraq. US and Iraqi forces have attacked key targets following the initial invasion, most notably in Falluja. This has resulted in an unknown number of civilian fatalities. The long-term impact of the action in the region is difficult to predict. The risk of global terrorism serves to justify any military action that America wishes to take.

The end of containment

In a speech made at the graduation ceremony at the US Military Academy at West Point, President George W. Bush stated:

> Containment is not possible when unbalanced dictators, with weapons of mass destruction, can deliver those weapons on missiles, or secretly provide them to terrorist allies. We cannot defend America by hoping for the best. We cannot put our faith in the words of tyrants, who solemnly sign non-proliferation treaties, and then systematically break them. If we wait for threats to fully materialise, we will wait for too long. (cited in Schultz and Vogt, 2003: 386)

President Bush laid the foundations for the new national security doctrine. The central core of the policy was deterrence, since containment was no longer a viable option. In the battle against the new form of globalised terrorism, America has shown its preparedness for pre-emptive action against terrorism. Such determined rhetoric seems to be distant from any discussion of the law and global governance based upon democratic principles.

One possible interpretation of events leading to military action in Iraq is that the USA is moving towards a form of global unilateralism. It is probably the case that the USA was intent on invading Iraq without a second UN mandate for a considerable time before hostilities began (Schultz and Vogt, 2003). Whether or not this is the case, the events of 11 September have been presented to the public on both sides of the Atlantic as posing a new risk which is so immense that it warrants actions beyond the rules normally guiding diplomatic behaviour.

In the second debate on Iraq in the House of Commons on the 18 March 2003, Tony Blair spoke of the changing psychology of the USA, and possibly of the world, following the attacks on the World Trade Center and Washington, DC. There are major risks emanating from this policy stance. As was mentioned in Chapter Nine, there is the risk that this new strategy will lead to a form of 'defensive' pre-emptiveness that will not end with Iraq and Afghanistan, but could extend to other states in the Middle East region. An aggressive, unilateral, global form of governance, dominated by the USA, risks inflaming tensions in sensitive areas such as the Middle East and Africa. The notion that the USA has the right to act pre-emptively in order to protect itself against threat has yet to be convincingly made. It is unclear whether the war in Iraq was legal, since UN Resolution 1441 did not contain a trigger for war. There is the possibility that the action taken over Iraq is in breach of international law.

Other disputes in the region, most notably that which exists between Israel and Palestine, must be resolved in order to lessen the risk of conflict in the Middle East.

How domestically acceptable it would be for the USA to become a global police force is debatable given the experience of loss of American life in Iraq and the memory of the conflict in Vietnam in the 1960s, in which many thousands of American and Vietnamese lives were lost. The risk of uncontrollable costs of warfare might make such an expansionist risk less likely. Some signs indicate that the Bush administration has retreated from the idea of pre-emptive strikes (*Guardian*, 2004a). The re-election of George W. Bush for a second term with 51 per cent of the total vote would indicate that support for pre-emptive attacks splits the USA. However, internationally, as Cornwell (2003) has argued, it may well be that fury has given way to resignation, as the realisation grows that it is futile to attempt to resist American might. The current approach to the foreign policy adopted by the USA will not prevent further isolated attacks, such as occurred in a Bali nightclub in October 2002 (Cornwell, 2003). At the time of writing, civilians, members of the police and military authorities in Iraq risk death or serious injury in an extremely unstable postwar situation.

Conclusion

The new, pre-emptive and aggressive unilateral stance adopted by the USA over Iraq was taken within a set of complex and conflicting international debates, which has at its foundation interlocking ideas about hypothetical risk. It also reinforces an exclusivity which further divides the Christian and the Muslim worlds. In the *Exclusive Society* (1999), Young has argued that insiders are more clearly distinguishable from outsiders, and that good and evil are constantly juxtaposed. The insane and the sane, the violent and the non-violent, dangerous activity and safe activity are all now reduced to simplistic, unproblematic certainties. Such a society is dominated by essentialist transactions that are attractive to the 'ontologically insecure' (Young, 1999). Perceived risks to security create exclusivist responses within international relations.

Recent international events have contained all the elements described by Young. They have emphasised risks posed by outsiders and reduced complex international relations to unproblematic certainties. The failure of nations to create unanimity could lead to a greater risk of global catastrophe though war. Interwoven in the idea of the impossibility of containment is the global and ever-present risk of fanatical mass destruction. The constant risk of terrorism has been accentuated, particularly by the USA, to justify the creation of a concerted military campaign. At the time of writing, Osama Bin Laden has become an international figure of terror. The risks posed by Al-Queda and other groups are used as a justification for greater vigilance, more intelligence gathering and more sophisticated surveillance. Since the 1990s, the role of the United Nations in global risk management has diminished, as gaps between the European and the American view of the world become more evident. The unilateralism demonstrated in the invasion of Iraq appeared to lay the basis for a new national security doctrine, the core of which was zero-tolerance towards the risks posed by terrorists and rogue states.

Further reading

David Held has described the disjunctures between the authority of the nation state and the realities of the emerging global system in his *Democracy and Global Order* (Polity Press, 1995). Robert Kagan, in his influential *Paradise and Power* (Atlantic Books, 2003), analyses a growing and risk-laden rift between postmodern Europe and a pragmatic, exclusivist and expansionist USA. Howard and Sawyer's edited volume, *Terrorism and Counter-Terrorism* (McGraw-Hill/Dushkin, 2003), contains a number of useful contributions on the impact of 11 September on international relations. John Kampfner's *Blair's Wars* (The Free Press, 2004) is a well-researched and detailed account of the relationship between the British Prime Minister and military intervention, examining the five occasions within six years when Tony Blair has gone to war. Coverage of the build-up to the Iraq War and the US neo-conservative doctrine of pre-emption are particularly helpful.

FOURTEEN   The Risk Society: An Assessment

Outline

One of the unintended consequences of modern capitalism is that it has increased uncertainties in the areas of health, employment, technology and communications. It has also been argued that a new security doctrine, led by the USA, has increased the risk of military intervention, and possibly also the risk of terrorist attack. All these developments appear to have been based upon insecurity and a desire to reduce risk. This chapter examines some of the attempts that have been made to synthesise approaches to risk analysis. The chapter also considers some of the central themes that have emerged from the book.

The management of risk

The management of risk has become a central problem of late modern society. All individuals and organisations develop a framework for dealing with perceived risks, based upon routines, procedures and behavioural responses. All these efforts, according to Giddens (1991), concentrate on an attempt to colonise the future by looking back at the past. Risk assessment is based upon an attempt to use knowledge of past risks and project that knowledge into the future in an attempt to create security by controlling events.

Although the idea of the risk society can assist in understanding the ascendancy of risk at many levels within the social structure, the examples in this book demonstrate that different groups within communities do not experience risk in the same way. The idea of a monolithic risk society fails to take into consideration the subtle differences in the way people experience and explain ontological insecurity. Risk can also be politically expeditious at certain times, creating a consensus against enemies, real and imagined. Risk changes in form and content over time, and is sometimes undetectable. Although risk and the desire for security appear to be critical goals, it is very difficult to argue that they have replaced older divisions based upon race, age, class and gender.

It has been suggested in Chapter Nine that a sense of impending risk has formed the basis for justifying a form of 'joined up' governance that combines the efforts of different arms of the state. Postmodern theory has informed this approach to understanding the ways in which the state has used risk to justify its complex social interventions (Chapter Two). It is the linkages made by those who have the power to define risk which enable actions to be taken by governments and which can create risks on a huge scale. Yet these risks are presented as being designed to reduce risks to citizens. The connections made by politicians between weapons of mass destruction, particularly in Middle Eastern states, and terrorist groups formed the basis for military intervention in Afghanistan and Iraq following the events of 11 September 2001. At the time of writing, the extent to which these linkages have been constructed with respect to the possession of weapons of mass destruction is still being debated.

At the local level, social control agencies more usually associated with the creation of consensus, such as social services, probation and education, work more closely with agencies such as the police, which has, in the traditional society, tended to use more coercive forms of social control. Groups within the population (and not individuals) are linked to policies designed to reduce the risk of crime within communities.

The theoretical positions described in Chapter Two constitute discrete views of risk. The examples of risk with respect to 'real-life' situations reflect a continuum of understanding, ranging from individualism to unspecific relativism. It would be misleading in the 'joined up' world of risk to give the impression that they were unconnected.

Synthesising theoretical positions

Attempts have been made to span the rift between absolutism, which characterises individualist actuarialised forms of risk assessment and the relativism of the culturalist explanations, and the work of some of the postmodern thinkers. Such a synthesis is built upon the growing consensus that risk contains two common elements. First, there is the reality of a potential danger or hazard. Secondly, there is the possibility of that danger or hazard actually occurring.

Working from this broad, emergent consensus, Rosa (1998) has identified a number of emergent sub-themes. While scientific positivistic research is required to identify and estimate risk, it is no longer sufficient in itself as a form of analysis. There still remains considerable work to be done in understanding how individuals perceive identifiable risks. The definition and estimation of risk is often removed from the lay individual. In order to democratise procedures for the management of risk assessment, research and management must be defined within interdisciplinary terms. This will require the separation of fact from opinion or, in other words, what we know about risks and what we might feel about them. Rosa attempts to construct a conceptual framework which allows risk judgements to be made with respect to prevailing cultural understandings.

Rosa describes different levels of 'risk judgement', which incorporate problem-solving strategies:

1 At the level of high ostensibility and high outcome stakes, Rosa locates what she refers to as grounded realism. An example of such a risk would be that created by accidents and emergencies. Knowledge about the outcome of such risks is high, and specific examples are numerous. At this level, traditional methods of risk assessment, based upon the natural sciences, are adequate.

2 As the decision stakes become higher and levels of uncertainty as to the nature of risk increases, a second level of risk can be described which draws on a wide range of professional consultancy. The most obvious example of this is the development of the relationship between the physician and the patient. The diagnosis of potentially life-threatening disease is an example of such a risk.

3 A third level of problem-solving strategy is characterised by high decision stakes and high levels of uncertainty. At this level, The basis of knowledge claims about outcomes stakes are low, with few available concrete examples. Problems require scientific understanding but are too uncertain to be explained entirely by positivistic science. The natural sciences are ill-equipped to deal with uncertainty. Rosa claims that, because decision-making takes place in a value-laden world, this order of risk inevitably requires that value judgements are made with respect to the nature of risk. One of the best examples of what she refers to as 'post-normal science' is the problem of global warming. Although global warming and rising sea levels are scientific issues, the levels of the increase, the cost and the different global impacts of such phenomena are contested by natural scientists (Dresner, 2002). Post-normal science, for Rosa, can include culturalist and phenomenological positions when defining both the nature of the risk and its possible impact. Exposure to environmental risks and, specifically, individual experiences of toxic waste exposure, provides an example in which lay perceptions and understandings are invaluable.

Rosa is not envisaging a situation in which laboratories are staffed by those without the necessary knowledge and skills. She argues that the assessment of risk can incorporate a democratisation of risk assessment procedures and bring the experiences of individuals affected by risk into public 'post-normal' scientific debates.

The democratisation of policy related to risk presupposes a form of regulated autonomy in which mature consumers, who are able to access and assess expert advice on risk, are available. This 'regulated autonomy' has an important implication. In a society which defines the citizen as being at risk from an ever-increasing number of external and internal sources, the messages given to consumers from a bewildering number of sources must concomitantly become complex and detailed.

Concluding themes

The conclusion of a book is meant to point the reader to some answers. A concept such as risk, which is rooted in uncertainty, renders any such attempt futile since, as has been evident in all chapters, unanswerable questions about risk are constantly being asked. Although the work of Beck has been criticised, his ideas have been pertinent to the way in which questions have been examined.

Part I examined the competing theoretical discourses from which the analysis of risk can be made in contemporary society. Although each theoretical position presents a framework for understanding risk, there are a number of points at which they intersect and diverge. The work of Douglas, Beck, Giddens and Foucault have been relevant throughout, although no conclusive answers are provided theoretically. Individualising risk may in some cases be necessary, yet risks, some would argue, are impossible to describe or quantify. Is it the case that other attempts to conceptualise risk (which do not rely on quantification) are too broad to have meaning? Does the idea of the 'risk society' reduce our understanding of the world to an over-reductionist historical logic? Has technology created or reduced risk? Has globalisation changed the nature of risk? How does a consciousness of risk affect daily life? How far has the development of a new form of global unilateralism been made possible by the risk society?

What is particularly unclear is how far the risk itself is related to public perception. Have risks been intensified, or have perceptions of risk changed with modernity? Some partial answers to some of these questions have been suggested. Housing risks can be linked to global markets and financial institutions (Chapter Three). A managed self-governance of risk has been evident in a number of examined aspects of daily life. These relate to food and health (Chapter Four) and crime (Chapter Eight). In Chapter Five it was argued that in the 'risk society' professional status has been eroded. Professional domination is under more scrutiny than ever before in managerially dominated organisations in which professionals once enjoyed almost unquestioned power. Despite this erosion of professional status, the media are heavily reliant on professional and expert validation when attempting to create controversy around risk (Chapter Six). Chapter Nine showed how internal and external conceptualisations of risk have been merged in order to conceptualise the battle against an ill-defined risk as a superordinate, national and international goal. Governmental reactions to the risks damaging the environment have reflected a chaos which permeates attempts at global regulation (Chapter Eleven). Some reactions to terrorist attacks have shown a lack of regard for human rights and international law, justified by risk. An international climate, in which insecurity and fear dominates, provides fertile ground for risky military interventions (Chapter Thirteen).

A number of themes have recurred in this book:

- There is no consensus as to what constitutes risk. This is particularly evident with regard to expert opinions which are often in conflict.
- The need for 'joined-up governance' has been justified on the basis of risk, yet this joining up can create risk. Risks can be used by governments to justify particular policies which infringe human rights.
- A new form of 'model citizenship' has emerged, based upon the abilities of individual citizens to engage with risks 'constructively'. The role of the state is to facilitate this self-governance rather than manage the risk directly (Draper and Green, 2002).
- One of the most serious criticisms of psychometric risk perception research is that it records snapshots of risk judgements outside specific social contexts. Wilkinson (2001a) has argued that perceptions of risk are by no means constant but change in relation to new knowledge and perception. Knowledge is embedded in social practices which can profoundly influence understandings of risk.
- Risks are often invisible, based upon supposed causal relationships and interpretation. They exist only in terms of the knowledge that individuals have about them. Risks can therefore be exaggerated, dramatised or minimised, and are open to social construction and political manipulation.
- Scientific definitions of risk appear to dominate in the creation of government policy and in media presentations of risk.
- The consequent proliferation of risk management in almost all aspects of social interaction has yet to be justified. Awkward questions as to the usefulness and efficacy of risk management are not asked, since the need for such institutional activity is presumed to be a moral imperative. The impact of risk assessment and management in many areas, such as social welfare and criminal justice, has yet to be fully researched.

- Technology has created a stressful and speedy realisation of risks which hitherto would have been unknown and undetectable. This is evident with respect to medical technology and its ability to predetermine certain risky conditions. Technology creates many solutions to problems while simultaneously creating risks.
- Risks are a cultural and symbolic product of the community in which people live.
- Risk knows no national boundaries. As Giddens and others have noted, human experience is 'disembodied' in that human experience is susceptible to the actions of others who can be located at a distance and are often unknown (Giddens, 1991).
- The blurring of 'internal' and 'external' risk has led to the convergence of civil and military authority across nations. The risk of terrorism and the risks posed by particular states have justified the suspension of human rights and aggressive militaristic policies, which ultimately could put world peace at risk.
- One of the most significant factors in the creation of risk is economic growth. The constant imperative to create global economic growth creates demands on infrastructure, which can also create risks. For example, the extraction of raw materials for the development of manufacturing has created an environmental risk. The constant struggle for economic growth has also placed particular pressure on specific systems. Transport systems, for instance, cannot safely respond to extra volume without sufficient investment in integrated infrastructure.
- Risk constitutes only one aspect of the social world. Risk societies have differentiated origins and manifestations. It is dangerous to regard the current condition as the inevitable result of an all-encompassing historical logic. Risk has been uppermost in the minds of citizens and policy-makers throughout history (O'Malley, 2000).

Having acknowledged the dangers in exaggerating the increasing dominance of risk as a template for social action, it cannot be seen simply as the extension or technicisation of previous practices. The avoidance of risk is not a defensive strategy; it has become a duty placed upon individuals, organisations and governments. Such a position has justified the breaking of international law, the ever-increasing use of surveillance and the inexorable rise and dominance of risk technology. This has often served to accentuate rather than diminish social division.

Further reading

There are relatively few over-arching, accessible accounts of competing discourses within the area of risk. Rosa's 'Meta theoretical Foundations for Post-Normal Risk' in *Journal of Risk Research* (1998) 1: 15–44 incorporates the notion of problem-solving within her analysis of risk. Rosa offers the hope of the democratisation of policy with respect to risk. Beck's chapter, 'Risk Society Revisited: *Theory, Politics and Research Programmes'*, in Adam, Beck and Van Loon's edited volume *The Risk Society and Beyond* (Sage, 2000a), provides a reassessment of his theories in the light of more recent economic and political developments following the publication of his seminal work in 1992. Wilkinson provides an excellent critical account of risk in his *Anxiety in a Risk Society* (Routledge, 2001b).

Bibliography

Abbott, D. and Quiglers, D. (2001) 'Managing the Risk of Unemployment', in R. Edwards and J. Glover (eds), *Risk and Citizenship*. London: Routledge.

Acheson, D. (1998) *Independent Inquiry into Inequalities in Health*. London: Stationery Office.

Adam, B. and Van Loon, J. (2000a) 'Re positioning Risk: The Challenge for Social Theory', in B. Adam, U. Beck and J. Van Loon (eds), *The Risk Society and Beyond: Critical Issues for Social Theory*. London: Sage.

Adam, B., Beck, U. and Van Loon, J. (eds) (2000b) *The Risk Society and Beyond: Critical Issues for Social Theory*. London: Sage.

Adams, J. (1995) *Risk*. London: UCL Press.

Akers, L. and Dwyer, P. (2002) *Senior Citizenship? Retirement, Migration and Welfare in the European Union*. Bristol: Policy Press.

Alaszewski, A., Harrison, L. and Manthorpe, J. (eds) (1998) *Risk, Health and Welfare*. Buckingham: Open University Press.

Albrow, M. (1996) *The Global Age*. Cambridge: Polity Press.

Aldridge, M. (1994) *Making Social Work News*. London: Routledge.

Aldridge, M. (1999) 'Poor Relations, State Social Work and the Press in the UK', in B. Franklin (ed.), *Social Policy the Media and Misrepresentation*. London: Routledge.

Allen, C.D., Barker, T., Newton, J.T. and Thorogood, N. (1992) 'Public Perceptions of the Funding of NHS Dental Services', *British Dental Journal* 173: 175–6. Also in J. Green and N. Thorogood (eds), *Analysing Health Policy*. London: Longman.

Amann, R. (2000) 'Foreword', in H. Davies, S. Nutley and P. Smith (eds), *What Works: Evidence-based Policy Practice in Public Services*. Bristol: Policy Press.

Anderson, R.M., Donnelly, N.M., Ferguson, N.M., Woolhouse, M.E.J., Watt, C.J., Udt, H.J. and Mahoney, S. (1996) 'Transmission Dynamics and Epidemiology in British Cattle', *Nature* 382: 779–88.

Andrews, D. (1995) 'The Psychology of Criminal Conduct and Effective Treatment', in J. McGuire (ed.), *What Works: Reducing Offending*. Chichester: Wiley.

Anthias, F. (1999) 'Theorising Identity: Difference and Social Divisions', in M. O'Brian, S. Penna and C. Hay (eds), *Theorising Modernity: Reflexivity, Environment and Identity in Social Theory*. London: Longman.

Baldock, J. (1997) 'Social Care in Old Age – More than a Funding Problem', *Social Policy and Administration* 31(1): 73–89.

Barclay, C. and Sleator, A. (1997) *Update on BSE and CJD* (Research Paper 97/27). London: House of Commons Library.

Barton, H. (ed.) (2000) *Sustainable Communities*. London: Earthscan.

Baudrillard, J. (2002) *The Spirit of Terrorism*. London: Verso.

Bauman, Z. (1992) *Limitations of Postmodernity*. London: Routledge.

Beachy, R.N. (1999) 'Facing Fear of Bio-Technology', *Science* 285: 335. Also cited in G. Marchant (2001) 'The Precautionary Principle: An "Unprincipled" Approach to Biotechnology Regulation', *Journal of Risk Research* 4(2): 143–57.

Beaumont, B. (1999) 'Assessing Risk in Work with Offenders', in P. Parsloe (ed.), *Risk Assessment in Social Care and Social Work*. London: Jessica Kingsley.

Beck, U. (1992) *Risk Society: Towards a New Modernity*. London: Sage.

Beck, U. (1994) 'The Re-invention of Politics: Towards a Theory of Reflexive Modernisation', in U. Beck, A. Giddens and S. Lash (eds), *Reflexive Modernisation: Politics Tradition and Aesthetics in the Modern Social Order*. Cambridge: Polity Press.

Beck, U. (1995) *Ecological Politics in an Age of Risk*. Cambridge: Polity Press.

Beck, U. (1996) 'World Risk Society as Cosmopolitan Society'. *Theory, Culture and Society* 14(54): 1–33.

Beck, U. (1997) *The Reinvention of Politics: Rethinking Modernity in the Global Social Order*. Cambridge: Polity Press.

Beck, U. (1998) *Democracy without Enemies*. Cambridge: Polity Press.

Beck, U. (1999) *World Risk Society*. Cambridge: Polity Press.

Beck, U. (2002a) 'Risk Society Revisited: Theory, Politics and Research Programmes', in B. Adam, U. Beck and J. Van Loon (eds), *The Risk Society and Beyond: Critical Issues for Social Theory*. London: Sage.

Beck, U. (2000b) 'The Cosmopolitan Position: Sociology of the Second Age of Modernity', *British Journal of Sociology* 51(1): 79–107.

Beck, U. (2001) 'Cosmopolis and Risk: A Conversation with Ulrich Beck', *Theory, Culture and Society* 18(4): 47–63.

Beck, U. (2002b) 'The Terrorist Threat: World Society Revisited', *Theory, Culture and Society* 19(4): 39–55.

Beck, U. (2002c) 'The Cosmopolitan Society and its Enemies', *Theory, Culture and Society* 19(1–2): 17–44.

Beck, U. (2004) *A Critical Introduction to the Risk Society*. London: Pluto Press.

Beck, U., Giddens, A. and Lash, S. (1994) *Reflexive Modernisation: Politics Tradition, and Aesthetics in the Modern Social Order*. Cambridge: Polity Press.

Becker, G. and Nachtigall, R. (1994) 'Born to be a Mother: The Cultural Construction of Risk in Infertility in the US', *Social Science and Medicine* 39(4): 507–18.

Bell, D. (1960) *The End of Ideology*. Glencoe, IL: The Free Press.

Bernstein, P.L. (1996) *Against the Gods: The Remarkable Story of Risk*. Chichester: John Wiley.

Beveridge, W. (1942) *Social Insurance and Allied Services* (Cmd 6404). London: HMSO.

Biernatzki, W. (2002) 'Terrorism and Mass Media', *Communication Research Trends* 21(1): 1–19.

Bloor, M. (1995) 'A User's Guide to Contrasting Theories of HIV-related Risk Behaviour', in J. Gabe (ed.), *Medicine, Health and Risk.* Oxford: Blackwell.

Boden, D. (2002) 'Worlds in Action: Information, Instantaneity and Global Futures Trading', in B. Adam, U. Beck and J. Van Loon (eds), *The Risk Society and Beyond: Critical Issues for Social Theory.* London: Sage.

Bourne, J. and Sivanandan, A. (1980) 'Cheerleaders and Ombudsman: The Sociology of Race Relations in Britain', *Race and Class* 21: 331–52.

Boyne, R. (2003) *Risk.* Buckingham: Open University Press.

Bradac, J. (2001) 'Theory Comparison: Uncertainty Reduction, Problematic Integration, Uncertainty Management and Other Constructs', *Journal of Communication* 51(3): 456–76.

Bradley, T. and Walters, R. (2002) 'Prevention and Community Safety: The New Zealand Experience', in G. Hughes, E. McLauglin and J. Muncie (eds), *Crime Prevention and Community Safety: New Directions.* London: Sage.

Brearley, C.P. (1982) *Risk and Social Work: Hazards and Helping.* London: Routledge.

Brewer, C. and Lait, J. (1980) *Can Social Work Survive?* London: Maurice Temple Smith.

Brindle, D. (1999) 'Media Coverage of Social Policy: A Journalistic Perspective in Social Policy', in B. Franklin (ed.), *The Media and Misrepresentation.* London: Routledge.

British Broadcasting Corporation (1999) 'One in Five "Mentally Ill"' (3 February). www.bbc.co.uk

British Broadcasting Corporation (2002a) 'Graduate Job Prospects Slide' (11 March). www.bbc.co.uk

British Broadcasting Corporation (2002b) 'Fifteen Million Ethiopians Face Starvation' (*Today Programme*, 11 November). www.bbc.co.uk

British Broadcasting Corporation (2002c) *One O'Clock News* (7 June). www.bbc.co.uk

British Broadcasting Corporation (2003a) 'BT Opens Indian Call Centres' (7 March). www.bbc.co.uk

British Broadcasting Corporation (2003b) 'Warning on Gene "ID Cards"' (4 March). www.bbc.co.uk

British Broadcasting Corporation (2003c) 'Flight 587: Horizon' (8 May). www.bbc.co.uk

British Broadcasting Corporation (2003d) 'The Day Britain Stopped' (13 May). www.bbc.co.uk

British Broadcasting Corporation, (2003e) 'Top Ten Terrorist Targets' (19 August). www.bbc.co.uk

British Broadcasting Corporation (2003f) 'Blair in Washington' (*News 24*, 17 July). www.bbc.co.uk

British Broadcasting Corporation (2004) 'At a Glance: Butler Report' (14 July). www.bbc.co.uk

British Entertainment and Discothèque Association (1995) 'Memorandum of Evidence', in Home Affairs Select Committee, *The Private Security Industry*, HL 17–2. London: HMSO.

Broad, B. and Denney, D. (1996) 'Users Rights and the Probation Service: Some Opportunities and Obstacles', *Probation Journal* 35(1): 61–76.

Brouwer, E. (1998) 'Sheep to Cows to Man: A History of TSEs', in S. Ratzan (ed.), *The Mad Cow Crisis*. London: UCL Press.

Brown, G. and Davidson, S. (1978) 'Social Class, Psychiatric Disorder of Mother, and Accidents to Children', *Lancet* i: 378–80. Also in J. Green (1997) *Risk and Misfortune*. London: UCL Press.

Brown, M. (2000) 'Calculations of Risk in Contemporary Penal Practice', in M. Brown and J. Pratt (eds), *Dangerous Offenders: Punishment and Social Order*. London: Routledge.

Brown, P. (1995) 'Popular Epidemiology, Toxic Waste and Social Movements', in J. Gabe (ed.), *Medicine, Health and Risk*. Oxford: Blackwell.

Brown, R., Bute, S. and Ford, P. (1986) *Social Workers and Risk: The Prevention and Management of Violence*. London: Macmillan.

Bruntland, G.H. (1987) *Our Common Future, World Commisssion on Environment and Development*. Oxford: Oxford University Press.

Brysk, A. (2002) *Globalization and Human Rights*. Berkeley, CA: University of California Press.

Buckerman, O. (2001) 'Am I Going Down?', *The Guardian*, 28 May: 15.

Bunton, R. and Burrows, R. (1995) 'Consumption and Health in the "Epidemiological" Clinic of Late Modern Medicine', in R. Bunton, S. Nettleton and R. Burrows (eds), *The Sociology of Health Promotion: Critical Analyses of Consumption Lifestyle and Risk*. London: Routledge.

Burrel, I. (2003) 'TV Dramas Put Lives at Risk with Misleading Medical Advice', *The Independent*, 30 July.

Business (2001) '10 Risks Businesses Must Take To Succeed', *Business*.

Butler, Rt Hon the Lord (2004) 'Review of Intelligence on Weapons of Mass destruction'. Report of a Committee of Privy Counsellors. London: The Stationery Office.

Cabinet Office (2004) 'Framework for Risk Based Decision Making'. www.cabinet office.gov.uk

Cahill, M. (2002a) *The Environment and Social Policy*. London: Routledge.

Cahill, M. (2002b) 'The Implications of Consumerism for the Transition to a Sustainable Society', in M. Cahill and T. Fitzpatrick (eds), *Environmental Issues and Social Welfare*. Oxford: Blackwell.

Cahill, M. and Fitzpatrick, T. (eds) (2002) *Environmental Issues and Social Welfare*. Oxford: Blackwell.

Caplan, P. (2000) 'Eating British Beef with Confidence: A Consideration of Consumers' Responses to BSE in Britain', in P. Caplan (ed.), *Risk Revisited*. London: Pluto Press.

Cappannari, A. (2002) 'American College Students Graduate with Record Levels of Debt', (22 April) www.wsws.org/articles/2002

Carling, A. (2000) 'New Labour's Polity: Tony Giddens and the Third Way', *Journal of Analytical Socialism* 3(3): 214–42. Also cited in B. Jordan and C. Jordan

(2000), *Social Work and the Third Way: Tough Love as Social Policy.* London: Sage.

Carson, R. (1962) *Silent Spring.* Boston, MA: Houghton Mills.

Carter, R., Goddard, A., Reah, D., Sanger, K. and Bowring, M. (1997) *Working with Texts.* London: Routledge.

Castel, R. (1991) 'From Dangerousness to Risk', in G. Burchell, C. Gordon and P. Miller (eds), *The Foucault Effect: Studies in Governmentality.* Chicago: University of Chicago Press.

Cebulla, A., Abbott, D., Ford, J., Middleton, S., Quiglars, D. and Walker, R. (1998) 'A Geography of Insurance Exclusion – Perceptions of Unemployment Risk and Actuarial Risk Assessment'. Paper presented to the Second European Urban and Regional Studies Conference, University of Durham, September 1998.

Clark, J. (2003) *Worlds Apart: Civil Society and the Battle for Ethical Globilisation.* London: Earthscan.

Clarke, J. and Newman, J. (1997) *The Managerial State.* London: Sage.

Clear, T.R. and Cadora, E. (2001) 'Risk and Correctional Practice', in K. Stenson and R. Sullivan (eds), *Crime, Risk and Justice.* Cullompton: Willan.

Cohen, S. (1972) *Folk Devils and Moral Panics: The Creation of the Mods and Rockers.* London: McGibbon and Kee.

Cohen, W. (1997) Speech to Conference on Terrorism, Weapons of Mass Destruction and the US, in J. Stern (1999) *Getting and Using the Weapons of Mass Destruction,* in R. Howard and R. Sawyer (eds) (2003) *Terrorism and Counter-Terrorism: Understanding the New Security Environment.* Guilford, CT: McGraw-Hill/Dushkin.

Colledge, R.G. and Stimpson, R.J. (1997) *Spatial Behaviour: A Geographical Perspective.* New York: Guilford Press.

Commission on Global Governance (1995) *Our Global Neighbourhood,* The Report of the Commission on Global Governance. Oxford: Oxford University Press.

Connor, S. (2003) 'The Diseases from Nowhere Which Strike with a Venom', *The Independent,* 25 April: 4.

Cooper, A., English, J. and Thakur, R. (eds) (2002) *Enhancing Global Governance.* Tokyo: United Nations University Press.

Cooper, D. (2002) 'Boundary Harms: From Community Protection to a Politics of Value – The Case of the Jewish Eruv', in G. Hughes, E. McLauglin and J. Muncie (eds), *Crime Prevention and Community Safety: New Directions.* London: Sage.

Cornwell, R. (2003) 'Has the War Left the World a Safer Place?', *The Independent,* 16 April: 4.

Cox, S. and McKellin, W. (1999) '"There's This Thing in Our Family": Predictive Testing and the Construction of Risk for Huntington Disease', in P. Conrad and J. Gabe (eds), *Sociological Positions on the New Genetics.* Oxford: Blackwell.

Crawford, A. (2001) 'Joined up but Fragmented: Contradictions, Ambiguity and Ambivalence at the Heart of New Labour's "Third Way"', in R. Matthews and J. Pitts (eds), *Crime and Disorder and Community Safety.* London: Routledge.

Crawford, A. (2002a) 'The Growth of Crime Prevention in France, as Contrasted with the English Experience: Some Thoughts on the Politics of Insecurity', in

G. Hughes, E. McLauglin and J. Muncie (eds), *Crime Prevention and Community Safety: New Directions*. London: Sage.

Crawford, A. (ed.) (2002b) *Crime and Insecurity: The Governance of Safety in Europe*. Cullompton: Willan.

Crawford, A. (2002c) 'Introduction: Governance and Security', in A. Crawford (ed.), *Crime and Insecurity: The Governance of Safety in Europe*. Cullompton: Willan.

Croall, H. (1998) *Crime and Society in Britain*. London: Longman.

Croft, J.A. (2001) 'Risk or At Risk: Conceptualising Housing Debt in a Risk Society', *Housing Studies* 16(6): 737–53.

Crombie, H. (1995) *Sustainable Development and Health*. Birmingham: Public Health Alliance.

Daily Mail (2002a) 'Chips May Cause Cancer', Friday 28 June: 2.

Daily Mail (2002b) 'Alert as GM Pollen Spreads', Friday 28 June: 2.

Dealer, S. (1998) 'Can the Spread of BSE and CJD Be Predicted?', in S. Ratzan (ed.), *The Mad Cow Crisis*. London: UCL Press.

Dealer, S.F. and Kent, J.T. (1995) 'BSE: An Update on the Statistical Evidence', *British Food Journal* 97(8): 22–34.

Dean, M. (1997) 'Sociology after Society', in D. Owen (ed.), *Sociology after Post Modernism*. London: Sage.

Dean, M. (1999) 'Risk Calculable and Incalculable', in D. Lupton (ed.), *Risk and Sociocultural Change: New Directions and Positions*. Cambridge: Cambridge University Press.

Denney, D. (1992) *Racism and Anti-racism in Probation*. London: Routledge.

Denney, D. (1998) *Social Policy and Social Work*. Oxford: Oxford University Press.

Denney, D. and O'Beirne, M. (2003) 'Violence to Probation Staff: Patterns and Managerial Responses', *Social Policy and Administration* 37(1): 49–65.

Department of Environment, Transport and the Regions (1998) *A New Deal for Transport* (Cm 3950). London: HMSO.

Department of Social Security (1998) *A New Contract for Welfare: Partnership in Pensions*. London: HMSO.

Dingwall, R. (2000) '"Risk Society": The Cult of Theory and the Millennium', in N. Manning and I. Shaw (eds), *New Risks, New Welfare: Signposts for Social Policy*. Oxford: Blackwell.

Dingwall, R., Eekelar, J.M. and Murray, T. (1983) *The Protection of Children: State Intervention and Family Life*. Oxford: Blackwell.

Douglas, M. (1966) *Purity and Danger: An Analysis of Concepts of Pollution and Taboo*. London: Routledge and Kegan Paul.

Douglas, M. (1973) *Natural Symbols: Explorations in Cosmology* (2nd edn). London: Barrie and Jenkins.

Douglas, M. (1985) *Risk Acceptability According to the Social Sciences*. New York: Russell Sage Foundation.

Douglas, M. (1992) *Risk and Blame: Essays in Cultural Theory*. London: Routledge.

Douglas, M. and Wildavsky, A. (1982) *Risk and Culture*. Berkeley, CA: University of California Press.

Drake, C.J.M. (1998) 'The Role of Ideology in Terrorists' Target Selection', *Terrorism and Political Violence* 10(2): 53–85.

Draper, A. and Green, J. (2002) 'Food Safety and Consumers: Constructions of Choice and Risk', *Social Policy and Administration* 36(6): 610–25.

Dresner, S. (2002) *The Principles of Sustainability.* London: Earthscan.

Driver, S. and Martell, L. (2002) *Blair's Britain.* Bristol: Policy Press.

Durham, F.D. (1998) 'News Frames as Social Narratives: TWA Flight 800', *Journal of Communication* 48(4): 100–18.

Dwyer, P. and Wynn, J. (2001) *Youth Education and Risk.* London: Routledge.

Earth Government (2003) Press Release (27 March). Available at: www.shaw.ca/earthgov/Ecbewketters,htm

Economist (2002) 'George Bush's Plan for Peace', *Economist,* 29 June.

Edelman, M. (1993) 'Contestable Categories and Public Opinion', *Political Communication* 10(3): 231–42.

Edwards, A. and Hughes, G. (eds) (2002) *Crime Control and Community.* Cullompton: Willan.

Edwards, R. and Glover, J. (eds) (2001) *Risk and Citizenship.* London: Routledge.

Elderidge, J. (1999) *Risk, Society and the Media: Now You See It, Now You Don't.* Harlow: Longman.

Elkin, T., McLaren, D. and Hillman, M. (1991) *Reviving the City: Towards Sustainable Urban Development.* London: Friends of the Earth.

Elston, M.A., Gabe, J., Denney, D., Lee, R. and O' Brian, M. (2002) 'Violence Against Doctors: A Medicalised Problem? The Case of National Health Service General Practitioners', *Sociology of Health and Illness* 24(5): 575–98.

Ericson, R. and Carriere, K. (1994) 'The Fragmentation of Criminology', in D. Nelken (ed.), *The Future of Criminology.* London: Sage.

Ericson, R. and Haggerty, K. (1997) *Policing the Risk Society.* Oxford: Clarendon Press.

Esping-Anderson, G. (1996) *Welfare States in Transition: National Adaptations in Global Economics.* London: Sage.

Evers, L. (2003) '*PLCs Not Acting in the Spirit of Turnbull',* *Accountancy Age,* 22 April. Available at: www.accountancyage.com

Ewald, F. (1991) 'Insurance and Risks', in G. Burchell, C. Gordon and P. Miller (eds), *The Foucault Effect: Studies in Governmentality.* Chicago: University of Chicago Press.

Falk, R. (1995) 'The World Order between Inter-state Law and the Law of Humanity', in D. Archibugi and D. Held (eds), *Cosmopolitan Democracy.* Oxford: Blackwell.

Feeley, M. and Simon, J. (1992) 'The New Penology: Notes on the Emerging Strategy of Corrections and its Implications', *Criminology* 30: 449–74.

Ferguson, E. (2001) 'The Roles of Contextual Moderation and Personality in Relation to the Knowledge–Risk Link in the Workplace', *Journal of Risk Research* 4(4): 323–40.

Ferguson, E., Farrel, K., Lowe, K.C. and James, V. (2001) 'Perception of Risk of Blood Transfusion: Knowledge, Group Membership and Pervaded Control', *Transfusion Medicine* 11: 129–35.

Ferguson, I. and Johnstone, C. (2001) 'Postmodernism and Social Welfare: A Critique', in M. Lavalette and A. Pratt (eds), *Social Policy: A Conceptual and Theoretical Outline,* (2nd edn). London: Sage.

Fernando, S. (ed.) (1995) *Mental Health in a Multi-ethnic Society: A Multi-disciplinary Handbook*. London: Routledge.

Fisher, M., Newton, C. and Sainsbury, E. (1984) *Mental Health Social Work Observed*. London: National Institute of Social Work.

Fiske, J. (1994) *Reading the Popular*. London: Routledge.

Ford, J. (2000) 'Risk in a Flexible Labour Market', in P. Taylor-Gooby (ed.), *Risk, Trust and Welfare*. London: Macmillan.

Ford, J., Burrows, R. and Nettleton, S. (2001) *Home Ownership in a Risk Society*. Bristol: Policy Press.

Forrest, R. and Murie, A. (1992) *Selling the Welfare State*. London: Routledge.

Forrest, R. and Murie, A. (eds) (1995) *Housing and Family Wealth: Comparative International Positions*. London: Routledge.

Foster, P. and Wilding, P. (2000) 'Whither Welfare Professionalism?', *Social Policy and Administration* 34(2): 143–60.

Foucault, M. (1965) *Madness and Civilisation: The History of Insanity in the Age of Reason*. New York: Pergamon.

Foucault, M. (1972) *The Archaeology of Knowledge*. London: Routledge.

Foucault, M. (1977) *Discipline and Punish: The Birth of the Prison*. London: Routledge.

Foucault, M. (1989) *The Order of Things: An Archaeology of the Human Sciences*. London: Routledge.

Fox, N.J. (1999) 'Postmodern Reflections on "Risk" Hazards and Life Choices', in D. Lupton (ed.), *Risk and Sub Cultural Theory: New Directions and Positions*. Cambridge: Cambridge University Press.

Frankenburg, R. (1994) 'The Impact of HIV/AIDs on Concepts Relating to Risk and Culture within British Community Epidemiology: Candidates or Targets for Intervention', *Social Science* 38(10): 1325–35.

Fresco, L. (2001) *Genetically Modified Crops*, Keynote Speech Royal Swedish Academy of Agriculture and Forestry Conference on Crop and Biodiversity, Falkenberg, Sweden, 16–18 September.

Freudenburg, W.R., Coleman, C.L., Gonzales, J. and Hegeland, C. (1996) 'Media Coverage of Hazardous Events', *Risk Analysis* 16: 31–42.

Frewer, L., Hunt, S., Rowe, G., Nilsson, A., Mays, C. and Menard, M. (1998) 'Media Reporting of Risk in European Countries at the Time of the 10th Anniversary of the Chernobyl Accident', Reading: Institute of Food Research, in A.A. F. Wahlberg and Sjoberg, L. (2000), 'Risk Perception and the Media', *Journal of Risk Research* 3(1): 31–50.

Friedson, E. (1994) *Professionalism Reborn*. Cambridge: Polity Press.

Fukuyama, F. (1992) *The End of History and the Last Man*. New York: Basic Books.

Fukuyama, F. (2001) 'The West Was Won', *The Guardian*, 11 October.

Furedi, F. (1998) *Culture of Fear: Risk Taking and the Morality of Low Expectation*. London: Cassel.

Gabe, J. (ed.) (1995) *Medicine, Health and Risk*. Oxford: Blackwell.

Gabe, J., Denney, D., Lee, R., Elston, M.A. and O'Brian, M. (2002) 'Researching Professional Discourses on Violence', *British Journal of Criminology* 41: 460–71.

Garland, D. (1990) *Punishment and Modern Society: A Study in Social Theory.* Oxford: Clarendon Press.

Garland, D. (1999) 'The Commonplace and the Catastrpohic: Interpretations of Crime in Late Modernity', *Theoretical Criminology* 3(3): 353–64.

Garland, D. (2001) *The Culture of Control: Crime and Social Order in Contemporary Society.* Oxford: Oxford University Press.

Gerbner, G. and Gross, L. (1976) 'Living with Television: The Violence Profile', *Journal of Communication* 26: 173–99.

Giddens, A. (1990) *The Consequences of Modernity.* Cambridge: Polity Press.

Giddens, A. (1991) *Modernity and Self-Identity: Self and Society in the Late Modern Age.* Cambridge: Cambridge University Press.

Giddens, A. (1994) 'Living in Post Traditional Society', in U. Beck, A. Giddens and S. Lash, *Reflexive Modernity.* Cambridge: Polity Press.

Giddens, A. (1998) *The Third Way: The Renewal of Social Democracy.* Cambridge: Polity Press.

Giddens, A. (1999) *Runaway World.* London: Profile Books.

Giddens, A. (2000) *The Third Way and its Critics.* Cambridge: Polity Press in association with Blackwell.

Glasius, M. and Kaldor, M. (2001) 'The State of Global Civil Society Before and After September 11th', in M. Glasius, M. Kaldor and H. Achier (eds), *Global Civil Society.* Oxford: Oxford University Press.

Glasius, M., Kaldor, M. and Anheier, H. (eds) (2001) *Global Civil Society.* Oxford: Oxford University Press.

Glennester, H. (1995) *British Social Policy since 1945.* Oxford: Blackwell.

Goode, E. and Ben Yahuda, N. (1994) *Moral Panics: The Social Construction of Deviance.* Cambridge, MA and Oxford: Blackwell.

Gordon, C. (1991) 'Governmental Rationality: An Outline', in G. Burchell, C. Gordon and P. Miller (eds), *The Foucault Effect.* Chicago: University of Chicago Press.

Gordon, D. and Gibbons, J. (1998) 'Placing Children on Child Protection Registers: Risk Indicators and Local Authority Differences', *British Journal of Social Work* 28: 423–36.

Gostin, L. (2000) *Public Health Law: Power, Duty, Restraint.* Berkeley, CA: University of California Press.

Gottfredson, S.D. and Gottfredson, D.M. (1986) 'Accuracy of Prediction Models', in A. Blumstein, J. Cohen, J. Royth and C. Visher (eds), *Criminal Careers and 'Criminal Careers'.* Washington, DC: National Academic Press.

Government Actuary's Department (2004) 'United Kingdom population set to pass 60 million next year', www.gad.gov.uk (accessed 30 September 2004).

Gramling, R. and Freudenberg, W.R. (1996) 'Environmental Sociology', *Sociological Spectrum* 16(4): 347–70.

Green, J. (1997) *Risk and Misfortune: The Social Construction of Accidents.* London: UCL Press.

Green, J. and Thorogood, N. (1998) *Analysing Health Policy: A Sociological Approach.* London: Longman.

Guardian (1994a) 'Death Ferry Sailed into the Baltic Storm with Faulty Door Seals', *The Guardian*, 29 September: 1.

Guardian (1994b) Leading Article: 'For Those in Peril of the Sea', *The Guardian*, 2 October: 23.

Guardian (2000) 'Paying Up for Dirty Tankers', *The Guardian*, 21 November: 18.

Guardian (2001a) 'Charities Uneasy about Street's Cancer Death', *The Guardian*, 19 June: 10.

Guardian (2001b) 'They All Failed Victoria', *The Guardian*, 13 January: 1.

Guardian (2002a) 'Fear of Tanker Disaster', *The Guardian*, 29 November: 15.

Guardian (2002b) '"Dirty Bomb" plot', *The Guardian*, 11 June: 12.

Guardian (2002c) 'Attack on Bagdad without New UN Resolution Illegal Says QC', *The Guardian*, 20 November: 16.

Guardian (2002d) 'Civil Wrongs Maya Jaggi', *The Guardian Weekend*, 22 June: 13.

Guardian (2003a) 'Taliban Captives Should Go Home Say Rights Group', *The Guardian*, 3 March: 5.

Guardian (2003b) 'Diplomacy Dies, Now Its War', *The Guardian*, 18 March: 2.

Guardian (2004a) 'Rebranding "Bush as a man of peace"', *The Guardian*, 3 January: 1.

Guardian (2004b) 'Why Limits Must Be Set on the Use of Science', *The Guardian*, 15 May: 11.

Guardian (2004c) 'There Were No Weapons of Mass Destruction in Iraq', *The Guardian*, 7 October: 1.

Guardian (2005a) 'Freed Britons Sent Home', 27 January: 1.

Guardian (2005b) 'Lawyers Criticise House Arrest Plan', 27 January: 4.

Hall, S. (1998) 'The Great Moving Nowhere Show', *Marxism Today*, Special Issue, November/December: 9–14.

Hall, S., Critcher, C., Jefferson, T. and Roberts, B. (1978) *Policing the Crisis: Mugging the State and Law and Order*. London: Macmillan.

Hallowell, N. (1999) 'Doing the Right Thing: Genetic Risk and Responsibility', in P. Conrad and J. Gabe (eds), *Sociological Positions on the New Genetics*. Oxford: Blackwell.

Hancock, L. (2001) *Community, Crime and Disorder: Safety and Regeneration in Urban Neigbourhoods*. Basingstoke: Palgrave.

Hargreaves Heap, S. and Ross, A. (eds) (1992) *Understanding the Enterprise Culture: Themes in the Work of Mary Douglas*. Edinburgh: Edinburgh University Press.

Harris, J. (1998) 'Bureau Professionals and New Managerialism: The Labour Process of State Social Work', *British Journal of Social Work* 28: 839–62.

Heelo, H. (2000) 'Campaigning and Governing', in N.J. Ornstein and T.E. Mann (eds), *The Permanent Campaign and its Future*. Washington, DC: American Enterprise Institute/Brookings Institute.

Heggen, K. and Dwyer, P. (1998) 'New Policies, New Options: Learning from Changing Student Transitions at Two Ends of the World', *Journal of Research in Compulsory Education* 3(3): 261–77.

Held, D. (1995) *Democracy and the Global Order*. Cambridge: Polity Press.

Hendrick, H. (1994) *Child Welfare in England, 1972–89*. London: Routledge.

Hertz, R. and Marshall, L. (2001) *Working Families*. Berkley, CA: University of California Press.

Heywood, F., Olman, C. and Means, R. (2002) *Housing and Home in Later Life*. Buckingham: Open University Press.

Hier, S. (2003) 'Risk and Panic in Late Modernity: Implication of the Converging Sites of Social Anxiety', *British Journal of Sociology* 54(1): 3–20.

Hobbs, D., Lister, S., Hadfield, P., Winlow, S. and Hall, J. (2000) 'Deceiving Shadows: Governance and Limitations of the Night Time Economy', *British Journal of Sociology* 51: 701–17.

Hoffman, B. (1998) 'Defining Terrorism', in R. Howard and R. Sawyer (eds) (2002), *Terrorism and Counter-Terrorism: Understanding the New Security Environment*. Guilford, CT: McGraw-Hill/Dushkin.

Hogarth, T., Elias, P. and Ford, J. (1996) *Mothers, Families and Jobs* (University of Warwick Institute for Employment Research). Warwick: University of Warwick.

Hogg, R. (2002) 'Criminology Beyond the Nation State: Global Conflicts, Human Rights and the "New World Disorder"', in K. Carrington and R. Hogg (eds), *Critical Criminology: Issues, Debates, Challenges*. Cullompton: Willan.

Home Office (1998) Supporting Families: a consultation document. London: HMSO.

Hood, C., Rothstein, H. and Baldwin, R. (2001) *The Government of Risk: Understanding Risk Regulation Regimes*. Oxford: Oxford University Press.

Hood, C., Rothstein, H., Spackman, M., Rees, J. and Baldwin, R. (1999) 'Explaining Risk Regulation Regimes: Exploring the "Minimal Feasibility Response" Hypothesis', *Health Risk and Society* 1(2): 151–66.

Hope, T. (2001) 'Crime Victimisation and Inequality in the Risk Society', in R. Matthews and J. Pitts (eds), *Crime Disorder and Community Safety*. London: Routledge.

Howard, R. (2002) 'Terrorism and Counter-Terrorism' (Preface), in R. Howard and R. Sawyer (eds), *Terrorism and Counter-Terrorism: Understanding the New Security Environment*. Guilford, CT: McGraw-Hill/Dushkin.

Howard, R. and Sawyer, R. (eds) (2003) *Terrorism and Counter-Terrorism: Understanding the New Security Environment*. Guilford, CT: McGraw-Hill/Dushkin.

Huby, M. (2001) 'The Sustainable Use of Resources on a Global Scale', *Social Policy and Administration* 35(5): 521–38.

Hudson, B. (2000) 'Human Rights, Public Safety and the Probation Service: Defending Justice in the Risk Society', Bill McWilliams Memorial Lecture Imprint, 28 June. Cambridge: Cambridge University Press.

Hudson, B. (2001) 'Punishment Rights and Difference: Defending Justice in the Risk Society', in K. Stenson and R. Sullivan (eds), *Crime Risk and Justice*. Cullompton: Willan.

Hughes, G. (1998) *Understanding Crime Prevention, Social Control, Risk and Late Modernity*. Buckingham: Open University Press.

Hughes, G. and Edwards, H. (eds) (2002) *Crime Control and Community: The New Politics of Public Safety*. Cullompton: Willan.

Hughes, G., McLauglin, E. and Muncie, J. (eds) (2002) *Crime Prevention and Community Safety: New Directions*. London: Sage.

Huxley, P. (1993) 'Case Management and Care Management in the Community', *British Journal of Social Work* 23(4): 365–81.

Huxley, P. (1997) 'Mental Illness', in Davies, M. (ed.), *The Blackwell Companion to Social Work*. Oxford: Blackwell.

Irvine, D. (2003) *The Doctor's Tale*. Abingdon: Radcliffe Medical Press.

Irwin, A. and Wynne, B. (1996) *Misunderstanding Science? The Public Reconstruction of Science and Technology*. Cambridge: Cambridge University Press.

Jaeger, C., Renn, O., Rosa, E. and Webler, T. (2001) *Risk Uncertainty and Rational Action*. London: Earthscan Publications.

Jain, J. and Guiver, J. (2002) 'Turning the Car Inside Out: Transport, Equity and Environment', in M. Cahill and T. Fitzpatrick (eds), *Environmental Issues and Social Welfare*. Oxford: Oxford University Press.

Jones, D.R. (1986) 'Flying and Danger, Joy and Fear', *Aviation, Space and Environmental Medicine* 57: 131–6.

Jordan, B. (1998) *The New Politics of Welfare*. London: Sage.

Jordan, B. and Jordan, C. (2000) *Social Work and the Third Way: Tough Love as Social Policy*. London: Sage.

Kagan, R. (2003) *Paradise and Power: America and Europe in the New World Order*. London: Atlantic Books.

Kampfner, J. (2004) *Blair's Wars*. London: The Free Press.

Kasperson, R.E. (1992) 'The Social Amplification of Risk: Progress in Developing an Integrative Framework', in D. Krimsky and D. Golding (eds), *Social Theories of Risk*. Praeger: Westport.

Kay, H. (1999) *Futures-Promoting Childrens and Young Peoples Mental Health*. London: The Mental Health Foundation.

Kellner, D. (2002) 'September 11th: Social Theory and Democratic Politics', *Theory, Culture and Society* 19(4): 147–60.

Kemp, J. (1993) *The Philosophy of Kant*. Bristol: Thoemmes Press.

Kemshall, H. (1997) 'Sleep Safely: Crime Risks May Be Smaller than You Think', *Social Policy and Administration* 31(3): 247–60.

Kemshall, H. (2000) 'Researching Risk in the Probation Service', *Social Policy and Administration* 34(4): 465–78.

Kemshall, H. (2002) *Risk, Social Policy and Welfare*. Buckingham: Open University Press.

Kemshall, H., Patron, N., Walsh, M. and Waterson, J. (1997) 'Concepts of Risk in Relation to Organisational Structure and Functioning within the Personal Social Services and Probation', *Social Policy and Administration* 31(43): 213–33.

Kendrick, D., Marsh, P. and Williams, E.I. (1995) 'General Practitioners, Child Accident Prevention and the Health of the Nation', *Health Education Research* 10: 345–53.

Kikbusch, I. (1988) 'New Positions for Research in Health Behaviour', in R. Anderson (ed.), *Health and Behaviour Research and Health Promotion*. Oxford: Oxford University Press.

Laming, H. (2003) *The Victoria Climbie Inquiry*. London: Stationery Office.

Lane, J. (2000) *New Public Management*. London: Routledge.

Lane, K. (1994) 'Birth as Euphoria: The Social Meaning of Birth', in D. Colquhoun and A. Kellehear (eds), *Health Research in Practice*. London: Chapman and Hall.

Lane, K. (1995) 'The Medical Model of the Body as a Site of Risk', in J. Gabe (ed.), *Medicine Health and Risk*. Oxford: Blackwell.

Lang, T. (1998) 'BSE and CJD: Recent Developments', in S. Ratzan (ed.), *The Mad Cow Crisis*. London: UCL Press.

Lang, T., Barling, D. and Carather, M. (2002) 'Food, Social Policy and the Environment: Towards a New Model', in M. Cahill and T. Fitzpatrick (eds), *Environmental Issues and Social Welfare*. Oxford: Oxford University Press.

Langan, J. (1999) 'Assessing Risk in Mental Health', in P. Parsloe (ed.), *Risk Assessment in Social Care and Social Work*. London: Jessica Kingsley.

Larana, E. (2001) 'Reflexivity, Risk and Collective Action over Waste Management: A Constructive Proposal', *Current Sociology* 49(1): 23–48.

Lash, S. and Wynne, B. (1992) 'Preface', in U. Beck, *The Risk Society*. London: Sage.

Lee, D. and Newby, H. (1981) *The Problem of Sociology*. London: Hutchinson.

Le Grand, J. (1997) 'Knights, Knaves or Pawns? Human Behaviour and Social Policy', *Journal of Social Policy* 26(2): 149–69.

Leisering, L. and Leibfried, S. (1999) *Time and Poverty in Western Welfare*. Cambridge: Cambridge University Press.

Lèvi-Strauss, C. (1966) 'The Culinary Triangle', *Partisan Review* 33: 586–95.

Loader, I. (1997) 'Private Security and the Demand for Protection in Contemporary Britain', *Policing and Society* 7: 143–62.

Lodge, D. (1981) *Working with Structuralism*. London: Routledge.

Lombroso, C. (1897) *L'Uomo Delinquente* (5th edn). Turin: Bocca.

London Stock Exchange (1992) *Report of the Committee on Financial Aspects of Financial Governance*. London: The London Stock Exchange.

Lowe, R. (1993) *The Welfare State in Britain since 1945*. London: Macmillan.

Luhmann, N. (1991) *Risk: A Sociological Theory*. Berlin: Walter de Guyter.

Luhmann, N. (2000) *The Reality of the Mass Media*. Cambridge: Cambridge University Press.

Lupton, D. (1993) 'Risk as Moral Danger: The Social and Political Functions of Risk Discourse in Public Health', *International Journal of Health Services* 23(3): 425–35.

Lupton, D. (1999a) *Risk*. London: Routledge.

Lupton, D. (ed.) (1999b) *Risk and Socio-Cultural Theory: New directions and Positions*. Cambridge: Cambridge University Press.

Lupton, D. (2000) 'The Heart of the Meal: Food Preferences and Habits among Rural Australian Couples', *Sociology of Health and Illness* 22: 94–109.

Lupton, D. and Tulloch, J. (2000) 'Theorizing Fear of Crime: Beyond the Rational–Irrational Question', *British Journal of Sociology* 50(3): 507–23.

Lupton, D. and Tulloch, J. (2002) 'Risk is Part of Your Life: Risk Epistemologies among a Group of Australians', *British Journal of Sociology* 36(2): 317–34.

MacDonald, K. and MacDonald, G. (1999) 'Perceptions of Risk', in P. Parsloe (ed.), *Risk Assessment in Social Care and Social Work*. London: Jessica Kingsley.

McGuire, J. (ed.) (1995) *What Works: Reducing Re-offending*. Chichester: Wiley.

Macintyre, S., Reilly, J., Miller, D. and Eldridge, J. (1998) 'Food Choice, Food Scare and Health: the Role of the Media', in A. Murcott (ed.), *The Nations Diet: The Social Science of Food Choice*. London: Longman.

McLaughlin, E. (2002) 'Same Bed, Different Dreams: Postmodern Reflections on Crime Prevention and Community Safety', in G. Hughes and A. Edwards (eds), *Crime Control and Community*. Cullompton: Willan.

Macnaughten, P. (2000) 'Trust, Risk and the Environment', in F. Tonkiss, A. Passey, N. Fenton and L. Hems (eds), *Trust and Civil Society*. London: Macmillan.

McMichael, A.J. (1993) *Planetary Overload: Global Environmental Change and the Health of Human Species*. Cambridge: Cambridge University Press.

McQuaid, J. (1998) Guest Editorial: 'The Future of Risk Research', *Journal of Risk Research* 1(1): 3–6.

Macey, M. (2002) 'Interpreting Islam: Young Muslim Men's Involvement in Criminal Activity in Bradford', in B. Spalek (ed.), *Islam, Crime and Criminal Justice*. Cullompton: Willan.

Mair, G. (2001) 'Technology and the Futures of Community Penalties', in A. Bottoms, L. Gelsthorpe and S. Rex (eds), *Community Penalties: Change and Challenges*. Cullompton: Willan.

Maley, W., Sampford, C. and Thakur, R. (eds) (2002) *From Civil Strife to Civil Society*. Tokyo: United Nations University Press.

Manthorpe, J. (2000) 'Risk Assessment', in M. Davies (ed.), *The Blackwell Encyclopaedia of Social Work*. Oxford: Blackwell.

Marchant, G. (2001) 'The Precautionary Principle: An "Unprincipled" Approach to Biotechnology Regulation', *Journal of Risk Research* 4(2): 143–57.

Matthews, R. and Pitts, J. (2001) *Crime, Disorder and Community Safety*. London: Routledge.

Meikle, J. (1998) '"Food Poisoning", *The Guardian*, 14 January: 15', in M. Cahill (2002) *The Environment and Social Policy*. London: Routledge.

Milburn, M.A. and McGrail, A.B. (1992) 'The Dramatic Presentation of News and Its Effect on Cognitive Complexity', *Political Psychology* 13: 613–32.

Moores, S. (2000) *Media and Everyday Life in Modern Society*. Edinburgh: Edinburgh University Press.

Mullard, M. and Spicker, P. (1998) *Social Policy in a Changing Society*. London: Routledge.

Muncie, J. (1999) 'Exorcising Demons: Media, Politics and Criminal Justice', in B. Franklin (ed.), *Social Policy, the Media and Misrepresentation*. London: Routledge.

Munro, E. (1996) 'Avoidable and Unavoidable Mistakes in Child Protection Work', *British Journal of Social Work* 26: 793–808.

Munro, E. and Rumgay, J. (2000) 'Role of Risk Assessment in Reducing Homicides by People with Mental Illness', *British Journal of Psychiatry* 176: 116–20.

Munro, M. (2000a) 'Labour Market Insecurity in the Owner-Occupied Housing Market', *Environment and Planning* 32(8): 175–89.

Munro, M. (2000b) 'Riding the Roller Coaster: Household Responses to Changing Housing Market Risk', in P. Taylor-Gooby (ed.), *Risk, Trust and Welfare*. London: Macmillan.

Mythen, G. (2004) *Ulrich Beck: A Critical Introduction to the Risk Society*. London: Pluto.

National Institute for Social Work (1999) *Violence Towards Social Care Staff* (an Internal Discussion Paper). London: National Institute for Social Work.

National Research Council. 'Understanding Risk: Informing Decisions in Democratic Society', in L. Gostin (2000) *Public Health Law: Power, Duty, Restraint*. Berkeley, CA: University of California Press.

Nellis, M. (2001) 'Community Penalties in Historical Position', in A. Bottoms, L. Gelsthorpe and S. Rex (eds), *Community Penalties: Change and Challenges*. Cullompton: Willan.

Newburn, T. and Hayman, S. (2002) *Policing, Surveillance and Social Control*. Cullompton: Willan.

Nye, J. (2002) *The Paradox of American Power*. Oxford: Oxford University Press.

O'Malley, P. (2000) 'Risk Societies and the Government of Crime', in M. Brown and J. Pratt (eds), *Dangerous Offenders*. London: Routledge.

O'Malley, P. (2001) 'Risk, Crime and Prudentialism Revisited', in K. Stenson and R. Sullivan (eds), *Crime, Risk and Justice*. Cullompton: Willan.

O'Malley, P. (2002) 'Drugs, Risks and Freedoms', in G. Hughes, E. McLauglin and J. Muncie (eds), *Crime Prevention and Community Safety: New Directions*. London: Sage.

Observer (2001a) 'League Table for Surgeons: Track Records and Success Rates to be Published', *The Observer*, 21 October: 13.

Observer (2001b) 'The Terror Crisis: So Are Civilisations at War? Interview with Samuel Huntingdon', *The Observer*, 21 October: 28.

Observer (2002) 'How Oil Slick Will Bring Black Death to Coast's Way of Life', *The Observer*, 24 November: 18.

Ontario Commission on Systematic Racism in the Criminal Justice System (1995) Ontario: Queen's Printer for Ontario.

Pahl, J. (1999) 'Coping with Physical Violence and Abuse', in J. Balloch, J. McClean and M. Fisher (eds), *Social Services Working Under Pressure*. London: Policy Press.

Parsloe, P. (ed.) (1999) *Risk Assessment in Social Care and Social Work*. London: Jessica Kingsley.

Parton, N. (1998) 'Risk, Advanced Liberalism and Child Welfare: The Need to Rediscover Uncertainty Ambiguity', *British Journal of Social Work* 28: 5–27.

Petts, J., Horlick-Jones, T., Murdock, G. (2001) *Social Amplification of Risk: The Media and the Public* (Health and Safety Executive). London: HMSO.

Phillips, L. (2000) 'Mediated Communication and the Privatisation of Public Problems: Discourses on Ecological Risks and Political Action', *European Journal of Communication* 15(2): 171–207.

Pidgeon, N. (1999) 'Risk Communication and the Social Amplification of Risk: Theory, evidence and policy implications', *Risk Decision and Policy* 4(2): 145–59.

Pilgrim, D. and Rogers, A. (1993) *A Sociology of Mental Health and Illness*. Buckingham: Open University Press.

Plant, M. and Plant, M. (1993) *Risktakers, Alcohol, Drugs, Sex and Youth*. London: Routledge.

Power, M. (1997) *The Audit Society*: Oxford: Oxford University Press.

Press Association (2003) 'Potters Bar Disaster', 12 June.

Rahman, M., Palmer, G., Kenway, P. and Howarth, C. (2000) *Monitoring Poverty and Social Exclusion 2000*. York: Joseph Rowntree Foundation.

Ratzon, S. (ed.) (1998) *The Mad Cow Crisis*. London: UCL Press.

Raynor, P. (2001) 'Community Penalties and Social Integration: Community as a Solution and as a Problem', in A. Bottoms, L. Gelsthorpe and S. Rex (eds), *Community Penalties: Change and Challenges*. Cullompton: Willan.

Reder, P., Duncan, S. and Grey, M. (1993) *Beyond Blame: Child Abuse Tragedies Revisited*. London: Routledge.

Reiner, R., Livingstone, S. and Allen, J. (2001) 'Casino Culture: Media and Crime in a Winner–Loser Society', in K. Stenson and R. Sullivan (eds), *Crime, Risk and Justice*. Cullompton: Willan.

Rhodes, R.A.W. (1997) *Understanding Governance: Policy Networks, Governance, Reflexivity and Accountability*. Buckingham: Open University Press.

Ring, P. (2003) 'Risk and UK Pension Reform', *Social Policy and Administration* 37(1): 65–82.

Robbins, K. (1997) 'What is Globalisation?', *Sociology Review* 6(2): 2–6.

Rogers, A. and Pilgrim, D. (1995) 'The Risk of Resistance: Positions on the Mass Childhood Immunisation Programme', in J. Gabe (ed.), *Medicine, Health and Risk*. Oxford: Blackwell.

Rosa, E.A. (1998) 'Meta-Theoretical Foundations for Post Normal Risk', *Journal of Risk Research* 1: 15–44.

Rose, N. (1999a) 'Inventiveness in Politics', *Economy and Society* 28(3): 467–93.

Rose, N. (1999b) *Powers of Freedom: Reforming Political Thought*. Cambridge: Cambridge University Press.

Royal College of Nursing/National Health Service Executive (1998) *Safer Working in the Community: A Guide for NHS Managers and Staff on Reducing the Risks from Violence and Aggression*. London: Royal College of Nursing.

Royal Society (1992) *Risk: Analysis, Perception and Management. Report of a Royal Society Study Group*. London: The Royal Society.

Royal Society for the Prevention of Accidents (2004) 'Health and Safety at School: School Trips'. www.rospa.com (7 October).

Sargent, K. (1999) 'Assessing Risks for Children', in P. Parsloe (ed.), *Risk Assessment in Social Care and Social Work*. London: Jessica Kingsley.

Saussure, F. de (1974) *Course in General Linguistics*. London: Fontana.

Saward, M. (2003) *Democracy*. Cambridge: Polity Press.

Schultz, R. and Vogt, A. (2002) 'The Real Intelligence Failure on 9/11 and the Case for a Doctrine of Striking First', in D. Howard and R. Sawyer (eds) (2003) *Terrorism and Counter-Terrorism: Understanding the New Security Environment*. Guilford, CT: McGraw-Hill/Dushkin.

Schutz, A. (1964) *Collected Papers* (2 vols). The Hague: Martin Nijhoff.

Scott, A. (2002) 'Risk Society or Angst Society? Two Views of Risk Consciousness and Community', in B. Adam, U. Beck and J. Van Loon (eds), *The Risk Society and Beyond: Critical Issues in Social Theory*. London: Sage.

Scott, H. (1998) 'Risk and Community Care for People with Mental Illness', in B. Heyman (ed.), *Risk, Health and Health Care: A Qualitative Approach*. London: Arnold.

Scraton, P. (2002) *Beyond September 11th: An Anthology of Dissent*. London: Pluto Press.

Seidel, G. and Vidal, L. (1997) 'The Implications of "Medical" Gender in "Development" and "Culturalist" Discourses for HIV/AIDS Policy in Africa', in C. Shore and S. Wright (eds), *Anthropology of Policy*. London: Routledge.

Selden, R. (1989) *A Reader's Guide to Contemporary Literary Theory*. London: Harvester Wheatsheaf.

Sharkey, P. (1995) *Introducing Community Care*. London: Collins.

Sharlin, H.I. (1986) 'EDB: A Case Study in Communicating', *Risk Analysis* 6: 61–8.

Shaw, A. (1999) 'What Are "They" Doing to Our Food? Public Concerns about Food in the UK', *Sociological Research Online* 4(3).

Shaw, A. (2000) 'Public Understanding of Food Risks: What Do the Experts Say?', *Food Science and Technology Today* 14(3): 140–43.

She (2000) 'Cosmetic Surgery – Before and After', *She* (June).

Short, C. (1998) 'The Meaning of Globalisation for Development Policy', *Social Policy and Administration* 32(5): 456–63.

Slovic, P. (1986) 'Informing and Educating the Public about Risk', *Risk Analysis* 6: 403–15.

Slovic, P. (1987) 'Perception of Risk', *Science* 236: 280–5.

Slovic, P. (2000) *The Perception of Risk*. London: Earthscan.

Smiljanic, N. (2002) 'Human Rights and Muslims in Britain', in B. Spalek (ed.), *Islam, Crime and Criminal Justice*. Cullompton: Willan.

Smith, M.J. (2004) 'Mad Cows and Mad Money: Problems of Risk in the Making and Understanding of Policy', *The British Journal of Politics and International Relations* 6: 312–32.

Smith, W. and Torstensson, M. (1997) 'Gender Differences in Risk Perception and Neutralizing Fear of Crime: Towards Resolving the Paradoxes', *British Journal of Criminology* 37(4): 608–34.

Solomos, J. (1988) *Black Youth, Racism and the State: The Policies of Ideology and Polity*. Cambridge: Cambridge University Press.

Soumerai, S.B., Ross-Degnan, D. and Khan, J.S. (1992) 'Effects of Professional and Media Warnings about the Association between Aspirin Use in Children and Reyes Syndrome', *Millbank Quarterly* 70: 155–82.

Sparks, R. (1992) *Television and the Drama of Crime: Moral Tales and the Place of Crime in Public Life*. Buckingham: Open University Press.

Spicker, P. (1998) *Social Policy in a Changing Society*. London: Routledge.

Spicker, P. (2001) 'Social Insecurity and Social Protection', in R. Edwards and J. Glover (eds), *Risk and Citizenship*. Routledge: London.

Stanley, J. and Goddard, C. (2002) *In the Firing Line*. Chichester: John Wiley.

Stegman, M., Brownstein, J. and Temkin, K. (1995) 'Home Ownership and Family Wealth in the United States', in R. Forrest and A. Murie (eds), *Housing and Family Wealth: Comparative International Positions*. London: Routledge.

Stenson, K. (2001) 'The New Politics of Crime Control', in K. Stenson and R. Sullivan (eds), *Crime, Risk and Justice*. Cullompton: Willan.

Stenson, K. (2002) 'Community safety in Middle England – the local politics of crime control', in G. Hughes and A. Edwards (eds), *Crime Control and Community*. Cullompton: Willan.

Stenson, K. and Edwards, A. (2001) 'Crime Control and Liberal Government: The "Third Way" and the Return to the Local', in K. Stenson and R. Sullivan (eds), *Crime, Risk and Justice*. Cullompton: Willan.

Stenson, K. and Sullivan, R. (eds) (2001) *Crime, Risk and Social Justice*. Cullompton: Willan.

Stenson, K. and Watt, P. (1999) 'Governmentality and the "Death of the Social"? A Discourse Analysis of Local Government Texts in South-East England', *Urban Studies* 36(1): 189–201.

Stern, J. (1999) 'Getting and Using the Weapons', in R. Howard and R. Sawyer (eds) (2003) *Terrorism and Counter-Terrorism: Understanding the New Security Environment*. Guilford, CT: McGraw-Hill/Dushkin.

Stern, J. (1999) *The Ultimate Terrorists*. Cambridge, MA: Harvard University Press.

Stevenson, O. (1999) 'Old People at Risk', in P. Parsloe (ed.), *Risk Assessment in Social Care and Social Work*. London: Jessica Kingsley.

Strydom, P. (2002) *Risk, Environment and Society*. Buckingham: Open University Press.

Suzuki, M. (2002) 'Water in our Future', in H. Van Ginkel, B. Barret, J. Court and J. Velasquez (eds), *Human Development and the Environment*. New York: United Nations Press.

Taylor-Gooby, P. (2000) *Risk, Trust and Welfare*. London: Macmillan.

Taylor-Gooby, P. (2001a) 'Risk, Contingency and the Third Way. Evidence from the BHPS and Qualitative Studies', *Social Policy and Administration* 35(2): 195–211.

Taylor-Gooby, P. (ed.) (2001b) *Welfare Sates under Pressure*. London: Sage.

Taylor-Gooby, P., Dean, H., Munro, M. and Parker, G. (1999) 'Risk and the Welfare State', *British Journal of Sociology* 50(2): 182–91.

Tew, M. (1990) *Safer Childbirth: A Critical History of Maternity Care*. London: Chapman and Hall.

The Management of Health and Safety at Work Regulations (1999). London: HMSO.

Thomas, P. (2002) 'Legislative Responses to Terrorism', in P. Scraton (ed.), *Beyond September 11th: An Anthology of Dissent*. London: Pluto Press.

Thorogood, N. (1995) 'London Dentist in HIV Scare: HIV and Dentistry in Popular Discourse', *Primary Dental Care* 2(2): 59–60.

Tilley, N. (2002) 'Crime Prevention in Britain 1975–2010', in G. Hughes, E. McLauglin and J. Muncie (eds), *Crime Prevention and Community Safety: New Directions*. London: Sage.

Tullock, J. and Lupton, D. (2003) *Risk and Everyday Life*. London: Sage.

Turnbull, A. (1999) *Internal Control-Guidance for Directors on the Combined Code*, London: Institute of Chartered Accountants in England and Wales.

Turner, B. (1997) 'Forward from Governmentality to Risk: Some Reflections on Foucault's Contribution to Medical Sociology', in A. Peterson and R. Banton (eds), *Foucault, Health and Medicine*. London: Routledge.

Twigg, J. (1999) 'Social Care', in J. Baldock, N. Manning, S. Miller and S. Vickerstaff (eds), *Social Policy*. Oxford: Oxford University Press.

Underdown, A. and Ellis, T. (1998) *Strategies for Effective Offender Supervision*. London: Home Office.

Ungar, S. (2001) 'Moral Panic versus the Risk Society: The Implications of the Changing Sites of Social Anxiety', *British Journal of Sociology* 52(2): 271–91.

Vail, J. (1999) 'Insecure Times', in J. Vail, J. Wheelock and M. Hill, *Insecure Times: Living with Insecurity in Contemporary Society*. London: Routledge.

Van Ginkel, H., Barret, B., Court, J. and Velasquez, J. (eds) (2002) *Human Development and the Environment: Challenges for the New Millennium*. Tokyo: United Nations University Press.

Van Swaaningen, R. (2002) 'Towards a Replacement Discourse on Community Safety', in G. Hughes, E. McLauglin and J. Muncie (eds), *Crime Prevention and Community Safety: New Directions*. London: Sage.

Vandereen, G. (2002) 'Regarding Riskism: On the Primary Importance of Public Opinion on Safety and Security'. Paper given to Law and Society Conference, July 2002. Vancouver, Canada.

Wade, A. and Smart, C. (2002) *Facing Family Change: Children's Strategies and Resources*. York: Joseph Rowntree Foundation.

Wadham, J. (2002) 'Mental Health Bill, DSPDs', letter to the Editor, *The Guardian*, 26 June.

Wahlberg, A.A.F. and Sjoberg, L. (2000) 'Risk Perception and the Media', *Journal of Risk Research* 3(1): 31–50.

Walker, C. and McGuiness, M. (2002) 'Commercial Risk, Political Violence and Policing the City of London', in A. Crawford (ed.), *Crime and Insecurity: The Governance of Safety in Europe*. Cullompton: Willan.

Wall, D. (2002) 'Insecurity and the Policing of Cyberspace', in A. Crawford (ed.), *Crime and Insecurity: The Governance of Safety in Europe*. Cullompton: Willan.

Weber, M. (1949) *The Methodology of the Social Sciences*. Trans. E. Shils and A.M. Henderson. Glencoe, IL: The Free Press.

Wildavsky, A. (1988) *Searching for Safety*. New Brunswick, NJ: Transaction Publishers.

Wiles, P. and Pease, K. (2001) 'Distributive Justice and Crime', in R. Matthews and J. Pitts (eds), *Crime Disorder and Community Safety*. London: Routledge.

Wilkinson, I. (2001a) 'Social Theories of Risk Perception: At Once Indispensable and Insufficient', *Current Sociology* 49(1): 1–22.

Wilkinson, I. (2001b) *Anxiety in a Risk Society*. London: Routledge.

Wimbledon, Mitcham and Morden Guardian (2002) 'Ethnic Groups at Risk', *Wimbledon, Mitcham and Morden Guardian*, 11 June.

Wittenberg, R., Comas-Herra, A., Pickard, L. and Hancock, R. (2004) *Future Demand for Long-term Care in the UK: a summary of projections of long-term care finance for older people to 2051*. York: Joseph Rowntree Trust.

World Commission on the Environment and Development (1987) *Our Common Future*. Oxford: Oxford University Press.

World Health Organisation (1989) *European Charter on Environment and Health*. Geneva: World Health Organisation.

Wright, A. (2002) *Policing*. Cullompton: Willan.

Wynne, B. (1992) 'Risk and Social Learning: Reification to Engagement', in S. Krimsky and D. Golding (eds), *Social Theories of Risk*. Westport, CT: Praeger.

Young, J. (1999) *The Exclusive Society*. London: Sage.

Zey, M. (1998) *Seizing the Future: The Dawn of the Macindustrial Era* (2nd edn). New Brunswick, NJ: Transaction Publishers.

Zveric, U. (1998) 'Criminal Victimisation in Countries in Transition: Rome UNICRI', in R.I. Mawby (ed.), *Burglary*. Cullompton: Willan.

Index